THE SHAPING OF AMERICAN GRADUATE EDUCATION

DANIEL COIT GILMAN AND THE PROTEAN Ph. D.

Dec. 21 _____ 1875

Professor F. J. Child,

My dear Sir;—

Yours of the 19th reached me this morning. I appreciate the difficulties which you encounter when you think of removing from Cambridge,—and I do not wonder that Pres. Eliot objects to your departure. As you still incline favorably to the suggestion of coming here, annually, in the month of February, I would propose the following basis,—to which if you assent, I will ask the assent of our Trustees. I hope you will see your way clear to an early and favorable response. As I said in my note yesterday I will meet you 'half way,' if you desire a personal conference,—I regret very much that we cannot induce you to make your permanent home here,—but we shall, confidently, hope for your partial cooperation. If you can suggest a better arrangement than I have planned, speak freely. The trustees meet Jan. 3, & I should like to have the acceptance then; the details can be deferred. Yours very truly

D. C. Gilman

Daniel Coit Gilman to Professor Francis J. Child, December 21, 1875.
Original in Houghton Library, Harvard University. See pp. 102-106.

THE SHAPING OF AMERICAN GRADUATE EDUCATION

DANIEL COIT GILMAN
AND THE PROTEAN Ph.D.

BY

FRANCESCO CORDASCO

ROWMAN AND LITTLEFIELD
TOTOWA, NEW JERSEY

Library of Congress Catalog Card No. 72-93393

ISBN 0-87471-161-4

Originally published 1959, 1960 as
Daniel Coit Gilman and the Protean Ph.D.
The Shaping of American Graduate Education

PRINTED IN THE UNITED STATES OF AMERICA

IN MEMORY OF MY BROTHER

MICHAEL CORDASCO (1915-1959)

But now farewell. I am going a long way ...
Where falls not hail, or rain, or any snow,
Nor ever wind blows loudly; but it lies
Deep-meadow'd, happy, fair with orchard lawns
And bowery hollows crown'd with summer sea,
Where I will heal me of my grievous wound.

Tennyson

The object of the university is to develop character—to make men. It misses its aim if it produces learned pedants, or simple artisans, or cunning sophists or pretentious practitioners. Its purport is not so much to impart knowledge to the pupils, as to whet the appetite, exhibit methods, develop powers, strengthen judgement, and invigorate the intellectual and moral forces. It should prepare for the service of society a class of students who will be wise, thoughtful, and progressive guides in whatever department of work or thought they may be engaged. Universities easily fall into ruts. Almost every epoch requires a fresh start.

Daniel Coit Gilman, *Inaugural Address*, The Johns Hopkins University, February 22, 1876.

TABLE OF CONTENTS

PREFACE

American higher education has in the last decade endured more stress than most other social institutions; its goals are vigorously debated; its newly defined societal responsibilities (cast in the matrix of the new awareness of the 1960s, and America's "discovery" of poverty and disenfranchisement) have shattered its fragile structure, and have taken it to the edge of chaos; and its leadership (often in exile) has, in a multiplicity of publications, attempted the differential diagnosis of the *malaise,* and has proposed widely varying therapies.

Jacques Barzun, in his acidulous commentary on the American university, has capsuled this disaffection:

> The university is now receiving the harshest criticisms it has ever had to endure. Never so trusted, never so challenged. Government (both the legislative and the executive branch) is suspicious of its management of research. Foundations accuse it of conservatism and inability to change. Students who attend it regard it as another establishment to be brought down by violence and revolutionized. Benefactors and paying customers shake their heads over rising costs and low productivity. And inside the house the scholars, who repeat that *they* are the university, complain of the work and the pay like wage earners, while declaring that their allegiance is not to the particular place but to their subject of specialization, their 'discipline.'[1]

Graduate education has not been immune to the difficulties which have overwhelmed higher education, and some critics have attributed to the success of graduate schools and the "Ph.D. Octopus" (with its specialization) a concomitant decline in the liberal arts college[2]; but Allan Cartter has noted (correctly in my view) that "graduate education, once considered an expensive luxury by many university administrations . . . , is today the heart of the institutions that have achieved full university status. The prestige of these institutions in academic circles,

---

[1] Jacques Barzun, *The American University: How it Runs, Where it is Going* (New York: Harper & Row, 1968), p. 6.

[2] See Earl J. McGrath, *The Graduate School and the Decline of Liberal Education* (New York: Bureau of Publications, Teachers College, Columbia University, 1959); and for a different point of view, see Bernard Berelson, *Graduate Education in the United States* (New York: McGraw-Hill, 1960); and Allan M. Cartter, *An Assessment of Quality in Graduate Education* (Washington: American Council on Education, 1966).

their ability to attract outstanding students at both the undergraduate and graduate levels, their support through grants from private foundations and government agencies, come primarily from the strength of their graduate schools. The trend is not without its problems and is viewed as a not unmixed blessing by many, but graduate education is truly the signature of the university today."[3]

The era of the giants in university administration came to an end with the passing of Nicholas Murray Butler of Columbia University ("Still in the saddle [1945], 'Nicholas Miraculous' had dominated the scene since 1902, having directed all things himself like a virtuoso conductor, without crisis or rebellions.");[4] yet the study of the classical period in American higher education is not without benefit, and in many ways provides insights (if not solutions) into many of the problems which plague us in higher education. A study of the long administrative tenures of Charles W. Eliot (Harvard), Daniel C. Gilman (Johns Hopkins), Nicholas Murray Butler (Columbia), William Rainey Harper (Chicago), David Starr Jordan (Stanford), inter alia, delineates the origins of our disaffection and, hopefully, suggests the strategies of reconciliation with the articulation of new roles.

It is appropriate (to our myriad concerns) that the present monograph is again made available. Originally published in the Netherlands, it has long been out of print.[5] Daniel Coit Gilman was not without problems at Johns Hopkins University; and he came to these challenges from a strengthening experience at Yale University and at the University of California. And if Gilman was the "patron saint" of American graduate education, he was above all a university administrator of con-

---

[3] Allan M. Cartter, "Graduate Education and Research in the Decades Ahead," in Alvin C. Eurich, ed., Campus 1980 (New York: Delacorte Press, 1968), p. 255.

[4] Jacques Barzun, op. cit., p. 7. I cannot help but wonder how Butler (or any of his contemporaries in university administration) would have handled the application of "affirmative-action" criteria to faculty recruitment in the colleges and universities by the U.S. Department of Health, Education, and Welfare (Executive Order 11246; Title VI, Civil Rights Act, 1964). See Paul Seabury, "HEW and The Universities," Commentary (February 1972), pp. 38-45 and correspondence, Ibid. (May 1972). Affirmative action criteria propose increased numbers of members of minority groups within instructional ranks. (Seabury writes: "Compliance with demands from the federal government would compel a stark remodeling of [universities'] criteria of recruitment, their ethos of professionalism, and their standards of excellence.")

[5] Francesco Cordasco, Daniel Coit Gilman and the Protean Ph.D.: The Shaping of American Graduate Education (Leiden: E. J. Brill, 1960). This new printing has allowed me the opportunity to append to the bibliography selected references for higher education which have appeared since 1960.

summate skill who remains instructive to our own age, and temper-
amentally akin to our enervating apprehensions: his admonition, on
assuming the presidency at Johns Hopkins University, augured the
cautions which his heirs chose not to make: "Universities easily fall
into ruts. Almost every epoch requires a fresh start."

Since the publication of this monograph, Gilman's main writings
have been republished, and are now conveniently available.[6] The scope
of his writings reveals the eclectic and comprehensive concerns which
ranged beyond the administrative role at Hopkins, and probed all facets
of the educational scene.

May 1972

---

[6] Daniel Coit Gilman, *University Problems in the United States*. With A New
Introduction by Francesco Cordasco (New York: Johnson Reprint Corporation,
1971) [Originally, New York: The Century Company, 1898]; Daniel Coit Gilman,
The Launching of A University. With A New Foreword by Francesco Cordasco
(New York: Garrett Press, 1969) [Originally, New York: Dodd, Mead & Com-
pany, 1906].

INTRODUCTION

The aim of the present study has been to place Daniel Coit Gilman (1831-1908) in the historical framework of the development of graduate education in the United States. Although Gilman's importance in the history of graduate education is usually acknowledged briefly in the general histories of American education, this study attempts the first comprehensive treatment of Gilman giving historical dimension to all his educational service including his presidency of the Johns Hopkins University, 1876-1902. Under the leadership of Gilman, the Johns Hopkins University fulfilled a half-century of American graduate aspiration; essentially, it was the culmination of a long, indigenous educational evolution. If the German *Wissenschaftslehre*, the history of whose influence on American education remains to be written, had any influence on Gilman and his Hopkins, it was mainly subordinate to native impulses.

I have incurred many obligations during the progress of this work, and it is a pleasant duty to thank the many individuals who have so kindly lent me their assistance without which I should indeed have been much at a loss. Mr. Mulford Martin of the New York University Libraries made available the *Will S. Monroe Collection of Henry Barnard Manuscripts* which are deposited at Washington Square. At Yale University I studied the *Gilman Family Papers* with the courteous help of Professor James T. Babb, Librarian of Yale University, and reference librarians Dorothy W. Bridgwater and Barbara Simison. Miss May Dornin, in charge of the Department of Archives of the University of California at Berkeley, made available letters and manuscripts of Daniel Coit Gilman deposited in the Doe Memorial Library. At the Johns Hopkins University I had the invaluable assistance of Frieda C. Thies, Chief Reference Librarian, and of J. Louis Kuethe of the library's staff in making my way through the labyrinthian deposits of the *Gilman Papers*. My enquiries to those who have worked in the history of higher education in the United States received prompt and helpful answer. I owe obligation to Professor Richard J. Storr of the University of Chicago, to Dr. Willis Rudy of State Teachers College of Worcester, Massachusetts, and to Professor William Jackson of Harvard University. My perspective in the appreciation of the problems of the present-day Ph. D. has been much sharpened by materials furnished by Professor Jacques Barzun of Columbia University. Outside the academic world, my talks with Mrs. Elizabeth L. Anderson, Daniel Coit Gilman's grandniece, have been very stimulating and I owe Mrs. Anderson particular obligation for allowing me to use restricted materials in the Historical Manuscripts Room of Yale University.

I am indebted to Professor John C. Payne of New York University for the preliminary reading he made of the manuscript and his painstaking removal of many blemishes which would have otherwise marred the text. I can only inadequately express my obligation to my dear friend, Professor William W. Brickman of New York University, whose discerning criticism and rich store of knowledge immeasurably improved the text and encouraged its completion. It is hardly necessary to add that any shortcomings in the *éclaircissement* of the materials made available must be charged to me and not to those who have so graciously assisted.

F. C.

ACKNOWLEDGEMENTS:

Grateful acknowledgement is made to the following for permission to quote from books which they published: to The Johns Hopkins Press, from *A History of the University Founded by Johns Hopkins*; to Dodd, Mead & Company, from *The Life of Daniel Coit Gilman*; to the University of Chicago Press, from *The Beginnings of Graduate Education in America*. Permission to reproduce letters from *The Gilman Papers* at the Johns Hopkins University was extended by the University librarian, Mr. John H. Berthel.

CHAPTER ONE

DANIEL COIT GILMAN AND THE GRADUATE PRONAOS: THE HISTORICAL BACKGROUND OF THE PROBLEM

On the twenty-fifth anniversary of Daniel Coit Gilman's inauguration as President of the Johns Hopkins University, President Charles W. Eliot of Harvard, one of the main speakers, paid tribute to Gilman in these words:

> President Gilman, your first success and achievement here . . . has been the creation of a school of graduate studies, which not only has been in itself a strong and potent school, but which has lifted every other university in the country in its departments of arts and sciences. I want to testify that the graduate school of Harvard University, started feebly in 1870 and 1871, did not thrive until the example of Johns Hopkins forced our faculty to put their strength into the development of our instruction for graduates. And what was true of Harvard was true of every other university in the land which aspired to create an advanced school of arts and sciences. [1]

The quarter century had witnessed tremendous changes in education in the United States, and great strides had been made in graduate studies in American universities. Between the foundation of the Johns Hopkins University in 1876, and the celebration of its twenty-fifth anniversary in 1902, a veritable revolution in American higher education had taken place. "No other short period (1865-1900) in the history of American higher learning witnessed so many significant changes as that which encompassed the last three decades of the nineteenth century. During this time three major forces were at work: European influence, represented principally by the German university; world trends affecting the higher education of all nations, such as the growing prestige of scientific methods and the increasing preoccupation with materialist technology; and lastly, native American social forces, which produced a notable democratization of knowledge and widening of opportunities for higher education." [2] A fourth force should be added as an impelling agency, that which

---

[1] *Celebration of the Twenty-Fifth Anniversary of the Founding of the University and Inauguration of Ira Remson as President of the University*, p. 105.

[2] S. Willis Rudy, "The Revolution in American Higher Education, 1865-1900," *The Harvard Educational Review*, 21 (Summer, 1951), pp. 169-170.

Ryan has called the force of "individual personality." One ". . . inevitable question in all this has to do with the individuals who headed . . . universities in their pioneering days. To what extent was the success of each of these institutions due to the leadership exerted by Gilman at the Johns Hopkins, Hall at Clark, and Harper at the University of Chicago? It goes almost without saying that each of these universities could hardly have developed in the particular form it did if it had had some other individual as president. Experts in university administration have said that Daniel Coit Gilman was probably the best equipped man to head a pioneering university that could have been found; that the success of the Johns Hopkins University was in considerable measure due to the happy circumstance that a great educational gift fell into the hands of a man who by training and experience was in close touch with the education and scholarship of his day." [1] In the academic year beginning in 1871, graduate enrollment stood at 198; by 1890 it was 2382; and by 1910, it had reached the huge figure of 9370. [2]

DANIEL COIT GILMAN, 1831-1908

In the career of Daniel Coit Gilman [3] the presidency of the Johns Hopkins University was not the first or the last service of an educator whose connections with American education ranged from his instructorship at Yale College in the 1850's to his presidency of the newly-founded Carnegie Institution in 1902. Gilman, himself, capsuled his career in these words:

I am a veteran of fifty years standing who has taken part in many an academic discussion and witnessed many a contest; who has seen a school of science grafted upon one of the oldest and most conservative classical colleges; who has helped rescue a state university from the limitations of a college of agriculture and enlarge it to meet the requirements of a magnificent commonwealth; who has watched over the infancy of an institution planned to provide advanced opportunity for American youth akin to those offered in the best foreign universities; and finally

---

[1] W. Carson Ryan, *Studies in Early Graduate Education*, p. 144.

[2] Walton C. John, *Graduate Study in Universities and Colleges in the United States*, Chapters I and II.

[3] This study is not chiefly biographical but a brief life of Gilman to serve as a focal point of reference for the study is best included in this chapter. The biography of Gilman by Fabian Franklin (1910) was a memorial biography paid for by Gilman's widow. See Franklin to Mrs. Elizabeth Gilman, January 8, 1909, and Mrs. Elizabeth Gilman to Fabian Franklin, January 10, 1909. *Gilman Papers*, Lanier Room, Johns Hopkins University Library.

who has seen a munificent fund set apart for the encouragement of investigation and the pursuit of knowledge without the restrictions of a school or college. [1]

This is a modest recital. Only four years after Gilman's death, Monroe's *A Cyclopedia of Education* characterized Gilman as "... one of the leading influences in American educational development during the greater part of his career." [2]

Daniel Coit Gilman graduated from Yale College in 1852. [3] At Yale College he formed an intimate friendship with his fellow student, Andrew D. White, later to become president of Cornell University. The lives of these two men were henceforth to interact. [4] Following graduation, Gilman studied for a few months at Harvard College, living in the home of Professor Arnold Guyot, the eminent geographer. [5] Late in 1853, Gilman and Andrew D. White sailed for Europe as attachés of the American legation at St. Petersburg. After an absence of two years, [6] Gilman returned to America. For the next seventeen years, his life revolved around Yale College. Professor James D. Dana (whose life Gilman was later to write) enlisted his aid in drawing up a plan for what was to become the Sheffield Scientific School, and this was published in 1856 as *A Proposed Plan for a Complete Organization of the School of Science Connected with Yale College*; and Gilman's notes on the European schools of science, published the same year, disclose how ob-

---

[1] *The Jubilee of the University of Wisconsin*, p. 64.

[2] Fabian Franklin, "Gilman," *loc. cit.*, III, p. 111.

[3] *Record of the Class of 1852, Yale College* (1878). See also *Fasciculi of the Memorial Symposium of the Class of 1852 ... D. C. Gilman* (1910). Gilman was enrolled in the "classical" course.

[4] In 1904, White wrote: "At the close of my undergraduate life at Yale I went abroad for nearly three years, and fortunately had, for a time, one of the best of companions, my college mate, Gilman, later President of Johns Hopkins University, and now of the Carnegie Institution, who was then, as he has been ever since, a source of good inspirations to me,—especially in the formation of my ideas regarding education." *Autobiography*, I, p. 34.

[5] There were few graduate facilities. Many years later Gilman wrote: "Opportunities for advanced, not professional, studies were then scanty in this country. In the older colleges certain graduate courses were attended by a small number of followers—but the teachers were for the most part absorbed with undergraduate instruction, and could give but little time to the few who sought their guidance." *Launching of a University*, p. 8.

[6] Gilman's letters to Henry Barnard in *The Will S. Monroe Collection of Henry Barnard Manuscripts* deposited in the Washington Square Library of New York University belong to this period.

servant he had been while abroad. [1] In the Sheffield Scientific School, Gilman served as librarian, as secretary, and as professor of physical and political geography. In the same period he served as a member of the New Haven Board of Education. When Senator Morrill visited New Haven, he was the guest of Gilman; and Chittenden notes that the Sheffield Scientific School was the first institution to put into actual use funds derived from the Morrill Act (1862). [2] In 1867, Gilman declined a call to the presidency of the University of Wisconsin, [3] as well as one in 1870 to the presidency of the University of California. In 1872, however, upon a second call, Gilman became the president of the University of California. On his way West, he visited President White of Cornell, discussed with Governor Baker of Indiana the plan of Purdue University, and at Urbana studied the formative plan of the University of Illinois. In San Francisco, he discussed with Louis Agassiz the place of science in the American schools. [4] Although Gilman was hampered by political difficulties at the University of California, he succeeded in laying the groundwork for a modern university as he conceived it. [5] In January, 1875, Gilman, after several invitations, accepted the presidency of the university which was to be founded in Baltimore by the beneficence of the Quaker merchant, Johns Hopkins.

The prominence of Daniel Coit Gilman in 1875 is attested to by the statement of President James Angell of the University of Michigan who, with President Eliot of Harvard and President White of Cornell, had recommended Gilman for the presidency of the Johns Hopkins University. "And now I have this remarkable statement to make to you; that,

---

[1] This first appeared in Henry Barnard's *American Journal of Education*, I, pp. 315-328. At Barnard's suggestion, Gilman visited most of the French and German technical schools with William M. Gillespie, a professor of Civil Engineering at Union College, who was traveling in Europe at the same time. Gilman wrote to Barnard: "I was very glad to make the acquaintance of that [Gillespie] gentleman, & during his stay in Paris, I met him frequently. . . . His attention to scientific schools will only be, I presume, attention to Schools of Engineering & of these he means only to visit the principal." Gilman to Barnard, May 29, 1855. Letter 3674, *Will S. Monroe Collection, loc. cit.*

[2] *The Sheffield Scientific School*, vol. I, p. 70.

[3] Gilman's letter declining the offer is very brief and is addressed to N.B. Van Slyke, Chairman Exec. Comm., Madison, Wisconsin. *Gilman Family Papers*, Yale University. The incident is not mentioned in Merle Curti and Vernon Carstensen, *The University of Wisconsin: a history*, 1848-1925.

[4] Gilman's itinerary westward can be fixed by reference to a notebook he kept during the trip. *Gilman Papers*, Lanier Room, Johns Hopkins University Library.

[5] W. W. Ferrier, *Origin and Development of the University of California*, p. 43.

without the least conference between us three, we all wrote letters . . .
that the one man was Daniel C. Gilman of California." [1] During his long
tenure, Gilman stamped the university with his own personality. Research
was the soul of the whole organism. [2] Many lands and many ages contributed to the achievement of the university, for Gilman was familiar
with many educational institutions in Europe and America; but all their
results were passed through the experience and thinking of Gilman
himself, so that the final product was not like any university system that
one might label German, English, or American. In 1902, on the occasion
of Gilman's retirement as President of the Johns Hopkins University,
Woodrow Wilson (Ph.D., Johns Hopkins, 1886, and then a professor
at Princeton University) presented Gilman with an address of "affection
and congratulation," with the signatures of more than a thousand of
the alumni and faculty of the university. "If it be true," said Wilson,
"that Thomas Jefferson first laid the broad foundations for American
universities in his plans for the University of Virginia, it is no less true
that you were the first to create and organize in America a university in
which the discovery and dissemination of new truth were conceded a
rank superior to mere instruction, and in which the efficiency and value
of research as an educational instrument were exemplified in the training
of many investigators." [3]

When Andrew Carnegie endowed the institution in Washington
which was to bear his name, he insisted that Daniel Coit Gilman be its
first president. Although Gilman accepted, he resigned at the end of
three years, apparently because he did not have a free hand in unifying
the forces of the Institution.

During the period of almost thirty years of Gilman's presidency of
the Johns Hopkins University, and of the Carnegie Institution of
Washington, he was engaged in a multitude of other educational activi-

---

[1] *Celebration of the Twenty-Fifth Anniversary of the Founding of the University* . . . ,
p. 133.

[2] "We often hear discussions as to the relation of instruction to research. Sterile
intellects attribute their non-production to overwork, when a more acute diagnosis
detects a lack of will-power. Will-weakness is as common as neurasthenia. None of
our college faculties are perfectly immune from this infection. It must be admitted
that serious administrative duties are impediments to prolonged work in the laboratory
or the library; but instruction is not administration. Sylvester, the great mathematician,
said that his mind was never so fertile as when excited by the queries and criticisms
of his pupils." *Launching of a University*, pp. 243-244.

[3] *Celebration of the Twenty-Fifth Anniversary of the Founding of the University* . . . ,
p. 37.

ties. He was president of the American Social Association in 1879. In 1882, he was made one of the original trustees of the John F. Slater Fund, an office that he held until his death. In 1893, he became a trustee of the Peabody Education Fund, and in 1903 a member of the General Education Board. In 1907, when he was in his seventy-sixth year, he was appointed a trustee of the Russell Sage Foundation. [1]

When Sir William Osler, who was then Regius Professor of Medicine at Oxford University, and who had been one of the great medical luminaries at Hopkins from 1889 to 1904, read of Gilman's death on October 13, 1908, he wrote to Mrs. Gilman as follows:

Paris, October 16, 1908.

> I have just seen in the *Times* the announcement of the death of my dear friend—or rather Mrs. Osler read it out—and I exclaimed from my heart, My father! My Father! the chariots of Israel and the horsemen thereof! My next feeling was one of gratitude that he should have been able to do so much for higher education in America and for medical education. A splendid life and a splendid work! We of the medical profession owe him an everlasting debt of gratitude. Not of us, he was always with us, heart and soul, and it was always a great satisfaction to me to feel that he knew we appreciated his efforts on behalf of the Medical School. The start on sound lines which he gave the Hospital was one of the best things he ever did. What memories of those happy days come up! Little did we think that so much would be accomplished in so short a time. [2]

THE ANTE-BELLUM COLLEGE

Rudy has written that "The early American college, whatever its shortcomings, had all the advantages of a logical and unified view of life. In essence, this may be said to have been based on Christianity." [3] There were nine colonial colleges: Harvard (1636), the College of William and Mary (1693), Yale (1701), the College of New Jersey

---

[1] There were other activities which lie outside the scope of this study. Gilman was President of the American Oriental Society from 1893 until 1906, and President of the National Civil Service League from 1901 to 1907; in 1896 he became a Vice-President of the American Bible Society and in 1903 its President. In 1896 he was asked by President Cleveland to be a member of the commission appointed "to investigate and report upon the true divisional line between the Republic of Venezuela and British Guiana."

[2] *Gilman Papers*, Johns Hopkins University. Franklin (*The Life of Daniel Coit Gilman*, pp. 426-27) prints an excerpt from this letter and dates it "1909", but this is error as the holograph, *loc. cit.*, clearly shows.

[3] *Op. cit.*, p. 156.

[Princeton] (1746), the College of Philadelphia [University of Pennsylvania] (1753), King's College [Columbia] (1754), Brown University (1764), Rutgers (1766), and Darthmouth (1769). [1] All of these colleges, with the exception of the College of Philadelphia, grew out of religious motives and all followed closely upon English models until late in the nineteenth century. [2] The religious impulse followed the college westward with the moving frontier. Tewksbury has written, "The American College was typically a frontier institution. It was designed primarily to meet the needs of pioneer communities, and was established in most cases on the frontier line of settlement. ... the colleges which were established during the period before the Civil War served as agents of a cultural and religious advance on a wide front ... a unique institution, destined to play a significant and dramatic role in the development of American life." [3] The classical curriculum, tersely summarized by Harvard President Henry Dunster in 1640, [4] persisted until the first quarter of the nineteenth century.

By the first quarter of the nineteenth century the curriculum of the American College had been standardized into some four divisions: (1) the classics, (2) rhetoric and belles-lettres, (3) mathematics and natural philosophy, and (4) mental and moral philosophy. Greek and Latin formed the backbone of the course. [5] Yale, "the mother of colleges," exported this system to new colleges in the South and West. In the seventy-five colleges operating before 1840, thirty-six presidents came from Yale, twenty-two from Princeton, and only eight from Harvard. [6] There were attacks on the system, and attempts were made to modify it, but to little avail. The famous *Yale Report* (1828) was a sweeping denunciation of the critics and of all attempts, even at mild change. [7] The Yale course of instruction for 1824 may serve as an illustration. Taught by a faculty composed of the President, five professors, and eight tutors, it consisted of the following:

---

[1] Edgar W. Knight, *Education in the United States*, pp. 115-116.

[2] *Ibid.*, p. 116.

[3] Donald G. Tewksbury, *The Founding of American Colleges and Universities before the Civil War*, pp. 1-2. The affinity with the Turner frontier thesis has particular interest.

[4] "Primus annus Rhetoricam docebit, secundus et tertius Dialecticam, quartus adiungat Philosophiam." Quoted in George P. Schmidt, *The Old Time College President*, p. 95.

[5] Louis F. Snow, *The College Curriculum in the United States*, p. 141.

[6] E. Merton Coulter, *College Life in the Old South*, pp. 15-16.

[7] Schmidt, *op. cit.*, p. 54. A summary of the report is in Snow, *op. cit.*, pp. 145-154.

Freshmen: Livy, Xenophon, Herodotus, Thucydides, a text on "Roman Antiquities" and algebra, geography, and grammar.
Sophomores: Horace, Demosthenes, Xenophon, Herodotus, Plato, Aristotle, Cicero, Euclid, geometry, trigonometry, rhetoric.
Juniors: Cicero, Homer, Tacitus, spherical trigonometry, Enfield's text on natural philosophy, astronomy, a text on history, Hebrew (optional), and lectures in natural philosophy.
Seniors: Paley on moral philosophy, natural theology, and evidences of Christianity, Stewarts' *Philosophy of the mind*, rhetoric, logic, Locke's *Essays*, and lectures on Chemistry, minerology, geology, and natural philosophy.

The *Graeca Majora* was also read through the first three years. [1] There were everywhere minor variations of this essential structure. The fundamental argument of the Yale faculty was "the one always advanced in favor of subjects of little demonstrable value—that is, mental discipline. It is based on the now discredited psychological principle of transfer of training." [2] It was into this academic world that Daniel Coit Gilman entered when he matriculated at Yale College in 1848, as a member of the class of 1852.

Gilman entered Yale College two years after the election of Theodore Dwight Woolsey to the presidency. Woolsey's administration (1846-1871) was marked by some advance in the scientific and scholarly quality of Yale College. [3] Among the members of the faculty whom he added—men whom Gilman knew as students, and whom he was later to know as colleagues—were Elias Loomis and Denison Olmsted in natural philosophy, Thomas A. Thacher in Latin, James D. Dana in geology, the Sillimans—father and son—in chemistry, James Hadley in Greek, William D. Whitney in philology, George J. Brush in metallurgy, J. Willard Gibbs in mathematics. A fellow student of Gilman was Timothy Dwight, who in 1886 succeeded Noah Porter as president of Yale. Here, too, he had as a fellow student, Andrew D. White, who was to remain a life long friend. [4]

In none of Gilman's writings is found the deprecation of the *ante-*

---

[1] Richard Hofstadter and C. DeWitt Hardy, *The Development and Scope of Higher Education in the United States*, p. 11. For illustrative curricula, see Louis F. Snow, *op. cit., passim.*

[2] Ernest Earnest, *Academic Procession*, p. 24.

[3] Franklin Bowditch Dexter, *Sketch of the History of Yale University*, pp. 63-65.

[4] Abraham Flexner, *Daniel Coit Gilman*, pp. 5-6; Franklin, *op. cit.*, pp. 8-15. See also Timothy Dwight, *Memories of Yale Life and Men, passim.*

bellum college that is typical of Andrew D. White [1] and of Henry P. Tappan. [2] Instead of being "critical of [his] own narrow undergraduate training," [3] Gilman recognized that the college was not to be radically changed; rather, its scope was to be broadened, and its true function was to serve as introduction to the advanced studies implicit in the "university idea." Gilman had no sympathy for the sweeping reform of Henry P. Tappan: "In a large city there was no substitute for a university, particularly as a humanizing influence. Therefore, the local colleges should abolish the four-year course and absorb the grammar school, to become something like the German gymnasia. A university should then be created on a scale commensurate with the requirements and the magnificence of the city." [4] In his inaugural address as President of Johns Hopkins University, Gilman said:

> The College implies, as a general rule, restriction rather than freedom; tutorial rather than professorial guidance; residence within appointed bounds; the chapel, the dining hall, and the daily inspection. The college theoretically stands *in loco parentis*; it does not afford a very wide scope; it gives a liberal and substantial foundation on which the university instruction may be wisely built. [5]

And in a speech at Western Reserve University in 1882, he reiterated the idea:

> The college and the school of science need not give up their dignity and independence because they are affiliated in a university. There must be a plan akin to that worked out in political life, a balance of powers, so that while local rights are preserved, the general interests are promoted. The problem is not easy, but its solution suggests far fewer difficulties than those which beset our national government. May not the parallel be carried further? As this nation began with local institutions, then proceeded to confederated action, and finally reached the idea of a federal republic, in which the rights of States were protected and the wider advantages of a union were secured; so may it be in our educational progress. There will be many colleges grouped under the aegis of a true university. [6]

---

[1] *Autobiography*, I, pp. 27-29. "From classical studies the gerund-grinding and reciting by rote had completely weaned me." *Ibid.*, p. 30.

[2] *University Education*, pp. 50 ff. "A facile system of education full of pretension and fair promises, but containing no philosophical or manly discipline." *Ibid.*, p. 67.

[3] George P. Schmidt, *The Liberal Arts College*, p. 168.

[4] Quoted by Storr, *op. cit.*, p. 82.

[5] *Addresses at the Inauguration of Daniel C. Gilman as President of the Johns Hopkins University*, p. 32.

[6] *Launching of a University*, p. 273.

In the organization of the Johns Hopkins University, Gilman provided for undergraduate instruction, although this fact is not mentioned by Horton, [1] by Ryan, [2] or in the general histories of Thwing, [3] Earnest, [4] or Schmidt. [5] "Because of [the] insistence on the European conception of a university, it has more than once been asserted, and rather widely believed, that the institution [Johns Hopkins] as planned and begun had at first no undergraduates; and that President Gilman's design of a wholly graduate university was thwarted by later changes. The fact is quite otherwise." [6] In his *Annual Report* for 1880, Gilman wrote:

> We have thought from the outset that the youth of Baltimore and the adjacent region had peculiar claims upon this university, for our founder was a Baltimore merchant who gave his fortune to build up in this place the institutions of charity and of education. His gifts were too generous to be restricted by any geographical consideration and they are administered in a most liberal spirit; at the same time it would not be reasonable that the boys of Baltimore should be obliged to go away from the city of their residence in order to secure the requisite preparation for university work. A kindred foundation for the education of young women is also much to be desired. [7]

Gilman's "group system of studies" was, to be sure, an innovation, but it did not attempt, or propose, the destruction of the collegiate curriculum. [8]

THE GERMAN UNIVERSITY AND AMERICAN GRADUATE STUDIES

Rudy has observed that "The impact of German Scholarship and university life upon nineteenth century American university ideas is one of the most important phenomena in modern intellectual history." [9] The history of this influence remains to be written. [10] Writing in 1928,

---

[1] Byrne J. Horton, *The Graduate School*, "The Origin and Development of Johns Hopkins University," pp. 47-72.

[2] *Op. cit.*, "The Johns Hopkins," pp. 15-46.

[3] Charles Franklin Thwing, *A History of Higher Education in America*.

[4] *Op. cit.*, pp. 164-168.

[5] *Op. cit.*, "The Emergence of the University," pp. 146-167.

[6] John C. French, *A History of the University Founded by Johns Hopkins*, p. 64.

[7] *Fifth Annual Report of the Johns Hopkins University*, 1880, pp. 8-9.

[8] The "group system" which Gilman initiated at the Sheffield Scientific School is discussed in Chapter II, and in Chapter V. Its full development was to come at Hopkins.

[9] S. Willis Rudy, *op. cit.*, p. 165.

[10] Nothing approaching a full study has been made. Charles F. Thwing, *The American and the German University* attempts a comprehensive study of institutional, personal, and scholarly influences, but remains superficial. John A. Walz, *German Influence in*

Thwing fixed the number of American students who had attended German universities as 10,000. He further observed:

> The influence of the German university in America has taken on, in the course of a hundred years, at least three special and distinct forms; first, the advantage it has given to American youth matriculating in its classes; second, the influence which native Germans,—doctors of their universities,—have had as teachers in American Colleges; and, third,—of a wholly different zone—the influence of German university methods, forces, and conditions, over the teaching given and over the methods and conditions prevailing in American institutions. [1]

The first four American students who matriculated at a German university were the New Englanders G. Edward Everett, George Ticknor, George Bancroft, and Joseph Green Cogswell. They went to Göttingen, which was to be an educational mecca for American students in the first half of the nineteenth century. [2] "Beginning with Ticknor at Harvard, early in the nineteenth century, followed by Agassiz in the Lawrence Scientific School in 1846, J. P. Norton and J. A. Porter at Yale in the middle decades, Tappan during his presidency at the University of Michigan from 1852 to 1863, Andrew D. White during his professorship at Michigan from 1856 to 1862 and afterwards in the foundation of Cornell, a host of American scholars trained in German universities brought to bear on American University and college problems some of the methods and ideas with which they had become imbued while studying in Europe." [3] Essentially, the ideas were the educational concepts of *Lernfreiheit* and *Lehrfreiheit*, and the methods were what Friedrich Paulsen called "the German principle of the union of scientific investigation and scientific teaching." [4] For scientific investigation and scientific teaching there were few facilities in the American *ante-bellum* college, and it has been cautiously observed that in any assessment of the German influence on

---

American Education and Culture is only an essay. Some information is in Henry A. Pochmann, *German Culture in America*. A valuable discussion of the German educational concepts of *Lehrfreiheit* and *Lernfreiheit* is in Richard Hofstadter and Walter P. Metzger, *The Development of Academic Freedom in the United States*, pp. 383-407.

[1] Charles F. Thwing, *The American and German University*, pp. 10-11.

[2] See William Goodwin, "Remarks on the American colony at Göttingen," *Proceedings of the Massachusetts Historical Society*, XII, (Second Series) 1897-99, pp. 366-69. An incomplete but valuable list of the names of American students attending Halle, Berlin, Leipzig and Göttingen is in B. A. Hinsdale, "Notes on the History of Foreign Influences upon education in the United States," *Report of the Commissioner of Education*, I (1897-98), pp. 610-13.

[3] Mary Bynum Pierson, *Graduate Work in the South*, pp. 16-17.

[4] *German Universities: Their Character and Historical Development*, p. 15.

the American college of this period, it must be remembered that "The denominational college was neither eager for German-trained scholarship nor ready for German-trained scholars. German theology was too skeptical, German philology too specialized, German *Wissenschaftslehre* too strenuous." [1] Rudy's statement that "Familiarity with the advanced methods and materials to be found at Heidelberg or Berlin acted as a catalytic agent in speeding up the processes of university reform in the United States" [2] needs modification. Each of the colleges adapted, if at all, German ideals of graduate work to the situation peculiar to itself. "Institutional and faculty backgrounds varied as much as the insights and generalship of their leaders, and each faced a different combination of economic, political, sectarian and other cultural pressures." [3] Daniel Coit Gilman's experience happily illustrates the indigenous development and adaptation of the German ideal.

Gilman had known the German university at first hand. On July 20, 1854, he wrote to Henry Barnard from Berlin:

> The city however is now so warm that I should prefer being away from it during the summer, if I could make a good arrangement for doing so, especially as it is my plan, unless I am otherwise advised in an interview with you, to spend next winter in attending upon some of the hundred-fifty lectures which will then be delivered in this university. I have made up my mind that during the next year or two it will be best to forego the pleasure of gratifying a traveler's curiosity, so far as making a tour of Europe is concerned, but that it will be well to spend the time in gaining as far as possible information which will be of service in America. [4]

In 1856, he prepared for Henry Barnard's *American Journal of Education* a brief article entitled *German Universities*, in which, although it was essentially statistical, he applauded the facilities for advanced work in the German universities. [5] German technical education had particularly impressed Gilman. In his "Scientific Schools in Europe" (also written for Henry Barnard's *American Journal of Education*) he observed:

> Granting that our common schools, our colleges, and our "professional" institutions are, for the most part, excellent, are there not great wants still unsupplied? Even with the good beginnings which have been made in

---

[1] Richard Hofstadter and Walter P. Metzger, *The Development of Academic Freedom in the United States*, p. 368.

[2] *Op. cit.*, p. 167.

[3] Ernest V. Hollis, *Toward Improving Ph.D. Programs*, p. 13.

[4] Letter 3493, *Will S. Monroe Collection, loc. cit.*

[5] Vol. I, pp. 402-404. Although the article is anonymous, its authorship can be fixed as Gilman's by Letter 3969, *Will S. Monroe Collection, loc. cit.*

several places, what have we in our whole land to compare with the Scientific Schools of European countries? [1]

Much of what he observed in Europe Gilman put to early advantage at the Sheffield Scientific School at Yale; but here, eminently, the German ideas were adapted to the existing collegiate structure. No drastic conflict ensued. Gilman, himself, many years later, at the semi-centennial celebration of the Sheffield Scientific School, said: ". . . no conflict of studies has been heard of; no hostility between science and letters; no warfare between science and religion. The Sheffield Scientific School has always stood for the idea of a liberal education . . . ." [2]

In his inauguration address as President of the Johns Hopkins University, Gilman makes further clear his eclectic use of his German experience:

> At a distance, Germany seems the one country where educational problems are determined; not so, on a nearer look. The thoroughness of the German mind, its desire for perfection in every detail, and its philosophical aptitudes are well illustrated by the controversies now in vogue in the land of universities. In following, as we are prone to do in educational matters, the example of Germany, we must beware lest we accept what is there cast off; lest we introduce faults as well as virtues, defects with excellence. [3]

For Johns Hopkins, Gilman recommended attention to the biological sciences, especially those basic to medicine, and what he called the modern humanities: ". . . the study of man in his relationship to society—history, jurisprudence, political economy, legislation, taxation; the study of the earth sciences: geodetical, typographical, meteorological, geological." [4] That these emphases were not copied from Germany is made quite clear from the observations of the great German democrat, Friedrich Paulsen, who had received the Ph.D. from the University of Berlin in 1870. He testifies to the narrow character of the graduate program at Berlin at that time:

> Convinced that I ought to cultivate at least some acquaintance with the natural sciences, I attended a course of lectures on physics by Helmholtz, who had recently accepted a call to Berlin. What I was out for—fundamental concepts and comprehensive ideas—he did not dispense. [5]

---

[1] Vol. I, pp. 326-27.

[2] *University Problems in the United States*, p. 132.

[3] *Addresses at the Inauguration of Daniel C. Gilman as President of the Johns Hopkins University*, pp. 28-29.

[4] *Ibid.*, pp. 43-44.

[5] *An Autobiography*, p. 214.

Although Paulsen fared somewhat better in chemistry and physiology, he continues:

> I should have liked to hear lectures on geography but the equipment of the University was extremely unsatisfactory. I tried to attend a course on German geography by Müller, but I found his lectures insufferably tedious, without any apparatus for purposes of demonstration—nothing but a bare enumeration of names. Nor were those of Kiepert, the learned historical geographer and designer of admirable maps, on a higher level.
> ... Generally speaking the equipment and program of the University left much to be desired. There were no lectures on history of modern art, nor even modern German literature—with the exception of a course of lectures on *Faust*. The other modern languages and literatures were no better off; it was not until the later 1870's that chairs began to be established for them. In those early days they were considered as lying outside the limits of strictly scientific work, Greek and Roman literature alone regarded as amenable to scientific treatment and worthy of it. [1]

It is significant to note that Gilman encountered at Johns Hopkins none of the difficulties which destroyed Tappan at Michigan, and hampered the efforts of Hall at Clark, White at Cornell, and Harper at Chicago. His use of the German *Minerva* was representative of his moderation and his eclecticism, both of which assured him success. ". . . the installation of a German university in Baltimore as such was neither desired nor attempted. What was desired and attempted, and also what was achieved, was the adoption of those elements of the German university which were, and are, worthiest, and which were adapted to the scholastic and other conditions of the new world." [2]

GRADUATE STUDIES IN ANTE-BELLUM AMERICA

The fullest account of graduate education in America before the Civil War is the monograph by Storr. [3] Storr found that "Of the efforts to found universities in the United States, those which provided in some way for graduate work fall into three distinguisable but overlapping classes." [4] The first of these advanced the idea of a university as a repository of all knowledge, the assemblage in one place of all the pre-eminent

---

[1] *Ibid.*, pp. 214-215. The deficiencies of the German universities seem to have been missed in George Haines, *German Influence Upon English Education and Science*, 1800-1866. The adulatory temper of Thwing (*The American and the German University*) precludes even an awareness of them.

[2] Franklin, *op. cit.*, p. 196.

[3] *The Beginnings of Graduate Education in America*.

[4] *Ibid.*, p. 131.

academic talent and some of the material resources which the multiplication of small colleges had scattered up and down the land. The second of these proposed that the university was to consist of an undergraduate college to which were added distinct graduate courses or graduate schools, possibly with facilities for undergraduate and graduate non-matriculated students. This resembled the German university and the German gymnasium but was comparable to neither. The third recommendation proposed an expansion of the subject matter of the liberal arts course and a loosening up of the machinery of instruction so as to give the college the intellectual stature and freedom of a university. "There was, however, no single, dominant idea of the American university." [1] Gilman subscribed to the second of these proposals, and this proposal was to prove pragmatically successful, despite the strident criticism leveled at it by Rudy:

> The result was most unfortunate. A German-type post graduate university granting the Ph. D. and having as its main purpose the training of scholars was super-imposed upon, and arbitrarily linked to, an English type undergraduate college granting the baccalaureate and seeking to provide a general education. Out of this has arisen the serious confusion of methods and purposes which bedevils American higher learning in the twentieth century. [2]

Yet, with some pertinency, Storr quotes Gilman's words at the outset of the Johns Hopkins experiment: "We begin our work ... after costly ventures of which we reap the lessons, while others bear the loss." [3]

Gilman's own experience, following his graduation from Yale College in 1852, is typical of the state of graduate education in *ante-bellum* America:

> Opportunities for advanced, not professional, studies were then scanty in this country. In the older colleges certain graduate courses were attended by a small number of followers—but the teachers were for the most part absorbed with undergraduate teaching, and could give but little time to the few who sought their guidance. After taking the degree of Bachelor of Arts in Yale College ... I remained a year at New Haven as a resident graduate. President Woolsey, whom I consulted, asked me to read Rau's political economy and come and tell him its contents; I did not accept the challenge. I asked Professor Hadley if I might read Greek with him; he declined my proposal. Professor Porter did give me some guidance,

---

[1] *Ibid.*, p. 130.

[2] *Op. cit.*, p. 169

[3] Storr, *op. cit.*, p. 134.

especially in German. I had many talks of an inspiring nature with Professor Dana—but, on the whole, I think that the year was wasted. [1]

The first earned Ph.D. degree was given at Yale in 1861 to candidates who had devoted at least two years to a course of work in the departments of philosophy and arts. In 1860, on appeal from the Sheffield Scientific School professors, the Yale Corporation took the pioneering step of authorizing the degree of Doctor of Philosophy so as "to retain in this country many young men, and especially students of Science who now resort to German Universities . . ." [2] In this action Gilman took no small part, and in the initiation of graduate studies, Gilman acknowledged the early example of Yale: "Here let me remind you of a fact not generally known, though clearly recorded. As far back as 1814 resident graduates were enrolled as a distinct class on the Yale catalogue, and in 1819 and 1820 the numbers so enrolled were thirty and thirty-one. This shows that the beginning of graduate studies in this university [Yale] antedates by more than thirty years the department of philosophy and the arts." [3] By 1873, Yale University had awarded twenty-three earned doctorates, above 90 per cent of the American total up to that time. [4] For the rest of the American academic world, the Ph.D. and the rise of graduate education were to be largely post Civil War matters, [5] and most were to await the example of Gilman at the Johns Hopkins University.

---

[1] *Launching of a University*, pp. 8-9.

[2] Quoted in George W. Pierson, *Yale College*, p. 50.

[3] *University Problems in the United States*, p. 125.

[4] Ernest V. Hollis, *op. cit.*, p. 10.

[5] At the University of Pennsylvania the Ph.D. was first conferred as an earned degree in 1870, and three years later Harvard conferred it and the doctor of science degree. Columbia first conferred the degree in 1875 in the School of Mines; Princeton gave the degree first in 1879, Brown University first in 1889. See Walton C. John, *op. cit.*, Chapter II. For graduate beginnings in the South, see Mary B. Pierson, *op. cit*

CHAPTER TWO

DANIEL COIT GILMAN AT YALE (1855-1872)

At the semi-centennial celebration of the Sheffield Scientific School of Yale University in October, 1897, Daniel Coit Gilman delivered the main address. In this commemorative address, Gilman acknowledged his own indebtedness to Yale, and particularly the formative influences he had known in his long tenure at the Sheffield Scientific School:

> For one such institution, now celebrating its majority, permit me to acknowledge with filial gratitude the impulses, lessons, warnings, and encouragements derived from the Sheffield Scientific School, and publicly admit that much of the health and strength of the Johns Hopkins University is due to early and repeated drafts upon the life-giving springs of New Haven. [1]

In line with his own interests, Gilman emphasized the contributions of Yale University and its Scientific School to American graduate education:

> Certainly Yale and Sheffield are entitled to the credit of introducing among American Institutions the degree of Doctor of Philosophy, demanding for it a high standard of attainments, and never bestowing the honor (not in a single case, so far as I can remember) by any irregular promotion. This degree has proved a powerful incentive to scholarship [graduate education] in this and other universities, and the list of *laureati Yalenses*, beginning, in 1861, with three distinguished names, soon followed by one of the highest renown, is a list to be proud of. [2]

For Gilman, the progress of science in America in the nineteenth century was capsuled in the history of the Sheffield Scientific School. With this progress, hand in hand, went the extension of educational facilities and the initiation of graduate studies. In the history of graduate instruction at Yale, [3] one was indistinguishable from the other, and Gilman was paying Sheffield the compliment it deserved. During the progress of the

---

[1] *University Problems in the United States*, pp. 146-147. The holograph ms. is in the *Gilman Family Papers*, Yale University Archive.

[2] *Ibid.*, pp. 134-135. The first three to receive the Ph. D. at Yale were Eugene Schuyler, James M. Whiton and Arthur W. Wright. The person of renown to whom Gilman refers was Josiah W. Gibbs (1839-1903), noted mathematical physicist, who took his doctorate in 1863.

[3] George W. Pierson, *op. cit.*, pp. 49-50.

scientific school at Yale, ". . . not a word was spoken in disparagement of classical culture, nor a word of religious controversy." [1] Looking forward to a second-half century of growth and advancement, with the typical scientific optimism of nineteenth century America, Gilman closed his discourse with a line from Laplace: "Ce que nous connaissons est peu; ce que nous ignorons est immense." [2]

Following his graduation from Yale in 1852, Gilman had traveled in Europe. [3] On his return to the United States in the latter part of 1855, he went immediately to New Haven. Until 1872 he was to be attached to Yale College in two official capacities, both in a measure interdependent. From 1856-1865 he served successively as assistant director and director of the Yale College Library. In 1863, he was appointed professor of physical geography which he held until his resignation in 1872 to accept the presidency of the University of California. Gilman's professorship was in the Sheffield Scientific School. Thus, almost fortuitously, Gilman found himself the double heir of educational change and advancement. It was in the sciences that instruction was undergoing change, and it was in the new schools of science that the graduate impulse was being strongly felt. [4] As librarian, he early sensed the need for the expansion of facilities, and worked tirelessly for a library that would permit practicable research and advanced studies.

The Yale College of Gilman was the Yale of President Theodore Dwight Woolsey (1801-1899) whose presidency extended from 1846 to 1871. By Woolsey's time, Yale had long since ceased to be a simple college. During President Ezra Stiles' administration (1778-1795), a "Plan of a University" had been proposed which would have added the four advanced schools of law, medicine, divinity, and the arts and sciences, and further proposed the creation of four professorships. Even though Stiles failed to get a single one, [5] his successor, Timothy Dwight (1795-1817), laid the foundation of the Medical Institution, the Law School, and the Department of Theology—thus providing for the three

---

[1] *University Problems in the United States*, p. 149.

[2] *Ibid.*, p. 148.

[3] See pp. 2-6, *supra*.

[4] Storr, *op. cit.*, pp. 46-47. "By the mid-Forties, Harvard and Yale thought they saw a way out in the creation of departments of arts and sciences independent of the undergraduate course but answerable to the college authorities. These departments did not immediately prosper and were eventually overshadowed by the scientific schools which developed from them."

[5] G. H. Nettleton, ed., *The Book of the Yale Pageant*, pp. 131-132.

professional schools of the traditional Continental university. [1] This was an important step forward.

Under Jeremiah Day (President, 1817-1846), with the assistance of Professors Benjamin Silliman and James L. Kingsley, further gains had been achieved. [2] In 1832 the completion of the Trumbull Gallery had established at Yale the first college-connected art museum in the United States. Between 1842 and 1846 the library collections had been strengthened by purchase from Europe, and Edward C. Herrick was appointed first full-time librarian.

Further gains were made during the administration of Theodore Dwight Woolsey. In early 1846, just before the inauguration of Woolsey, professorships of agricultural chemistry and applied chemistry were created "for the purpose of giving instruction to graduates and others not members of the undergraduate classes" [3] by the laboratory method. In 1847 a Department of Philosophy and the Arts was set up to include advanced work in the arts, together with the sciences not already being taught, and "their application to the arts." [4] From its opening the School of Applied Chemistry was included under Philosophy and the Arts, thus giving it responsibility at both the graduate and undergraduate levels. Although the instruction was at first individual and unsystematic, course programs were established and a School of Engineering was added in 1852. These scientific efforts were successful, and in 1854 the schools were grouped together and named the Yale Scientific School. In 1861, following the various endowments of Joseph Earl Sheffield, the name was changed to the Sheffield Scientific School. [5] The informal graduate instruction in philosophy, history, language, and pure science had attracted only a few students. In 1860, on appeal from the Scientific School professors, the Yale Corporation took the pioneering step of authorizing the degree of Doctor of Philosophy. [6] Thus, it was in the new science that graduate education first knew real development in New Haven, but George W. Pierson cautions that it was not to be "until the late 1880's that graduate instruction became important in New Haven." [7]

---

[1] George W. Pierson, *Yale College*, p. 49.

[2] *Ibid.*, pp. 49-50. See also, Franklin B. Dexter, *Sketch of the History of Yale University*, p. 81.

[3] Quoted in George W. Pierson, *op. cit.*, p. 49.

[4] *Ibid.*, p. 50.

[5] Russell H. Chittenden, *History of the Sheffield Scientific School*, II, pp. 88-91.

[6] *Ibid.*, II, pp. 35-38.

[7] G. W. Pierson, "American Universities in the Nineteenth Century: the Formative Period," *The Modern University*, ed. by Margaret Clapp, p. 74.

Why did Yale, which was to grant the first Ph. D. in 1861, lose its initiative? To this question there appears to be one answer: what Pierson has called "the conservatism of Noah Porter."[1] Throughout most of the administration of Theodore Dwight Woolsey there is easily discerned the gradual remaking of Yale College into a coordinated university. In 1871, the process, in essence, stopped. Noah Porter, who was to be President of Yale from 1871 to 1886, was the champion of the conservatives, whose traditional concepts of education he had defended in *The American Colleges and the American Public* (1869). "To Porter the word University sounded pretentious. Instinctively he preferred the modest old name, Yale College. With simple fervor he clung to the immemorial mission of educating young men to be citizens. Having offered graduate instruction himself, he questioned whether the American public was yet ready for real graduate schools. And he could not bring himself to a wholehearted belief in the Scientific School or the newer subjects of instruction."[2] Porter, himself, was willing to admit of the Sheffield Scientific School that "It has certainly done its share, as a constituent of the so-called department of philosophy and the arts to awaken an interest in and to provide instruction for an efficient post-graduate department, or a University proper in connection with Yale College," but he added, ". . .the practical spirit and the literary or scholastic spirit are both good, but they are incompatible. If commingled, they are both spoiled."[3] If Yale had hoped to develop its research and scholarship through postgraduate work, such plans had to await the retirement of President Porter. Without its own funds and professorships, unable to arouse the enthusiasm of Yale's graduates and its administration, and "not able at first to enlist the undergraduate faculties in much specialized investigation and instruction, the Graduate School proved slow to develop. . . . It lost the lead to Johns Hopkins and Harvard."[4] It is significant that Daniel Coit Gilman, who had worked tirelessly for the coordinated university in New Haven, chose to resign early in President Porter's administration. In a sense, Gilman's resignation was an augury of an administration which gave "the larger Yale a delayed and rather one-sided development."[5]

---

[1] George W. Pierson, *Yale College*, p. 57.

[2] *Ibid.*, pp. 57-58.

[3] *The American Colleges and the American Public*, pp. 261, 263.

[4] George W. Pierson, *Yale College*, p. 68.

[5] *Ibid.*, p. 60. In a letter (April 1, 1958) to the author, Professor Richard J. Storr of the University of Chicago writes: "It is striking that several of the men who are

GILMAN AS LIBRARIAN

Gilman became assistant librarian in the fall of 1856 [1]. The post of librarian was held by Edward Claudius Herrick (1811-1862), an entomologist and astronomer whose library duties were largely incidental to his teaching. [2] Herrick had become librarian in 1843, for the most part replacing James Luce Kingsley (1778-1852), professor of Hebrew, Greek, Latin, and ecclesiastical history, and who had served the library as director since 1805. [3] Although Kingsley had served the library well, a great deal remained to be done. [4] When Herrick resigned his post as college librarian in 1858, Gilman was appointed to take his place. From 1856 to 1865 Gilman struggled to improve the unsatisfactory conditions in the library, but in most respects, he failed.

A good contemporary picture of the library is given by Benjamin Silliman (1779-1864), first professor of chemistry and natural history at Yale. The library was open but five hours a day. The buildings consisted of one large hall for the college library proper, with two smaller halls for the Brothers and Linonian libraries connected with by corridors on either side. These society libraries in earlier days had been a very important factor in college life, and in Gilman's time, together outnumbered the college library proper by some eight thousand volumes. In the summer time, when both halls could be used, the building gave ample room for both librarians and readers. In winter, however, when the main hall was without heat, and only one of the corridors heated, this one room served both as a workshop for the librarian and assistant and as a reading room for professor and student alike. [5]

---

thought of as great university-builders (Gilman, White, and Harper) had roots in New Haven. One might argue that these men became university-builders in reaction against Yale, were it not that Gilman and Harper at least appear to have felt little or no alienation from Yale."

[1] There is no history of the Yale Library. Most of the materials of this section have been found in the *Gilman Family Papers* at Yale, and in the archives of the Yale Library made available to the author by Professor James T. Babb, director of the Yale Libraries.

[2] Harris E. Starr, "Edward Claudius Herrick," *Dictionary of American Biography*, XVIII, pp. 286-287.

[3] Harry M. Hubbell, "James Luce Kingsley," *Dictionary of American Biography*, IX, pp. 411-412.

[4] Kingsley was responsible for great gains. The library increased its holdings fivefold during his tenure. Most of 1845, Kingsley spent in Europe making further acquisitions for the library. Kingsley wrote about the library in articles published in the *American Quarterly Register*, August, 1835 and February, 1836; and in the *American Biblical Repository*, July, 1841 and January, 1842.

[5] George P. Fisher, *The Life of Benjamin Silliman*, II, pp. 46-47.

In every way, the library was hampered by the lack of funds, and its use was restricted by many regulations. The President, Fellows, members of the faculty, graduates resident at the college, members of the theological, medical, and philosophical departments, and Juniors and Seniors (these on Mondays and Thursdays) were allowed to use the library and draw books. Both graduate and undergraduate students had to pay for the use of books; twelve cents was charged for each folio or quarto volume, and six cents for an octavo or smaller volume. [1] No provision was made for an assistant, and the library budget was arbitrarily fixed, and usually most meagre. [2] The history of the library was a history of its championship by its curator. [3] Gilman championed many reforms both physical and fiscal, if with little success.

Most of Gilman's suggested reforms are contained in three reports he made to the Yale Corporation in 1862, 1864 and 1865. [4] He pointed out the complete lack of heat in the winter which made the library inhabitable six months of the year. He asked that he be relieved of paying the salary of his assistant, and he further noted and reaffirmed the need for the library's expansion and improvement to meet the faculty and student requirements. The imagination and leadership of Gilman are clearly seen in an extract from the last of these reports:

> For all these purposes [suggested reforms] we need to raise at least $ 100,000; $ 200,000 would not be too large a sum. To secure this amount we must appeal to enlightened friends of learning and especially to the pride and the interests of New Haven. The Library is the home of all our scholars, whatever their creed, residence, education or political principles. It is freely opened to all who wish to consult it without the slightest charge. The number who thus make use of it has already transcended our powers to accomodate, or our ability to supply the wants which the college and the library have created. The want is pressing. In scarcely any direction would an expansion of the college resources be so useful to the interests of learning, and the attractiveness of New Haven as a residence for literary men. [5]

Unfortunately, there was no response.

---

[1] Franklin B. Dexter, *Documentary History of Yale University*, p. 133.

[2] See *Report of the Treasurer of Yale College* for the years of Gilman's tenure (1856-65).

[3] Daniel C. Gilman, "Bishop Berkeley's gifts to Yale College," *Papers of the New Haven Historical Society*, I (1865), p. 153.

[4] Extracts from the *Corporation Records* are in the *Historical Register of Yale University*, 1701-1937.

[5] *Corporation Records*, July 1865.

Gilman recognized that a good, serviceable, and adequate library was indispensable. As early as 1860 he minutely described the resources of the Yale College Library and found it inadequate. [1] In 1869 (after his resignation as librarian) his interest was unabated; he wrote: "It is the scholars who make a college; not bricks and mortar. It is endowments which secure the time and services of scholars. Next to scholars books are essential, but Yale College has not a dollar on hand to buy books for the next two years, its scanty library income having already been expended in advance. Will not your discussions respecting the college lead some of the wealthy men of Norwich to look into the real defects of the college and devise some liberal measures for their removal?" [2]

When, in the autumn of 1864, Gilman found that the salaries of all the other officers of the college had been raised except that of the librarian, he decided to resign as librarian. He resigned reluctantly, and waited some months before sending official notice to President Woolsey:

> I presume it will not take you wholly by surprise to learn that I desire to be released from the office of College Librarian. I have come to this conclusion with hesitation and regret, but the truth is that after nine years' service in this capacity, I am quite discouraged.
>
> Improvements and changes which have long been talked of as essential to the progress of the library, the increase of funds for the purchase of books, the employment of permanent assistance, the introduction of a heating apparatus, the opening of a quiet reading room, the consolidation of the Society libraries, and other minor alterations, seem to be no nearer than when I entered on the office of Librarian. I am aware that the poverty of the College is a standing reason for the delay of improvements, but this does not lessen my disappointment.
>
> Moreover I am not able to support a family on the salary paid to the librarian, especially with the reduction in it, which I have felt compelled to make ever since my appointment, for the payment of an assistant. I am under the constant necessity of seeking other employment to meet my current expenses.
>
> On the other hand attractive and remunerative occupations of a literary

---

[1] "Yale College Library," *University Quarterly*, IV (October, 1860), pp. 131-34. Gilman estimated the holdings as 67.000 books and 7000 unbound pamphlets. The article also contains a description of the library's special collections, with a view toward possible research in these collections.

[2] "The Yale College Library," *Norwich Bulletin*, III (July, 1869), p. 80. For Gilman's awareness of the need of special libraries for university seminars, and for his conversant familiarity with library methods and terminology see his dedicatory address at the opening of the Sage Library of Cornell University. *University Problems in the United States*, pp. 237-261.

character are continually offering themselves for which I long to secure the necessary time. When I add to these considerations, that my health has already suffered and physicians remind me frequently that it will be still more impaired by continued exposure to the cold and dampness which prevail in the library much of the year,—I think you cannot wonder at my proposed withdrawal.

Will you therefore do me the favor to present my resignation of the office of librarian to the Corporation of the College at their next meeting. I trust it is unnecessary for me to assure you of my undiminished interest in the college and my sincere desire to promote its welfare. [1]

President Woolsey's acceptance of the resignation is interesting because it suggests that there is little likelihood of any changes being made in the library; its categoric rejection of Gilman's proposed changes further notes how pioneering some of Gilman's reforms were:

In regard to your leaving your place my thoughts have shaped themselves thus: the place [the library] does not possess that importance which a man of active mind would naturally seek; and the college cannot, now or hereafter, while its circumstances remain as they are, give it greater prominence. With the facilities which you possess of making your way in the world, you can in all probability secure for yourself, while yet young and enterprising, a more prominent and a more varied, as well as stirring [sic] employment. I feel sure that you will not long content yourself, with your nature, in your present vocation, and therefore I regard it better, if you must leave, to leave now, better I mean for yourself; for the college, of course, will be a loser, by losing your knowledge of books, and capacity to serve its interests. [2]

Gilman's resignation was officially accepted in July 1865, and in the same month he prepared, for presentation to the Yale Corporation, a faculty petition urging the formation of a committee which would study the reforms he had proposed. [3]

GILMAN AND THE SHEFFIELD SCIENTIFIC SCHOOL

Gilman's first connection with the Sheffield Scientific School was early in 1856 when he was employed to raise funds for the school. [4] Although he was not appointed as Professor of Physical Geography in the Sheffield Scientific School until 1863, his associations with Professor Benjamin Silliman and Professor James Dwight Dana were very

---

[1] Gilman to President Woolsey, June 1, 1865. *Gilman Family Papers.* Yale University Archive.

[2] President Woolsey to Gilman, June 10, 1865. *Ibid.*

[3] *Yale Corporation Records*, July 24, 1865.

[4] R. H. Chittenden, *op. cit.*, I, p. 41.

close, [1] and, from his strategic position in the library, he chose to serve the research needs of the new science. [2] From 1856 to 1872 Gilman served the Sheffield Scientific School in one capacity or another. In all of these years he served as apologist and educational theorist for the new science education; from 1863 to 1872 he served the school as its Professor of Physical Geography, and from 1866 to 1872 he was secretary of the school's governing board. [3] "Gilman transferred his ambition and fertile imagination from the stagnant librarianship of the College to the teaching of modern subjects and the particular promotion of the Scientific School. In this endeavor Brush, Treasurer of the School, proved an invaluable partner. Gilman was quick, eloquent, and ingenious; Brush had slow judgment and great tenacity. The one started the nails, the other drove them home." [4]

As educational theorist for the new science, Gilman published in 1856, largely at Professor Dana's behest, [5] a small pamphlet entitled, *Proposed Plan for the Complete Organization of the School of Science Connected with Yale College.* The appendix to this pamphlet, "Notes on the Schools of Science of Europe" is a verbatim reprint of his "Scientific Schools in Europe" which had appeared in Henry Barnard's *American Journal of Education.* [6] This important pamphlet, which seems to have been missed by Storr [7] and by Chittenden, [8] is a clear call for the expansion

---

[1] Gilman's brother, Edward, had married one of Professor Silliman's daughters. Professor Dana was Silliman's son-in-law. See Gilman, *Life of James Dwight Dana*, p. 152.

[2] See in this connection an interesting letter of Gilman to Andrew D. White on Gilman's acquisition of the Hillhouse library of mathematical books for the Yale College Library. Franklin, *op. cit.*, p. 91. Franklin cites no deposit for the letter, and it is not in the *Gilman Family Papers* at Yale.

[3] R. H. Chittenden, *op. cit.*, I, Chapter III. See also Charles H. Warren, "The Sheffield Scientific School from 1847 to 1947," *The Centennial of the Sheffield Scientific School*, ed. by George A. Baitsell, p. 158.

[4] George W. Pierson, *op. cit.*, p. 51. George Jarvis Brush had been appointed Professor of Metallurgy in 1855. He served as director of the Sheffield Scientific School from 1872 to 1898. See George P. Merrill, "George Jarvis Brush," *Dictionary of American Biography*, III, pp. 187-189.

[5] Franklin, *op. cit.*, pp. 41-42.

[6] Vol. I (1856), pp. 326-327. "What have we in our whole land to compare with the Scientific Schools of European countries?"

[7] Storr, *op. cit.*, p. 57. Storr does mention an article by Dana, "Science and Scientific Schools," *American Journal of Education*, II (1856), p. 374, which called for support of the Yale Scientific School and, in essence, repeats the arguments of Gilman's pamphlet. Gilman was responsible for the printing of the article. See Gilman to [Barnard], March 8 [1856], *Will S. Monroe Collection of Henry Barnard Mss.*, *loc. cit.* The letter is unfiled.

[8] R. H. Chittenden, *op. cit.*, I, Chapter III.

of the teaching in science at the Yale Scientific School, and for the establishment of the Ph. D. degree. Gilman asked that there be ". . . full and vigorous study through the relatively new Scientific School, under its professors and other instructors, of, viz: Mathematics, Civil and Dynamical Engineering, Analytical and Descriptive Geometry, Astronomy, Pure and Applied Chemistry, Agriculture, Mechanics, Physics, Metallurgy, Zoology, Botany, Geology, Paleontology, Physical and Political Geography, Linguistics, French and German, besides the English Language and Literature." [1] He further recommended that the two year course in the Scientific School be changed to a three year course in the undergraduate section, [2] and that the degree of Doctor of Philosophy be given only in cases "of high proficiency after a rigid examination." [3] In the pamphlet, too, he emphasizes the idea that it is important to gain a very thorough knowledge of what is being done in foreign institutions, not to copy their methods but to adapt them to local conditions and to the wants of America "as acknowledged by practical men." [4] He also proposed that the two undergraduate colleges (the Scientific School and the College) be put on the same footing. This last proposal was most radical, for as Pierson has pointed out: "But they [the students of the College] looked down on the Scientific School because it was scientific and because it was easy, because it had no dormitories or adequate social system, and its men were sometimes of lesser ability or from more limited backgrounds." [5]

Of course, Gilman's proposals were not immediately adopted. Yet, by 1871 most of the proposals of Gilman had been carried out. Direct acknowledgement of the achievement of Gilman's reforms was made by James Dwight Dana in 1871. "The scheme which has so far been carried out was presented by the writer, speaking for others, in an address before the Alumni, at Commencement in 1856—fifteen years ago, when the Scientific School was struggling on under a few unpaid professors." [6] And, the essence of Gilman's point in his *Proposed Plan*

---

[1] *Proposed Plan for the Complete Organization* . . . , p. 3.

[2] *Ibid.*, p. 5.

[3] Gilman does not elaborate on the amount of time to be spent in study for the degree, or the requirements for candidacy.

[4] *Proposed Plan for the Complete Organization* . . . , p. 6.

[5] George W. Pierson, *op. cit.*, p. 64.

[6] James Dwight Dana, *The New Haven University: What it is, and What it Requires*, p. 4. The *Address* which Dana mentions is reprinted in his article in Barnard's *American Journal of Education*, II (1856), p. 374. It is this article to which Storr refers, *op. cit.*, p. 57. Dana's phrase, "speaking for others," is obviously an allusion to Gilman.

for the Complete Organization . . ., that these reforms be adapted to local conditions and the wants of America, is reaffirmed by Dana: "Our action shows (and hence we need not hesitate to say it) that we regard this as the best University in the land; that is, the best, not for Germany, but for existing America." [1]

By 1871, three year undergraduate programs in agriculture, natural history, premedical studies, and a "Select Course in Scientific and Literary Studies" had been added to the applied chemistry and civil and mechanical engineering with which the Scientific School had started. [2] In 1861, endowed by Joseph Earl Sheffield, [3] the school was renamed the Sheffield Scientific School, and as Pierson observes: "While the need of the nation was for both scholars and engineers, the public response had been so one-sided that what had started as a department of graduate studies, with a chemical laboratory attached, had grown into a substantial undergraduate school of applied sciences, with only meagre graduate extensions." [4] Yet, the beginnings had been made and Gilman's advocacy of the institution of the Ph.D. degree was realized in 1860, when, on appeal from the Scientific School Professors, the Yale Corporation took the pioneering step of authorizing the doctorate.

It is strange, in view of the historical importance of the institution of the Ph.D. at Yale in *ante-bellum* American graduate education, that Pierson and Storr only most briefly quote from the appeal made to the Yale Corporation by Scientific School professors. [5] Only in its entirety can the full importance of the memorial (such it is called) be realized, for by instituting the Ph.D., Yale "systematized graduate study, thus realizing the original promise of the department opened in 1847." [6] In 1869, President Charles W. Eliot of Harvard University was willing to admit that it was in this action (the institution of the Ph.D.) that Yale parted company with Harvard. [7]

---

[1] *Ibid.*, p. 5. Dana was asking for the consolidation of the reforms, and there is, in the last paragraph of the pamphlet, an augury of Gilman's departure for the University of California. "Seven professors of the University have within two years been invited to other positions in the country . . . ." *Ibid.*, p. 8.

[2] Pierson, *op. cit.*, pp. 51-52. See also Chittenden, *op. cit.*, I, Chapter III.

[3] There is no biography of Sheffield. See *Papers of the New Haven Historical Society*, VII (1908), 313-323 for an important unsigned article. See also, Chittenden, *op. cit.*, I, Chapter III.

[4] George W. Pierson, *op. cit.*, p. 50.

[5] *Ibid.* Storr, *op. cit.*, p. 57.

[6] Storr, *op. cit.*, pp. 57-58.

[7] Charles W. Eliot, "The New Education," *Atlantic Monthly*, XXIII (1869), p. 208.

"To the President and Fellows of Yale College, the faculty of the scientific school respectfully recommend [sic] to your honourable body the institution of a more complete course of scientific instruction extending through the three years in the chemical section of the scientific school.

Candidates for admission to the chemical section are examined in arithmetic, algebra, geometry, plane trigonometry and the departments of natural philosophy and chemistry. Starting from this point it is proposed to devote the 1st year of the higher course which is now recommended to the further pursuit of natural philosophy and the mathematics, including surveying, descriptive geometry, and linear perspective with geometrical drawings, analytical geometry and mathematical crystallography and also to the study of French and German languages. The 2nd and 3rd years, physics, chemistry, minerology, crystallography, geology, and the application of science to the arts. A higher course in these branches than has hitherto been given will be rendered practicable by the mathematical and other training that the student will have acquired in the first year.

The faculty further request [sic] of the Board that the degree of *Doctor of Philosophy*, be installed and in accordance with the usage of the German universities be conferred on those students who have successfully pursued the above named higher course of scientific study. [1] It is also here suggested that the same degree of *Doctor of Philosophy* may hereafter with propriety and in accordance with the usage of foreign universities be conferred for high attainments in mathematics or philology or such other branches as may be taught in the Department of Philosophy and the Arts. [2]

This degree has acquired a value by long usage which no new degree

---

[1] It would appear that the A.B. was not considered prerequisite for the Ph. D. candidates. However, in the first published statement regarding the doctor's degree, the *Yale Catalogue* 1860-61, it is noted that "all persons who have not previously received a degree furnishing evidence of acquiantance with the Latin and Greek languages will be required before presenting themselves for the final examination for the doctor's degree to pass a satisfactory examination in these languages, or in other studies (not included in their advanced course) which shall be accepted as equivalent by the faculty." Obviously, it was assumed that in most cases students in the higher course of study leading to the Ph.D. would have had training equal to that which was required for the A.B.

[2] This is strange in view of the bitter feelings between the College and the Scientific School. See George W. Pierson, *op. cit.*, pp. 49-57.

would possess. [1] Its institution would remove a disadvantage under which our Department of Philosophy and the Arts labors in comparison with similar departments of German universities. The degree which they offer is an inducement which we do not present. Its establishment here would, in the opinion of the faculty, enable us to retain in this country many young men, and especially students of science who now resort to German universities for advantages of study no greater than we are able to afford. It is proposed that this degree of *Doctor of Philosophy* be conferred on students of the scientific school on the following conditions:

1) that they shall have pursued their studies for the year next preceding their examination for the degree in this institution.

2) That they should have passed a satisfactory examination in all of the studies of the above named higher course.

3) That they shall at the time of their examination present a written thesis which shall be approved by the faculty giving the results of an original chemical or physical investigation.

All of which is respectfully submitted by the faculty of the scientific school.

[signed] John A. Porter

Dean of the Faculty of the Scientific School

Yale College [2]
July 21, 1860

In view of the clarity and cogency of Gilman's proposed reforms in his *Proposed Plan for the Complete Organization . . .*, we can reasonably assume that he took part (perhaps, with James Dwight Dana, a major part) in the drafting of the above memorial. The memorial became a blueprint for the establishment of graduate programs in many agitated American faculties in the 1860's and the 1870's. [3] It was the blueprint which Gilman carried with him to the University of California and to the

---

[1] This may be an allusion to the Sc. D. which had been granted *causa honoris* at Yale and other universities. See Stephen E. Epler, *Honorary Degrees*, pp. 124-128.

[2] *Yale Corporation Records*, July 24, 1860. Porter (1822-1866) was Professor of Organic Chemistry. He had studied with Liebig at the University of Giessen. See Lyman C. Newell, "John Addison Porter," *Dictionary of American Biography*, XV, pp. 96-97.

[3] "Yale's success pointed the way to improvements 'which ought soon to be made at all the more important universities, which will then better deserve their ambitious title'." Storr, *op. cit.*, p. 58. Storr is quoting from Charles W. Eliot's "The New Education," *loc. cit.* See also Mary B. Pierson, *op. cit.*, p. 16.

Johns Hopkins, an influence which he felicitously termed "the early and repeated drafts upon the life-giving springs of New Haven." [1]

Gilman recognized that, if the graduate impulse had its origin in the new science, its total emphasis must not lie therein, and its orientation, perforce, had to be both scientific and humanistic. [2] He had made this point in his *Proposed Plan for the Complete Organization . . .*, and he made it again in 1867 in *Our National Schools of Science*. In this publication, after noting that the scientific schools were in a formative state and that nobody could foretell exactly what they would become, he cautiously observed that they [the schools of science] "were a very significant spirit of the age, a manifestation of the desire for an advanced education on some other basis than the literature of Greece and Rome." [3] But, if the "constant effort should be made to educate men of science, able to investigate, competent to teach, proficient in specialties, . . . the predominace which will of necessity be given to scientific studies renders it important to be watchful that the study of Latin, at least to the extent of reading Cicero and Virgil with ready accuracy, is, on many accounts, of great importance. The critical study of English is indispensable, and a scientific man is not equipped for his work in life without some knowledge of French and German. Heretofore, the complaint has been that the Classics were the only means of liberal education. Henceforward, science will offer its aids to intellectual culture in organized schools. Both classes of institutions will flourish side by side, and each will be strong in the other's strength." [4] Unfortunately, the *rapport* between Yale College and the Sheffield Scientific School which Gilman saw and advocated as the symbolic marriage of humanism and the new science did not take place at Yale until the great re-organization of 1918. [5]

In September, 1866, Gilman was elected by the governing board of the Sheffield Scientific School as their secretary. [6] In this capacity, he wrote seven reports, the last of which appeared in 1872, just before his departure for California. In these reports the constant theme is the struggle for funds, and Gilman well served an apprenticeship in money-raising which was to prove invaluable in the lean years at the Johns Hopkins University

---

[1] *University Problems in the United States*, pp. 146-147.

[2] Cf., on the other hand, Henry P. Tappen, *University Education*, Chapter III.

[3] Daniel C. Gilman, *Our National Schools of Science*, p. 10. This also appeared in the *North American Review*, CXX (1867), pp. 300-328.

[4] *Ibid.*, pp. 10-11.

[5] See George W. Pierson, *Yale College*, pp. 477-535.

[6] R. H. Chittenden, *op. cit.*, I, pp. 81-82.

when that institution's funds suffered serious depletion as the result of business reverses. [1] In the constant effort to economize, and to make fullest use of existing facilities, Gilman developed with his colleagues at the Sheffield Scientific School, a modified elective system which he called "the group system of studies." Gilman describes the system and its origin in his report for 1868.

> Before 1860 there were but two classes of students, those engaged in the chemical laboratory and those who were studying civil engineering. In 1868, in accordance with public demand, as our program of studies indicates, special professional or technical education is provided for chemists, metallurgists, civil, mining and mechanical engineers, agriculturists, geologists and naturalists. We are also called upon to provide a general disciplinary course closely corresponding to the academic course; and likewise higher courses of instruction suited to the wants of those who have already taken their first degree and are candidates for a second. Thus the students of the department are divided into not less than seventeen groups or squads, each having its prescribed curriculum, and there are also several independent students pursuing their special researches. All this involves a large corps of teachers, everyone of whom aims to be proficient in certain branches of study.... We are only kept back by the lack of a sufficient number of teachers from making the regular course extend through a period of four years. [2]

In the semi-centennial address which he delivered at the Sheffield Scientific School in 1897, Gilman further observed of the system: "It is one of the glories of the Sheffield Scientific School that, from the beginning, [3] students have here been permitted to choose a group of studies, the constituents of which were beyond their control. 'Freedom under control' has been the rule of the house." [4] Gilman's phrase, "freedom under control," clearly differentiates it from Charles W. Eliot's elective system. In speaking of the elective system *contra* the group system, Pierson writes: "Now Eliot did not invent this system, nor first use it. On the contrary, Jefferson, Ticknor, Nott, and Wayland had all preceded him. And in his own time the Sheffield Scientific School, Cornell, and Johns Hopkins (and later Stanford) all used it. But they used it as a device for letting students with different interests choose *on entering*

---

[1] John C. French, *op. cit.*, pp. 94-101.

[2] *Report of the Secretary of the Sheffield Scientific School of Yale College*, 1868, p. 43.

[3] This statement is not altogether accurate. See R. H. Chittenden, *op. cit.*, I, pp. 80-88. Gilman's memory is playing tricks on him. The group system was not actually put into effect until the mid-sixties.

[4] *University problems in the United States*, p. 133

between specialist programs, each of which was required and drawn up by the professors in advance. Eliot, on the other hand, encouraged college men to choose *after entering* and to keep on electing—even when a few chose entirely one-sided programs, and the majority elected programs so scattered and capricious, or so elementary and easy, that neither discipline nor mastery were obtained." [1]

Despite the multitude of his duties, Gilman managed to contribute to the scholarship of physical geography, a science comparatively new in his day. [2] As Professor of Physical Geography in the Sheffield Scientific School, he was imaginative and resourceful and highly regarded by his students. [3] Primarily, it was Gilman who succeeded in having Connecticut designate the Sheffield Scientific School as its College of Agriculture and the Mechanical Arts, thus enabling the school to receive aid under the Morrill Act of 1862, aid which it received from 1863 to 1895. [4] He touched education at all its levels, serving as Acting School Visitor for the New Haven Board of Education from 1856 to 1859, and as secretary of the Connecticut Board of Education for the school year 1865-1866. [5] In this latter capacity, he reported to the State Board of Education the dire need for good teachers in the state and recommended the expansion and more liberal subsidy of the State Normal School. [6] His friendship with Samuel B. Ruggles, the liberal trustee of Columbia College, brought him squarely to face with the problems of academic-freedom. [7]

THE CALL TO CALIFORNIA

Why did Gilman choose to leave New Haven in 1872 and accept the presidency of the University of California? By 1872 the Sheffield Scientific

---

[1] George W. Pierson, "American Universities in the Nineteenth Century: the formative Period," *loc. cit.*, pp. 86-87.

[2] He contributed many articles on physical geography to Silliman's *The American Journal of Science and the Arts*. See *Index to the First Series* (1874). The German geographer, A. Petermann, spoke of his work as "the best on geography in the New World." See Petermann to Gilman, August 4, 1860, *Gilman Family Papers, loc. cit.*

[3] See student estimates in Franklin, *op. cit.*, p. 74.

[4] Charles H. Warren, "The Sheffield Scientific School from 1847 to 1947," *loc. cit.*, p. 159.

[5] B. C. Steiner, *The History of Education in Connecticut*, p. 159.

[6] *Annual Report of the State Board of Education of Connecticut* (1866), pp. 131-138.

[7] Samuel B. Ruggles (1800-1881), as trustee of Columbia College, had defended the appointment of Oliver Walcott Gibbs as professor of chemistry at Columbia when the other trustees objected to Gibbs's Unitarianism. See Hofstadter and Metzger, *op. cit.*, pp. 269-273. For Gilman's agreement with Ruggles, see Gilman to Ruggles, April 21, 1864. *Gilman Family Papers, loc. cit.*

School was flourishing. [1] Gilman had seen the Ph.D. instituted, and some progress had been made in achieving the coordinated university at Yale. The answer to this question has already been suggested. [2] When Noah Porter became the eleventh president of Yale in 1871, the graduate work initiated in the Sheffield Scientific School was seriously arrested, and instruction in the new science was regarded with suspicion. [3] Porter and his supporters were determined to meet the need for the new subjects outside Yale College, and if Yale must become a university, it would become a federated university. "In a federated university each school could stand for a different thing, and insist on its own required courses. The students, in choosing between schools, would do their electing at the moment of entrance, not afterward. This meant that . . . the Scientific School would become the safety valve." [4] The historian of Yale has put it succinctly: "The 1871 election of Porter did, in fact, delay the progressive development of the scientific and professional schools, and restrain the more liberal elements in the College." [5] Gilman's fears are clearly seen in a letter to Andrew D. White. He writes:

> As to Yale matters, the tendency, right or wrong, is to diversity or duality in the undergraduate instruction-course rather than to unity; that is to say, the Sheffield Scientific School is bound to work out its notions in one way and the old College in another will carry out its plans. . . . Gradually all our instructions have become distinct from theirs and now not one of our classes goes to the old College for instruction. This is contrary to our original expectations and desires; we have rather been forced into these circumstances. [6]

It is clear that Gilman was apprehensive and uncertain.

Another factor may suggest further answer to why Gilman chose to leave Yale. It is useless to speculate what would have happened had Gilman become president of Yale, [7] but there is some point in enquiring whether Gilman seriously entertained aspirations to become president of Yale. In 1869-70, the Young Yale Movement had been in favor of

---

[1] See Gilman's seventh and last report as secretary, 1872.

[2] See pp. 18-20, *supra*.

[3] George W. Pierson, *Yale College*, pp. 63-65.

[4] *Ibid.*, p. 67.

[5] George W. Pierson, "The Elective System and the Difficulties of College Planning, 1870-1940," *Journal of General Education*, IV (April 1950), p. 169.

[6] Gilman to White, May 5, 1871. *Gilman Family Papers, loc. cit.*

[7] Storr, *op. cit.*, p. 170. In a letter to the author (April 1, 1958) Professor Storr writes: "I suspect that [Gilman] would have found it very hard to refuse the presidency of Yale." See also Wilbur L. Cross, *Connecticut Yankee*, pp. 153-154, for the same sentiment. Cross was Dean of the Graduate School of Yale from 1916 to 1930.

breaking the ministerial tradition and electing a layman to Yale's highest office. [1] Pierson suggests the movement's candidate was Daniel Coit Gilman. [2] That Gilman was seriously considered as a candidate is affirmed in the following excerpt from a letter written by a member of the governing board of the Sheffield Scientific School: "You do not do Gilman justice; he would be, I think, the best man selectable to put the California University through, as his loss would be the greatest we could endure. You know I told you last spring that I hoped to see him our president, and we certainly need the best man not less than do the Californians." [3]

No answers are suggested in Gilman's polite letter of resignation to President Porter:

> Since the last college term I have been chosen President of the University of California, and have been to San Francisco that I might become personally acquainted with the Regents and their plans. The prospects of the new institution are full of hope, and the opportunities for usefulness in its service are ample. Family considerations [4] had predisposed me to regard with favor a change of climate. Under all the circumstances, I have come with great reluctance to the decision that duty requires me to relinquish my work in the Scientific School and to sever the ties which have bound me to New Haven uninterruptedly since I came here as a student.
>
> I therefore beg leave to resign by this letter my office of a professor in Yale College, with all the duties growing out of it which have been entrusted to me by the Corporation. In taking this step it is a pleasure to believe that all the departments of the University are flourishing and that especially the Scientific School has attained to a position of strength and of growing influence.
>
> In communicating to the Corporation my resignation, will you be good enough to assure them of my undiminished interest in everything which will promote the welfare of Yale College; and you will accept for yourself my congratulations upon the auspicious opening of your administration. [5]

---

[1] George W. Pierson, *Yale College*, pp. 61-62.

[2] *Ibid.*, p. 61.

[3] Franklin, *op. cit.*, p. 101. Franklin's source is not given, and no place of deposit is cited. The original is not at Yale.

[4] Gilman is referring to the illness of a young daughter. See Franklin, *op. cit.*, p. 105.

[5] Gilman to Noah Porter, September 12, 1872. *Gilman Family Papers, loc. cit.*

CHAPTER THREE

DANIEL COIT GILMAN AT CALIFORNIA (1872-1875)

Daniel Coit Gilman's departure from New Haven in October, 1872 "was the cause of universal regret to his friends [who] felt not only their personal loss but also the loss the college sustained in his removal from its activities." [1] In 1873 the governing board of the Sheffield Scientific School wrote of his departure:

> None parted from him with more regret than those who had so long been associated with him in the management of the Scientific School; and they desire to express publicly here their appreciation of his earnest and constant efforts to promote the growth of this department, and their full confidence in and hope for his success in the new and broad field of labor upon which he has entered. [2]

The words, "new and broad field of labor," have a special connotation. Gilman's colleagues were, perhaps, thinking of what their former secretary could accomplish as president of the University of California. Certainly, Professor James Dwight Dana was thinking of the proposals voiced in his *The New Haven University: What it is, and What it Requires*, and of the great gains which could be made by Gilman, unfettered by tradition and the conservatism of the elements led by President Porter at Yale. It is reasonable to assume that Gilman, who had witnessed and assisted the institution of the Ph.D. at Yale and who had nurtured the new scientific study, should have carried these ideas with him to California. Gilman described his California years in the statement that he had "helped to rescue a state university from the limitations of a college of agriculture and enlarge it to meet the requirements of a magnificent commonwealth." [3] But, if it is relatively clear as to why Gilman left Yale, a corollary must be asked. Why did the Regents of the University of California invite Gilman to become president?

The answer to this question is twofold. By 1870 Gilman was widely known in New England, not only as a geographer and secretary of the

---

[1] Franklin, *The Life of Daniel Coit Gilman*, p. 108.
[2] *Report of the Secretary of the Sheffield Scientific School of Yale College*, 1873, p. 33.
[3] *The Jubilee of the University of Wisconsin*, p. 64.

Sheffield Scientific School, but as an individual identified with the progress of general education. [1] He was not a controversial figure, but in 1869-70 the Young Yale Movement, in Gilman's advocacy for the presidency of Yale University, had given him some wide prominence. [2] Pierson observes that "in 1871 not a few had been in favor of breaking the ministerial tradition and electing a layman—perhaps Daniel Coit Gilman—to Yale's highest office." [3] Of course, the Regents of the University sought outside recommendation, and in this second consideration, Gilman was particularly fortunate. He was personally acquainted with most of the educational *illuminati*. For years he had been a close friend and associate of Andrew D. White, who had become President of Cornell University in 1867. [4] His warm friendship with Charles W. Eliot of Harvard University had extended over many years, [5] and he had long known James Burrill Angell who was to become President of the University of Michigan in 1871. [6] The best index to Gilman's reputation in the early 1870's as an educator must remain the unqualified and independently formulated recommendation made by Messieurs White, Eliot, and Angell in 1875 that Gilman be made president of the proposed Johns Hopkins University. [7] There is still a further consideration which may have prompted the Regents of the University of California to select Gilman as their president. As a state college, the University of California had to act quickly to avail itself of the aid allowed under the Morrill Act of 1862. [8] Gilman's success, in obtaining aid under the Morrill Act for the Sheffield Scientific School, was widely known and must have

---

[1] B. C. Steiner, *The History of Education in Connecticut*, p. 110. See also Franklin, *op. cit.*, pp. 102-105.

[2] George W. Pierson, *Yale College*, p. 61.

[3] *Ibid.*

[4] See Andrew D. White, *Autobiography, passim. The Gilman Papers* in the Doe Memorial Library at the University of California include nine letters to White, a small fraction of the correspondence which must have passed between the two during Gilman's years at California.

[5] See Willis Rudy, "Eliot and Gilman: the History of an Academic Friendship," *Teachers College Record*, 54 (March 1953), pp. 307-318.

[6] See James B. Angell, *Reminiscences, passim.*

[7] At the retirement of Gilman as president of the Johns Hopkins University, President Angell of the University of Michigan observed: "And now I have this remarkable statement to make to you; that, without the least conference between us three, we all wrote letters . . . that the one man [for the presidency of Hopkins] was Daniel C. Gilman of California." *Celebration of the Twenty-Fifth Anniversary of the Founding of the University* . . . , p. 133.

[8] For the difficulties in qualifying for aid, see Edward D. Eddy, *Colleges for Our Land and Time*, pp. 23-46.

impressed the Regents. [1] All in all, it was not an unknown who was tendered the presidency of the University of California, but "one [whose nomination] has elicited favorable comments from the newspapers that reflect the best possible opinion and [whose] declination would be a calamity to the University and to the State." [2]

THE UNIVERSITY OF CALIFORNIA BEFORE GILMAN

As early as 1849 the Constitution of the Provisional Territorial Government of California included an article providing for education in the new territory. [3] In the matter of higher education the Constitution directed the Legislature to establish a university and to provide "effectual means for the improvement and permanent security of funds for said university." [4] It was not until 1868, however, that the California Legislature chartered an institution to be known as the University of California. [5] Before this date many plans had been put forward for an institution of higher learning, but none had succeeded. [6] The success, in 1868, was largely due to the efforts of Henry Durant, a Congregationalist minister, who had founded the College of California in 1855. [7] Durant was primarily interested in assuring a College of Letters in the new university with "a liberal course of instruction in languages, literature, and philosophy, leading at the end of the usual four years' course of study to the degree of Bachelor of Arts." [8] Durant and the faculty of the College of California offered to donate to the state university the Berkeley site of the College of California, and all the College's assets. [9] Accepting Durant's offer, the California Legislature passed the Organic Act in

---

[1] Franklin, op. cit., pp. 102-105.

[2] Copy of letter from Governor Booth of California to Gilman, August 1, 1872. Gilman Papers, Doe Memorial Library, loc. cit.

[3] College of California Documents. Case I, Doe Memorial Library, University of California Archives.

[4] Ibid.

[5] William W. Ferrier, Ninety Years of Education in California, p. 315. See also College of California Documents. Case I, loc. cit.

[6] See William W. Ferrier, Origin and Development of the University of California, Chapters II, III.

[7] For Durant see William W. Ferrier, Henry Durant. Durant told Gilman in 1873 that he [Durant] was "a New Englander who had come to California with college on the brain." Interview of D. C. Gilman with Henry Durant, March 3, 1873. Gilman Papers, loc. cit. Durant was an 1827 graduate of Yale.

[8] College of California Documents. Case I, loc. cit.

[9] Ibid. See also discussion in William W. Ferrier, Henry Durant, pp. 75-82.

1868, creating and organizing the University of California. [1] However, in 1865 the Legilature, to asssure itself funds under the Morrill Act, had created an Agriculture, Mining, and Mechanic Arts College. [2] Thus, California in 1868 found itself with a university composed of a young, religiously oriented liberal-arts college, and an agricultural college which had still to be developed. The situation, at best, was an anomaly which forebode serious difficulty. In a sense it presaged Gilman's failure at California.

The Board of Regents of the University gave early study to the selection of a president. In November 1868, they chose General George B. McClellan, but after some months of inaction, General McClellan declined.[3] The Board of Regents then appointed Professor John Le Conte Acting President. [4] Efforts were made to elect Henry Durant but Durant's ministerial connections made for apprehension and his supporters had no success. [5] After much deliberation the Regents, in June 1870, elected Gilman president of the university. [6] Edward Tompkins, the regent who had supported Gilman's candidacy wrote to the president-elect:

> The lowest consideration, money, will not prevent. We pay $ 6000 in gold, to which in due season a house will be added. I need not contrast that with any salary paid on your side of the continent. The opportunity to do good is vastly greater in a new, energetic, enterprising region poorly supplied with means of education, than in an old country where colleges and educated men abound. The promise for the future is much the greater on this side of the continent. Where you are, suppose you could be president of Yale! You would get it only after a controversy with 'old fogyism', and you would be one of a long line of presidents. Old ideas, if they did not defeat, would embarrass you. Here you would be the founder of a new dynasty—the first president and would forever be at the head. You would only be asked to relieve regents who are so hurried that they are glad to be left alone, and thus would shape everything to suit yourself.

---

[1] William W. Ferrier, *Origin and Development of the University of California*, pp. 204-207.

[2] *Ibid.*, p. 62.

[3] *College of California Documents*. Case I, *loc. cit.* The nomination of General McClellan touched off a controversy. See W. W. Ferrier, *The Origin and Development of the University of California*, pp. 301-304.

[4] *College of California Documents*. Case I, *loc. cit.* John Le Conte, with his brother Joseph, had come to California from South Carolina to accept professorships. See Joseph Le Conte, *Autobiography*, *passim*, for an interesting picture of the years described.

[5] William W. Ferrier, *Henry Durant*, pp. 83-85.

[6] Gilman received eleven out of fourteen votes. See copy of minutes for Board of Regents meeting, June 21, 1870. *Gilman Papers*, Doe Memorial Library, *loc. cit.*

I concede all that you claim for the society and surroundings of New Haven, but the educational interests of California are nearly all concentrated at Oakland, a faculty of high order is already gathered there, and you would soon be in a position to call around you the best culture in America. [1]

Gilman's declination was tersely but politely written. "I am strongly tempted to accept the unexpected and gratifying proposal that I should become identified with the great institution which California has established on so liberal a basis for the promotion of higher education . . . the opportunities for usefulness in guiding the foundation of a university on so generous a plan and in such an attractive State are certainly most ample and alluring. But after careful consideration I do not see how I can sever the ties by which I am at present bound to the Sheffield Scientific School, which is entering upon a new career of usefulness and power." [2] As an interim measure the Board of Regents chose Henry Durant president. [3] This election was, at best, a temporary measure for Durant was unacceptable to some of the Regents and his Congregationalism irritated those who felt that he might develop strong sectarianism in the university. [4] When the Regents were certain that Gilman was ready to accept the presidency, Durant conveniently resigned. [5]

On July 30, 1872, the Board of Regents again elected Gilman President of the University of California. [6] By mid 1872 Gilman's situation in New Haven had materially changed. Noah Porter had been elected eleventh President of Yale University and "within the portals of New Haven, Porter's administration gave the larger Yale a delayed and rather one-sided development. As an emerging university Yale was affected in its government, in its funds, in its organization, and in its ruling ideas." [7] There is reason to believe that the Regents of the University of California knew in advance that Gilman would not decline their

---

[1] Edward Tompkins to D.C. Gilman, June 22, 1870. *Gilman Papers*, Doe Memorial Library, *loc. cit.*

[2] D. C. Gilman to Governor Haight, August 12, 1870. *Ibid.*

[3] Durant was made president on August 16, 1870. See Ferrier, *Henry Durant*, p. 85.

[4] William W. Ferrier, *Origin and Development of the University of California*, pp. 303-305.

[5] Although Durant pleaded the infirmities of age (he was sixty-eight) as the reason for his resignation, it would appear that he knew he was unacceptable to most of the Regents. See Interview of D.C. Gilman with Henry Durant, March 3, 1873. *Gilman Papers*, Doe Memorial Library, *loc. cit.*

[6] There were no other nominations. Gilman received twelve votes of the seventeen. Five blank ballots were cast. See copy of minutes for Board of Regents meeting, July 30, 1872. *Gilman Papers*, Doe Memorial Library, *loc. cit.*

[7] George W. Pierson, *Yale College*, pp. 60-61.

second invitation. Gilman replied by telegram on August 2, 1872: "Regents' telegrams . . . received. I leave immediately for San Francisco prepared to accept the great responsibility." [1]

GILMAN'S PRESIDENCY OF THE UNIVERSITY OF CALIFORNIA

Gilman arrived in California with a definite university program in mind. Even before his inauguration (which was scheduled for November 7, 1872), he had publicly intimated his plans. On September 2, 1872, he addressed the San Francisco Academy of Sciences which was honoring Professor Louis Agassiz, who had recently arrived in San Francisco. As main speaker, Gilman took the occasion to speak of the modern university. He observed:

> I can echo his [Professor Agassiz] words in a faint way, and take up a few of the thoughts he has dropped. He has told you that the museum at Cambridge [Harvard] is distinguished as the museum of today. Should it not be so with the University? Should it not be a University for the wants of today? Should we not use it for the great problems which belong to this generation, for the great future that is opening upon us? Should we not all unite to gather up the best of the past experience of every nation, the accumulations of all men before us, to bring them to bear upon our society, and upon, I trust you will allow me to say it, our own State of California? One other thought I should like to re-echo. Professor Agassiz has told you that the great want of science is observers, and the great want of society is men. Now, the object of the University is to turn out men, not narrow specialists, though they may be as eminent as possible in this or that department which they may pursue, but men of honest and earnest purpose, men of true wisdom, and that is what the University has before it. I will not prolong these remarks, but let me trust that the true utterances you have heard from the distinguished orator who has spoken to you, that you need an institution for today, and an institution for the training of men, may sink deep into all your hearts and inspire us all for the work which is to come. [2]

At once preoccupied with the affairs of the university, Gilman was able

---

[1] *Gilman Papers*, Doe Memorial Library, *loc. cit.* The manuscript of a few pages of notes which Gilman made on his trip to California is also deposited in the *Gilman Papers*. He visited with President Andrew D. White of Cornell University, and in Indianapolis, he discussed with Governor Baker the plan of Purdue University and the proposed second Morrill Bill.

[2] Franklin, *op. cit.*, pp. 119-120. The chapter on Gilman's years at California in Franklin's biography was done by William Carey Jones, a member of the University of California Class of 1875. Jones was later Professor of Jurisprudence in the university. Ferrier mentions a *History of the University of California (Origin and Development* . . . . p. 181), by Jones.

in late September 1872 to obtain the university's first large benefaction from a private source. Gilman persuaded Regent Edward Tompkins, a State Senator, to deed the university a valuable piece of land which was to be sold when it would realize fifty thousand dollars. The money was to be used to endow a professorship of Oriental Languages and Literature, and in compliment to the great scientist then visiting California, it was to be called the "Agassiz Professorship." [1] In this early act, perhaps most graphically, Gilman's intentions were clear. The university, in order that it build correctly, must have "men of true wisdom" and the facilities which will allow for true growth and research. [2] Gilman's blueprint for the University of California was publicly stated in his inaugural address.

Gilman took as his theme "The Building of the University." [3] The address was a statement of policy, and Gilman was lucidly clear in its presentation. He posed the central consideration: "California, thus endowed by nature and thus organized by man, is to build a university. What shall it be?" [4] Gilman was quick to add, "Time alone can tell, but forethought and faith may be factors in the problem." [5] The forethought of Gilman was the long experience at Yale and its Sheffield Scientific School, and his study of the "great changes [which had] been made in the higher educational systems of this and other lands." [6] Gilman turned to the clarification of two points which, in essence, embodied his "university idea" and his philosophy of advanced [graduate] education. Briefly, these two points were (1) the definition of the "university" and its concomitant differentiation from other educational institutions, with its emphasis on advanced and "liberal culture in all the great depart-

---

[1] See copy of minutes for Board of Regents meeting, September 18, 1872. *Gilman Papers*, Doe Memorial Library, *loc. cit.* Tompkins was a graduate of Union College (1834), and had come to California in 1860. The land he donated was sold by the Regents in 1895 for $ 87,629.45. See Ferrier, *Origin and Development . . .* , p. 417.

[2] Gilman arrived in California with several thousand volumes for the library of the new university, including six hundred which he personally donated. See Ferrier, *op. cit.*, p. 413.

[3] The holograph draft of the address is deposited with the *Gilman Papers* in the Doe Memorial Library. Gilman retitled it and printed it with some modification in his *University Problems in the United States*, pp. 153-185.

[4] *University Problems in the United States*, p. 155. Since there are no essential differences between the holograph draft in the *Gilman Papers* and Gilman's published form, the published text is quoted from. In the published form the address was retitled "The University of California in its Infancy."

[5] *Ibid.*

[6] *Ibid.*, p. 153.

ments of learning; (2) the necessary indigenous character of any proposed university, "adapted to this people." So important are these pronouncements made in 1872, four years before the beginning of the Johns Hopkins University, and so elemental to Gilman's educational thought, that it is strange to find no notice of these points or of this inaugural address in the students of American graduate education. It is not noted by Ryan, [1] by Pierson, [2] by Hofstadter and Hardy, [3] or by Rudy, [4] or by Storr. [5] Flexner quotes from it very briefly, but his source appears to Franklin's *Life of Daniel Coit Gilman* which similarly makes cursory notice of the inaugural address without indicating the source of information. [6]

Before turning to the main tenets of his address, Gilman made some preliminary observations. These observations were historical and essentially basic to educational tenets which he was to propose and to propound. "Everywhere among civilized people, universities in their comprehensive scope are in this year of grace receiving impulses which are as creditable to the spirit of the age as they are hopeful for the ages yet to come." [7] That the spirit of the age must be met is clear, for Gilman continues, "Our State and national governments see that the questions of the higher education must be met in the public councils, and in many places are vying with one another to devise wise schemes of educational development; the builder's hammer is heard in many seats of learning, —at Harvard, at Yale, at Amherst, at Princeton, at Ithaca, at Philadelphia,—constructing the walls which shall furnish homes to successive generations of pupils; collections of books, maps, and charts, and works of art, museums of geology and natural history and archaeology, laboratories ... and researches are multiplying with a marvelous rapidity. ... Prizes and scholarships have been endowed, and fellowships sometimes provided for continued residence at the college, and sometimes for residence in foreign universities; to the traditional schools of law, medi-

[1] W. Carson Ryan, *Studies in Early Graduate Education*, pp. 3-14.

[2] Mary Bynum Pierson, *Graduate Work in the South*, pp. 18-22. For Pierson, the main source for Gilman is Franklin's *Life* which is used somewhat uncritically. See particularly pp. 18-19, *op. cit.*

[3] Richard Hofstadter and C. DeWitt Hardy, *The Development and Scope of Highe Education in the United States*, pp. 57-100.

[4] S. Willis Rudy, "The Revolution in American Higher Education, 1865-1900," *The Harvard Educational Review*, 21 (Summer, 1951), pp. 169-170.

[5] Richard J. Storr, *The Beginnings of Graduate Education in America*. See Chapter XI.

[6] Abraham Flexner, *Daniel Coit Gilman*, pp. 18-21.

[7] D.C. Gilman, *University Problems in the United States*, p. 154.

cine, and theology have been added schools of philology, of history, of the fine arts, of chemistry, engineering, agriculture, and mines—devises and arrangements to allure young men to higher attainments, and to aid them in their onward steps. . . . Such is the hopeful aspect of university education elsewhere." [1] Thus, in late 1872, Gilman recapitulated the forces and tendencies of American university education at the time. He recognized, as Storr observes of *ante-bellum* America, that "there was, however, no single, dominant idea of the American University. By 1861 it was apparent that to induce young men to undertake graduate study a practical incentive as well as a love of knowledge was required. Repeatedly, after 1850, educators pointed out the need for financial aid to advanced students, proposing fellowships on the English order but limiting them to a short term. This was one of the few proposals on which agreement was general. No single philosophy of education determined American thinking, nor did a single purpose give form to graduate study." [2]

In the light of these developments Gilman's definition of the "university," and his insistence on its indigenous character are truly significant. His eclectic approach to the problem of the university in America provided an answer to what Pierson has called "the period [the nineteenth century] of trial and failure, of discovering the elements that were essential to universities, and then assembling them in various patterns or distinctive combinations. By contrast with England and the Continent, the problem [in America] was one of creation, not capture or redirection." [3] What was the University of California to be? Gilman gave this answer:

> First, it is a *university* and not a high school, nor a college, nor an academy of sciences, nor an industrial school, which we are charged to build. Some of these features may, indeed, be included or developed with the university; but the university means more than any or all of them. The University is the most comprehensive term which can be employed to indicate a foundation for the promotion and diffusion of knowledge—a group of agencies organized to advance the arts and sciences of every sort, and to train young men as scholars for all the intellectual callings of life. Universities differ widely in their internal structure. The older institutions are mostly complex, including a great variety of faculties, colleges, chairs, halls, scholarships, and collections, more or less closely

---

[1] *Ibid.*, pp. 154-155.

[2] Storr, *op. cit.*, pp. 130-131.

[3] George W. Pierson, "American Universities in the Nineteenth Century: the Formative Period," *The Modern University*, ed. by Margaret Clapp, pp. 62-63.

bound together as one establishment, endowed with investments, privele-
ges, and immunities, and regarded as indispensable both to the moral
and material progress of the community, or, in other words, as essential
both to church and state." [1]

Gilman, however, observed that in America "the name [university]
is often misapplied to a simple college, probably with that faith which is
'the substance of things hoped for, the evidence of things not seen.'
We must beware lest we, too, have the name without the reality." [2]
If the university were to be complete, "around the nucleus of the traditional college which has been well maintained since the earliest days of
this State [3] . . . must [be] the schools of advanced and liberal culture in
all the great departments of learning. . . . We must at least begin to
recognize the various sciences by chairs which may be the nucleus of a
school or department." [4] Thus, Gilman formulated the plan of a coordinated university which he had helped emerge at Yale, only to see his
efforts thwarted by the educational federalism of Noah Porter.

Yet, even with the definition of the American university accepted,
Gilman demanded that his audience recognize that the American univer-
sity must be truly indigenous, that it respond to the needs of the people.
This was his second requirement for success. He cautioned:

> Second, the charter and the name declare that this is the University of
> California. It is not the University of Berlin nor of New Haven which we
> are to copy; it is not the University of Oakland nor of San Francisco
> which we are to create; but it is the university of this State. It must be
> adapted to this people, to their public and private schools, to their peculiar
> geographical position, to the requirements of their new society and their
> undeveloped resources. It is not the foundation of an ecclesiastical body
> nor of private individuals. It is "of the people and for the people"—not in
> any low or unworthy sense, [5] but in the highest and noblest relations to
> their intellectual and moral well-being. [6]

Gilman's University of California, then, was closely modeled on what

---

[1] *University Problems in the United States*, p. 156.

[2] *Ibid.*

[3] Gilman, unlike Hall at Clark or Harper at Chicago, was never antagonistic to
the liberal-arts college. He never attempted its complete metamorphosis. Almost
intuitively, he recognized the historical problems. See Pierson, "American Universities
. . .," *loc. cit.*, pp. 81-89.

[4] *University Problems in the United States*, p. 156.

[5] Gilman's use of Lincoln's phrase is interesting in noting its early wide currency.
His gloss is even more interesting in suggesting its possible inferior connotation.

[6] *University Problems in the United States*, p. 157.

he had known in New Haven. It was to consist of an undergraduate college to which were added distinct graduate schools or courses, with facilities for non-matriculated students. It resembled a combination of the German gymnasium and the German university, but was actually comparable to neither. But Gilman had profited from his experience at Yale, and he categorically stated that "The University is no place for sectarian controversy. It is a school of learning." [1] And, if Gilman had found the faculty impeded at Yale, and graduate studies belabored by "a borrowed faculty, . . . no full time men, and no formal administration," [2] in the University of California "It [was] on the faculty more than on any other body that the building of [the] university depends. . . . College work for college boys implies daily guidance under prescribed rules; professional work implies voluntary, self-impelled enthusiasm in the acquisition of knowledge." [3]

A careful reading of Storr's *The Beginnings of Graduate Education in America* makes one point eminently clear. In no individual, other than Gilman, had a practicable, eclectic plan been formulated which would gather up "the policies and the problems [of higher education] which the pre-Civil War generations passed down to guide the action and tax the ingenuity of later times." [4] This practicable eclecticism was absent in Tappan at the University of Michigan, [5] its compromise was absent in the inflexibility of what Henry James has called "the defects in Charles William Eliot's attitude toward graduate education," [6] and its absence in Andrew D. White may suggest the cause of many of his early difficulties at Ithaca. [7] But, why, then, did Gilman fail at the University of California? The answer to this question is mainly to be found in Gilman's inability to reconcile a conflict which antedated his arrival. Gilman, himself, has best defined the nature of the controversy. It was not the old problem of "the new education versus classical education" which Gilman knew

---

[1] *Ibid.*, p. 177.

[2] George W. Pierson, *Yale College*, p. 63.

[3] *University Problems in the United States*, p. 167.

[4] Richard J. Storr, *op. cit.*, p. 134. It is strange that Storr fails to see Gilman as his logical and chronological *terminus*.

[5] See Charles M. Perry, *Henry Tappan, Philosopher and University President*, Chapter III.

[6] Henry James, *Charles W. Eliot*, II, p. 15. Although Eliot had had the advice of Gilman in the preparation of his inaugural address as President of Harvard University in 1869, there is little of compromise in Eliot. See S.E. Morison, *Three Centuries of Harvard*, p. 329.

[7] See Walter P. Rogers, *Andrew D. White and the Modern University*, Chapter IV.

at first hand, and with which he had delt deftly at Yale; it was something quite different and unique. [1] Gilman capsuled it in these words:

> I believe that the real controversy which has been carried on during the last few months arises from a deep and radical difference of opinion as to the scope of the University of California. On the one hand are those who insist upon it [sic] that the chief object is to maintain an Agricultural College, or, as it is sometimes more liberally stated a College of Agriculture and the Mechanic Arts. They call for a large increase in the 'practical' elements of instruction, often going as far as to insist that instruction in carpentry, blacksmithing, and other manual and useful trades should be given in the University. On the other hand are those who insist upon it [sic] that the constitution and laws of the State, the condition of the endowments, and the highest interests of California demand a true University, in which indeed there should be maintained at least one college of agriculture and the mechanic arts, but where the best of every sort of culture should likewise be promoted. These claim that the most practical service which the University can render to the state is to teach the principles of science, and their application to all the wants of men—and at the same time to teach all that language and history have handed down as the experience of humanity. [2]

If at Yale, Gilman had fought a battle against the forces of educational conservatism, he found himself embattled in California with the advocates of the agriculture and 'mechanic arts' college. [3]

Actually, Gilman may have won against the agriculturists were it not for the intransigency of two of the faculty members whose motives for opposing Gilman are, at best, suspect. These were William Swinton, who had been appointed Professor of English in 1869, and Ezra S. Carr,

---

[1] Ouelette fails to see the problem correctly when he describes it as "differences in the point of view . . . between advocates of the new education and classical education." Ouelette's brief article (12 pp.) is largely derivative, based for the most part on the chapter in Franklin's *Life*. V.A. Ouelette, "Gilman at California," *Pacific Spectator*, VIII (1954), pp. 128-140.

[2] Daniel Coit Gilman to the Board of Regents, April 8, 1874. Copy in *Gilman Papers*, Doe Memorial Library, *loc. cit.*

[3] The situation of Andrew D. White, when he became President of Cornell University in 1868, was not actually the same. Although Ezra Cornell the founder, demanded that agricultural and industrial studies be provided for, he did not object to White's plan for dividing the university into two great divisions, the first to consist of agricultural and industrial studies; the second to be made up of several departments of general literary and scientific subjects. See Andrew D. White, *Report of the Committee on Organization, presented to the trustees of the Cornell University, October* 21, 1866. See also Walter P. Rogers, *op. cit.*, Chapter II. Gilman, too, may have similarly succeeded at the University of California.

appointed professor of agriculture in the same year. [1] These men enlisted the aid of Henry George, the single-tax advocate, who was then editing the San Francisco *Daily Evening Post*, and took advantage of every opportunity to discredit Gilman and the university. [2] George's charges of fraud and corruption [3] in the management of the University of California culminated in a special session of the State Legislature to which Gilman was summoned. As champion of the University, Gilman pleaded:

> I acknowledge that with all the success there are very great defects that come in the selection of teachers. There are the errors in marking out the course of study, the difficulties in moving to a new site ... but with all these drawbacks the State of California has got what it went for. *It has got a University.* ... It is still in its experimental stage. ... There are no religious bodies who control it or [would like] to see it die in order that separate denominational colleges might grow up instead. I should not be surprized if there were political bodies that would like to capture it because of [4] its success. ... Then come the theorists: there are men who want it to be a purely literary, classical college—the old-fashioned sort. There are men that don't want to have anything to do with the old-fashioned sort. They would like to capture it for the "new education." [5]

The special session of the Legislature took place on January 26, 1874 which graphically shows that most of 1873 had been spent in argument and controversy. The irony of the controversy was the fact that Gilman was never antagonistic to agricultural or industrial education. Later, Gilman was an enthusiastic member of the *Industrial Education Association* of which Nicholas Murray Butler was president. [6] Upon Gilman's request a Joint Committee of the Senate and the Assembly was appointed to investigate the charges brought by Professors Carr and Swinton and the public utterances of the *Daily Evening Post*. [7] The Joint Committee

---

[1] The *Gilman Papers* in the Doe Memorial Library contain four manuscripts of Gilman concerning the dismissal of Professors Carr and Swinton from the University. For the most part these manuscripts are made up of disconnected confidential comments, and notes. About Carr no information is available. For Swinton, see Thomas M. Spaulding, "William Swinton," *Dictionary of American Biography*, XVIII, pp. 252-253.

[2] There is no notice of George's attacks on the infant University of California by his biographers. See Henry George, Jr., *Henry George*.

[3] See Franklin, *op. cit.*, pp. 145-147 for quotations from the *Daily Evening Post*.

[4] An allusion to the Grangers. See Franklin, *op. cit.*, pp. 142-43.

[5] *Gilman Papers*, Doe Memorial Library, *loc. cit.* Case II. Most of the materials in Case II are undated and unfiled.

[6] Gilman wrote for the *Association* its first monograph, *A Plea for the Training of the Hand* (1888).

[7] This material is reconstructed from the data noted in footnote 1, *supra*. Ferrier, *Origin and Development of the University* ... , pp. 355-360, deals with the matter superficially.

placed all witnesses under oath and attempted the examination of four questions:

1   instruction in agriculture and the mechanic arts
2   management of the land grant funds
3   management of the general funds
4   all other matters relating to the University, upon which, in the opinion of the Committee, further information might be of use to the Legislature or the public

On March 26, 1874, the Joint Committee made its final report: "The Regents and Faculty have done well and . . . they deserve the sympathy and support of the people at large in the management of the University." [1] This amounted to a complete exoneration of Gilman and the Regents. In due time Professor Carr was dismissed, and Professor Swinton chose to resign. [2]

However, President Gilman was apprehensive about future difficulties. The long and bitter struggle had seriously shaken him, and he wrote to Andrew D. White: "There are dangers here which I could not foresee. I feel that we are building a superior structure but it rests over a mill which may blow up any day." [3] On April 8, 1874, Gilman presented his resignation to the secretary of the Board of Regents. In it he observed:

> The University of California is now organized on a comprehensive basis. Its plans are in accord with the best experience of modern institutions in other states and countries. *I believe in it as it stands*, rejoicing that in so short a time so much has been done, with some promise of good fruit ripening rapidly. I am heartily in sympathy with the introduction of science into higher educational establishments and eager to see also the wide diffusion of technical instruction. But because I cannot assent to some of the radical demands which would overthrow the University, abolish the Regents, and entirely change the present course of study, I am exposed to censure. . . . I have tried to the utmost of my ability to conciliate the various conflicting parties and beg them to sink the points on which they differ for the sake of the University and those on which they agree; to make a University of the most liberal, elevated and comprehensive sort, worthy of the 19th century, worthy to train up the future citizens of

---

[1] *Ibid.*

[2] Carr was dismissed on August 11, 1874. Swinton resigned as of March 3, 1874. Undated Mss. notes, *Gilman Papers*, Case II, Doe Memorial Library, *loc. cit.* "Swinton then turned to writing school textbooks, with such success that a gold medal was awarded to him at the Paris Exposition of 1878, and his royalties sometimes were $ 25,000 a year." T. M. Spaulding, "William Swinton," *loc. cit.*, p. 253.

[3] D.C. Gilman to Andrew D. White, April 5, 1874. *Gilman Papers*, Doe Memorial Library, *loc. cit.*

this great state. . . . Notwithstanding all this, and notwithstanding that my record as an advocate of technical instruction is clear and decided, it is probable that some one else will better serve you in the present difficulties. For University fighting I have had no training; in University work I delight. I therefore beg of you to release me from the post I hold, at the earliest day you can consistently do so. I only ask leave to present more fully for your consideration at another time the embarrassments to which I have been subjected from within as well as from without the University circle. [1]

The Regents quietly persuaded Gilman to withdraw his resignation, but it was apparent that Gilman had grave doubts about the future. On May 12, 1874, he wrote to Andrew D. White: "We seem to have come out in still waters,—and have a smooth prospect for the next two years, but I should not like to go through such a tussle again. . . . I often thought during the winter that I should quit at this time,—but the legislature did so well, and the Regents stand so firm, that I cannot resign here without some very strong reason presents itself for doing so." [2] The very strong reason—the invitation to the presidency of the Johns Hopkins University—was only a few months away.

GILMAN'S ACHIEVEMENT AT THE UNIVERSITY OF CALIFORNIA

The proposals which Gilman outlined in his inaugural address for the infant University of California were not achieved during his tenure. In the large sense Gilman failed; but some positive gains were made. The record of these positive gains is in the *Statement of the Progress and Condition of the University of California* which Gilman prepared at the request of the Regents in March 1875. [3] Essentially a progress report, the statement clearly establishes the solid basis for future growth which Gilman had provided in a little over two years.

The work of the university was organized into seven courses. "In addition to the original courses of study in Agriculture and Letters which were commenced in 1869, a course in Engineering was begun in 1871. Since then the courses in Mechanics, Mining, and Chemistry have been established, and the course in Letters has been separated into a classical

---

[1] *Gilman Papers*, Doe Memorial Library, *loc. cit.*

[2] D.C. Gilman to Andrew D. White, May 12, 1874. *Ibid.*

[3] Neither Ouelette, "Gilman at California," *loc. cit.*, nor Ferrier, *Origin and Development of the University of California*, mentions this report. It is, however, the only full statement of the condition of the university made by Gilman as president and was officially published by the university. A copy of the report is in the Doe Memorial Library at Berkeley.

and a literary course. ... These courses are commonly spoken of as 'colleges'. At the head of each of these seven departments of instruction is a professor, who acts under the President and Faculty as the director of the studies of the course." [1] Five courses (Agriculture, Mechanics, Mining, Chemistry, and Engineering) constituted the College of Science. Two of the courses (Classics, and Literature) constituted the College of Letters. [2] Gilman reproduced, in large measure, the curriculum of the Sheffield Scientific School in the five technical courses of the University of California. "In the five technical courses, the first two years are devoted chiefly to those studies which are fundamental and of general importance —to Mathematics, Elementary Chemistry, Physics, Natural History, and Modern Languages, including English. During the last two years, the special subjects of the several courses predominate, that is to say, Agriculture, Mechanics, Mining, Chemistry, or Engineering. The degree given at the conclusion of each of these courses is that of Bachelor of Philosophy in the college of agriculture, mechanics, etc., as the case may be." [3] In the College of Letters, Gilman organized the traditional classical course, and a literary course. This last was, in essence, the "Select Course in Scientific and Literary Studies" which Gilman had helped institute at Yale in 1871. "The Literary Course is quite new in our University. It corresponds during the first two years with the scientific courses above enumerated, and during the last two years provides a liberal training in modern languages, history, and literature, and in those departments of science taught in the University which are of the most general interest." [4]

Despite all attendant difficulties, Gilman provided for graduate education. It was at California that Gilman first introduced "graduate fellowships." Pierson rightly observes that at the Johns Hopkins University "Gilman closed the gap between need and demand for advanced studies by first 'hiring his students'." [5] This measure was dictated by necessity but Gilman recognized that it would provide a nucleus for further development. "In the Summer of 1874, the Regents determined to appoint as assistant instructors several young men who had recently graduated. The amount of their compensation was not to be large ($ 600 per year),

---

[1] D.C. Gilman, *Statement of the Progress and Condition of the University of California. Prepared at the Request of the Regents of the University*, pp. 22-23.
[2] *Ibid.*   [3] *Ibid.*, p. 23.   [4] *Ibid.*, p. 39.
[5] George W. Pierson, "American Universities in the Nineteenth Century: the Formative Period," *loc. cit.*, p. 75.

and it was not supposed that their duties would be responsible or onerous. But it was thought that they would be led to prosecute advanced studies under the direction of the Faculty, and would thus become better fitted for the duties of life. This plan, which is nearly equivalent to the establishment of graduate scholarships, has worked well." [1] Two other provisions assured the growth of graduate education. Mention has already been made of the large benefaction of Edward Tompkins. Gilman set up provisions for an Oriental College and observed in his *Statement* that "Letters have already been exchanged with an eminent scholar in Chinese, with reference to his acceptance of this chair [Oriental Languages]." [2] In the absence of funds to maintain a large graduate faculty, Gilman instituted the visiting lectureship, a devise which he was to use with great variation at the Johns Hopkins University. [3] And, as a former librarian, Gilman doubled the holdings of the library in his short tenure.[4] "It is intended that the main library of the University shall be chiefly a reference library, so that scholars in any department may be sure of finding upon the shelves the various treatises which they wish to consult."[5]

From the very first Gilman admitted women to all departments of the University, and he wryly observed: "Among the regular students the proportion of ladies who have been good scholars has been greater than that of young men." [6] Professional education was provided by absorbing the Toland Medical College of San Francisco, but Gilman pointed out that the medical department "[was] behind the other departments of the University, in its standards of requirements for admission, when it should be decidedly in advance." [7] Gilman also provided for the organization of a College of Pharmacy, a College of Dentistry, and a Faculty of Law whose formation was in progress at the time of the report. [8] The Statement also calls to attention proposals for advanced scientific foundations for which Gilman was soliciting funds. [9]

---

[1] D.C. Gilman, *Statement of the Progress and Condition of the University of California* . . . , p. 12.　　　　[2] *Ibid.*, pp. 43-44.

[3] For a list of the lectures for 1874-75, see *Ibid.*, pp. 41-42.

[4] *Ibid.*, pp. 47-50.　　　　[5] *Ibid.*, p. 48.　　　　[6] *Ibid.*, p. 47.

[7] *Ibid.*, pp. 42-43. In his inaugural address as President of the Johns Hopkins University, Gilman took up this theme again: "In some of our very best colleges the degree of Doctor of Medicine can be obtained in half the time required to win the degree of Bachelor of Arts." Gilman anticipated by thirty-five years the sensational charges which Abraham Flexner laid at the door of American medical education. See Abraham Flexner, *Medical Education in the United States and Canada* (1910).

[8] *Ibid.*, p. 56.

[9] The *Gilman Papers* contain a draft in holograph of a recommendation to James Lick to found a *San Francisco Union for the Advancement of Science, Literature and the Arts.*

Obviously, Gilman's departure arrested many of the developments outlined above. [1] Particularly, advanced studies and graduate education were impeded, [2] and the growth of the University between 1875 and 1900, if slow, was largely due to the careful foundations which Gilman had constructed. [3]

GILMAN'S RESIGNATION

As early as May 12, 1874, Gilman had indicated in confidence to Andrew D. White that he would resign as president of the University were a strong enough reason to present itself. [4] In three other letters to White, written before the year was over, it is clear that the strong reason had presented itself. [5] Gilman wrote to White on November 4, 1874:

> The Baltimore [the presidency of the Johns Hopkins] overtures have reached me an hour ago. . . . I feel much gratified by the confidence which so many of my friends have shown in me by saying a good word, at the opportune moment; but I must be very careful that the interests here do not suffer. We are apparently over the crisis; the answer to the Grangers has silenced them; our large increase of scholars, and general quiet and serenity surprizes us all; if I am to resign at all within two years, now is the moment. No legislature in thirteen months; and then the tidal wave of what sort of democracy? I have not mentioned your letter respecting the visit and talk of the Hopkins Trustees to anybody, by letter or orally; so I don't know how to proceed with their overture,—but I shall have a frank talk with some of our Regents. I think I shall resign,—resignation to take effect at a time to be mutually agreed upon. Then being free, I shall go East and look at the situation. It would seem to me unwise to accept such a post without having first a personal interview. I write on the spur of the moment. [6]

By early December, Gilman had made his decision. He wrote to Governor Booth: "It is my intention to inform the Regents at their next meeting that I have received letters from an institution of learning at [sic] the

---

[1] Ferrier, *Origin and Development* . . . , pp. 367-369.

[2] See in this connection the progress made at the University of Southern California which was founded in 1880. Allison Gaw, *Development of Graduate Work at the University of Southern California.*

[3] Ferrier, *Origin and Development of the University of California*, Chapter XXIII.

[4] D. C. Gilman to Andrew D. White, May 12, 1874, *Gilman Papers*, Doe Memorial Library, *loc. cit.*

[5] D.C. Gilman to Andrew D. White, September 30, October 18, and November 4' 1874. *Ibid.*

[6] D.C. Gilman to Andrew D. White, November 4, 1874. *Gilman Papers*, Doe Memorial Library, *loc. cit.*

East looking to my acceptance of the Presidency of the same. The overtures are so attractive that I feel bound to consider them and in order
that I may honorably do so, I shall present my resignation to the Board."[1]
The Regents accepted Gilman's resignation to take effect as of March
1875. That there was wide misgivings is apparent in a letter from one
of the Regents to Gilman. "You have a great opportunity in Baltimore,
that of organizing the first real American *university*. That you will do
it successfully, and thus place yourself at the head of your profession
in America, I have not the least doubt." [2]

Perhaps, Gilman felt, despite his early success at the University of
California, that progress in achieving the goals he had outlined in his
inaugural address would be too slow. Certainly, the bitter factionalism
had disenchanted him. The opportunity presented him by the Hopkins
Trustees was one "without parallel in the history of our country." [3]
In an address on April 2 [?], 1875, before leaving Berkeley, Gilman
observed:

> A wealthy citizen of Baltimore, who died a few months since, has left his
> fortune for the good of his fellow men. One large portion is devoted to a
> hospital; another to the maintenance of a university. Nearly seven millions
> of dollars are consecrated to these two objects.
>
> The trustees whom he has selected are responsible neither to ecclesiastical
> nor legislative supervision; but simply to their own convictions of duty
> and the enlightened judgment of their fellow men. They have not adopted
> any plan nor authorized, as I believe, any of the statements which have
> been made as to their probable course, —but they are disposed to make a
> careful study of the educational systems of the country, and to act in
> accordance with the wisest counsels which they can secure. Their means
> are ample; their authority complete; their purposes enlightened. Is not
> this opportunity without parallel in the history of our country? [4]

---

[1] D.C. Gilman to Governor Booth, December 9, 1874. *Ibid.*

[2] John W. Dwinelle to D.C. Gilman, February 12, 1874. *Ibid.*

[3] Undated manuscript in *Gilman Papers*. Doe Memorial Library, *loc. cit.*, Case II.

[4] *Ibid.* The date is uncertain but appears to be April 2, 1875, from a study of other
mss. in Case II. In Case II there is the ms. of an ode "The Departure of the Pilot,"
which signalizes the loss of Gilman. It was written by Edward R. Sill, Professor of
English. A typical stanza is reproduced:

> But the pilot-captain, lo!
> How serene in strength is he!
> Blithe as winds that dawnward blow,
> Fresh and fearless as the sea.

The full text of the poem was reprinted in the *Johns Hopkins Alumni Magazine*
(March, 1937).

CHAPTER FOUR

DANIEL COIT GILMAN AT HOPKINS: THE FIRST DECADE (1876-1886)

In *The Launching of a University*, Daniel Coit Gilman reminnisced, "Before a university can be launched there are six requisites: An idea; capital, to make the idea feasible; a definite plan; an able staff of coadjutors; books and apparatus; students." [1] To these six, Gilman may have added a seventh: the proper leader, or, put another way, that individual who gives the university requisite force and direction. Ryan has expressed it this way: "Experts in university administration have said that Daniel Coit Gilman was probably the best equipped man to head a pioneering university that could have been found; that the success of the Johns Hopkins University was in considerable measure due to the happy circumstance that a great educational gift fell into the hands of a man who by training and experience was in close touch with the education and scholarship of his day." [2]

Johns Hopkins (1795-1873), [3] the Quaker merchant of Baltimore who was to endow the university which bears his name, formed two corporations in 1867, one to maintain a hospital, the other to found a university. [4] By his will Hopkins left to the proposed university an endowment valued at $ 3,500,000, invested in 15,000 shares of the common stock of the Baltimore and Ohio Railroad, and Clifton, a rambling estate outside Baltimore. [5] He recommended to the trustees "not to dispose of the said capitol stock, but to keep the said stock as an investment." [6] Hopkins knew "that the success of his generous plans would depend in great measure on the judgment and the fidelity of his original trustees." [7] He chose with great care, and Gilman described his choice as "a capitol

---

[1] "Reminiscences of Thirty Years in Baltimore, 1875-1905," *loc. cit.*, p. 9. Gilman added tantalizingly: "I have the advantage of knowing more than anyone else of an unwritten chapter of history; the disadvantage of not being able or disposed to tell the half that I remember." *Ibid.*

[2] W. Carson Ryan, *Studies in Early Graduate Education*, p. 144.

[3] See Helen Hopkins Thom, *Johns Hopkins*. Some notices of Hopkins' life are in John C. French, *A History of the University founded by Johns Hopkins*.

[4] Thom, *op. cit.*, pp. 71-72.

[5] The will is published in full in Thom, *op. cit.*, pp. 91-120.

[6] *Ibid.*, p. 98.

[7] French, *op. cit.*, p. 17.

selection from among men, resident in Baltimore, in middle life, independent, and acquainted with affairs." [1] Hopkins chose fourteen trustees,
ten of whom served on both Boards. [2] Hopkins left great freedom to
his trustees. A careful reading of his will shows that only one passage
specifically presents any direct requests for the university which he
endowed, and these requests were not particularly restrictive. [3] Primarily,
the restrictions were financial admonitions. He enjoined the trustees to:

1 "not ... dispose of the said capital stock, or of any stock accruing
   thereon by way of increment or dividend stock, if any, as an invest-
   ment."
2 "maintain the said University, afterwards, out of its receipts from
   scholars, and out of the annual revenue derived from the devise and
   bequest hereby made, without encroaching upon the principal fund."
3 "to establish, from time to time, such number of free scholarships
   in the said University as may be judicious, and to distribute the said
   scholarships amongst such candidates from the States of Maryland,
   Virginia and North Carolina, as may be deserving of choice, because
   of their character and intellectual promise; and to educate the young
   men so chosen free of charge." [4]

He gave some further instructions regarding the hospital which might
equally be applicable to the university. For the hospital, he enjoined
the trustees "to obtain the advice and assistance of those, at home, or
abroad, who have achieved the greatest success in the construction and
mangement" [5] of like institutions. He particularly noted that "It is my
special request that the influence of Religion should be felt in and impressed on the whole mangement ...; but I desire, nevertheless, that
the administration ... shall be undisturbed by sectarian influence,
discipline, or control." [6] Thus, the trustees found themselves with the
largest single bequest ever left to a university up to that time, with little
or no restriction as to the type of institution of higher learning which
they were to create. [7] Yet, Hopkins had not acted rashly and without

---

[1] *The Launching of a University*, p. 29.

[2] See Thom, *op. cit.*, p. 70.

[3] See *Johns Hopkins University. Charter, Extracts of Will, Officers and By-Laws*,
pp. 5-6. The relevant passage is reprinted in French, *op. cit.*, pp. 463-464.

[4] French, *op. cit.*, pp. 463-464.

[5] *Letter of Johns Hopkins to the Trustees of "The Johns Hopkins Hospital."* Reprinted
in Thom, *op. cit.*, pp. 87-90.

[6] *Ibid.*

[7] "The sum of $ 3,500,000 is appropriated to a university .... So far as I can learn,
the Hopkins foundation, coming from a single giver is without a parallel in terms or
in amount in this or any other land." D.C. Gilman, *University Problems in the United
States*, pp. 3-4.

careful consideration. French observes: "When Mr. Hopkins took up the task of choosing trustees for his proposed foundation, he was on sure ground. Of the art and mystery of the teacher, the doctor of medicine, and the nurse he had no special knowledge; but he did know very well all about boards of trustees and directors, for he had shared in the management of many of the most important business and welfare organizations in Baltimore." [1]

THE HOPKINS TRUSTEES

Johns Hopkins chose fourteen trustees, ten of whom served on both the hospital and the university boards. [2] Of the trustees, Reverdy Johnson, Jr. (1826-1907), a Baltimore attorney with a Ph.D. from Heidelberg University, acted as correspondent of the University Board in the negotiations with Gilman for the presidency of the proposed university. [3] The trustees held their first meeting on June 13, 1870. [4] Since the university existed only on paper, the meeting was perfunctory and a formality. They did not meet again until February 6, 1874 following the death of Johns Hopkins and the proving of his will. They took under serious consideration the injunction of Johns Hopkins "to obtain the advise and assistance of those at home and abroad who had achieved the greatest success." They began a long serious of conferences which culminated in the election of Daniel Coit Gilman to the presidency of the new university. [5] In seeking the advice of those "who had achieved the greatest success" they turned, quite naturally, to Charles William Eliot, President of Harvard University from 1869 to 1909; [6] to Andrew D. White,

---

[1] French, op. cit., p. 17.

[2] These were Francis T. King (1819-1891); Lewis N. Hopkins (1834-1904); Thomas M. Smith (1810-1877); William Hopkins (1814-1881); John W. Garrett (1820-1884); Francis White (1825-1904); Charles J. M. Gwinn (1823-1894); Galloway Cheston (1806-1881); George W. Dobbin (1809-1891); Dr. John Fonerden (1804-1869); Reverdy Johnson (1826-1907); and George W. Brown (1812-1890). See French, op. cit., pp. 17-18. Six were Quakers; four were Episcopalians; one was a Presbyterian and one, a Swedenborgian.

[3] Johnson was the only one who had studied abroad.

[4] Trustee Minutes, June 13, 1870. The minutes of the early trustee meetings are in the President's Office, Johns Hopkins University.

[5] The fullest study of the trustees and their work on the university Board is Hugh Hawkins, The Birth of a University: A History of the Johns Hopkins University from the Death of the Founder to the End of the First Year of Academic Work (1873-1877). Unpublished Ph. D. Dissertation, Johns Hopkins University, 1954.

[6] See Henry James, Charles W. Eliot: President of Harvard University, 1869-1909. Also, Samuel E. Morison, The Development of Harvard University Since the Inaugura-

President of Cornell University from 1867 to 1885; [1] and to James B. Angell, President of the University of Michigan from 1871 to 1909. [2] The trustees were not totally without educational experience; four were also trustees of the Peabody Institute; ten had some college training, and one had studied abroad. [3]

The seriousness with which they approached the task of selecting a president for the new university is seen in the early action of Reverdy Johnson. Acting for the Executive Committee, Johnson bought a collection of books on education. As French notes, "Here was something unique in university history—a reading course for trustees, prerequisite to the assumption of their duties." [4] The list of titles is interesting in calling to attention the educational problems and concerns of 1874:

Matthew Arnold, *Higher Schools and Universities in Germany*, 1874.
E. H. Clarke, *Sex in Education*, 1874.
William Everett, *On the Cam*, 1867.
S. H. Tayler, *Classical Study*, 1870.
J. Orton, *The Liberal Education of Women*, 1873.
B. H. Hall, *College Words and Customs*, 1856.
Walter Smith, *Art Education*, 1873.
L. H. Bragg, *Four Years at Yale*, 1871.
Horace Mann, *Lectures and Reports on Education*, 1872.
James R. Rigg, *National Education*, 1873.
Noah Porter, *American Colleges and the American Public*, 1870.
Josiah Quincey, *History of Harvard University*, 1840.
C. A. Bristed, *Five Years in an English University*, 1873.
E. L. Youmans, *The Culture Demanded by Modern Life*, 1873.
B. G. Northrop, *Education Abroad*, 1873.
I. Todhunter, *The Conflict of Studies*, 1873.
Herbert Spencer, *Education*, 1873.
W. B. Hazen, *The School and the Army in Germany and France*, 1872.
L. B. Monroe, *Vocal and Physical Training*, 1873.
J. K. Rosenkranz, *Pedagogics as a System*, 1872.
S. D. Alexander, *Princeton College During the 18th Century*, 1872.
C. Durfee, *A History of Williams College*, 1860. [5]

---

tion of President Eliot: 1869-1929; and the same author's *Three Centuries of Harvard*: 1636-1936.
[1] See Andrew D. White, *Autobiography*; and Walter P. Rogers, *Andrew D. White and the Modern University*.
[2] See James B. Angell, *Reminiscences*; and Shirley W. Smith, *James B. Angell: An American Influence*.
[3] Hawkins, *op. cit.*, pp. 6-64. See also Hugh D. Hawkins, "Three University Presidents Testify," *American Quarterly*, vol. XI (Summer 1959), pp. 99-119.
[4] French, *op. cit.*, p. 24.
[5] *Accession Book: Johns Hopkins University*, 1-5000. Librarian's Office, Johns

The trustees were soon ready to act, and their decision was largely based on the recommendations they were prepared to hear from Presidents White, Eliot, and Angell. [1]

THE SELECTION OF GILMAN

The trustees conferred with President Eliot on June 4, 1874; [2] soon afterwards, on July 3, 1874, [3] they met with President Angell. Although White appears not to have come to Baltimore, most of his views were made known to Trustee James Carey Thomas. [4] For the most part, the trustees and the university presidents discussed the need and nature of university buildings, dormitories and dining halls, and student discipline. [5] Eliot's admonitions on student control are of particular interest: "I do believe in one sort of control—the indirect control which comes from good teaching, from good example, from the inculcation of good manners, from the encouragement of athletic sports and from keeping young men at work—steadily at work." [6] The discussions impinged on the problems of student admissions, on the questions of examinations, grades and class divisions, and on the admission of women to the proposed university. [7] On the last question all three presidents seemed to agree that co-education was wrong, and Eliot proposed that women be educated in their own institutions. [8] In the matter of what the university

Hopkins University. Johnson ordered the books on Many 21, 1874. See *Trustee Minutes*, May 21, 1874.

[1] The trustees also invited President McCosh of Princeton University but he declined. See Hawkins, *op. cit.*, p. 71.

[2] *Trustee Minutes*, June 4, 1874.

[3] *Ibid.*, July 3, 1874. Many years later, Angell recalled the interview: "I was shut up in a room with these Trustees and a stenographer, and what few ideas I had in these early days were squeezed out of me remorselessly." *Johns Hopkins University Celebration of the Twenty-Fifth Anniversary* . . . , p. 133.

[4] Andrew D. White to James Carey Thomas, March 13, 1874. *Daniel Coit Gilman Papers*, Lanier Room, Johns Hopkins University Library. This collection consists of about 13,000 incoming letters, notebooks, diaries, clippings, and Gilman's manuscript drafts of speeches and reports. About three-fifths of the material is catalogued. However, some material is kept in the library stacks.

[5] Besides the incomplete stenographic notes made at the meetings, the sources for the reconstruction of these early discussions is *Johns Hopkins University Miscellaneous Letters to Trustees*, 1874-1875, a collection in the Lanier Room, Johns Hopkins University Library. The material is sketchy, at best.

[6] C. W. Eliot to Reverdy Johnson, May 1, 1874, *loc. cit.* See also J. B. Angell to Reverdy Johnson, May 12, 1874; and A. D. White to Reverdy Johnson, May 1, 1874, *loc. cit.*

[7] *Ibid.*

[8] C.W. Eliot to Reverdy Johnson, May 1, 1874, *loc. cit.*

should teach, and how it should be organized, the discussion turned largely to "the new education" which Eliot had written of in his two articles in the *Atlantic Monthly*. [1] Eliot suggested that Yale had come closest to success with its Sheffield Scientific School; White stressed the necessary modification of the classical curriculum; and Angell advised that a separate polytechnic school be created. [2] All in all, the recommendations were hazy, inconsistent, and unimaginative. But in one respect they were sadly deficient.

In the discussions graduate education was only most peripherally mentioned. It was mentioned with reference to the feasibility of establishing fellowships which White heartily endorsed, urging the trustees to create "ten or twenty [fellowships], each one yielding a sum sufficient to maintain a young graduate at the University in a reasonable degree of comfort, while he pursues a more extended course of study under the general direction of the Faculty." [3] When one of the trustees asked Eliot if the proposed university "should be created as an institution which should attempt to give a higher degree of education than has heretofore been done . . .," Eliot retorted in what Hawkins has called "the worst prediction of educational history." [4] Eliot replied:

> The post-graduate course is a matter far off for you. Not until you have organized the whole of the College course, only in the fifth year of the existence of the College, could that question practically present itself. [5]

It appears that Eliot was merely noting that graduate work was a continuation of undergraduate work carried on in the same institution. He had not solved, for himself or Harvard, what Storr has called, "[The] problem raised by the concept of the American university as a composite institution with graduate departments superimposed on an undergraduate college with a single, prescribed course." [6] Angell noted the graduate work going on at the University of Michigan, but his remarks were quite insubstantial.

> We are at work upon the Post-Graduate system with a good deal of industry. It is supported warmly by the Professors. We have organized a specific post-graduate course, and generally have from ten to twenty

---

[1] *Atlantic Monthly*, XXIII (February, March 1869), 203-220, 358-367. For discussion see Henry James, op. cit., I, pp. 166-171.

[2] *Johns Hopkins University Miscellaneous Letters to Trustees*, 1874-1875, *loc. cit.*

[3] Andrew D. White to Reverdy Johnson, May 1, 1874. *Gilman Papers loc. cit.*

[4] Hugh Hawkins, *op. cit.*, p. 92.

[5] Quoted in Hawkins, *op. cit.*, p. 92.

[6] Richard J. Storr, *The Beginnings of Graduate Education in America*, p. 133.

persons and hope to increase that number. Our own students fall into the habit of remaining—among these one or two young ladies. [1]

Angell seemed to be completely unaware of the attempts by Henry Tappan to establish graduate work on the German model at the University of Michigan which Angell now headed. [2] Hawkins makes the point, and correctly, that it was the trustees, and not their advisers, who seemed to grasp the graduate idea. [3] One question asked of President Angell by Trustee Dobbin seems to clearly illustrate this:

> The first question, it seems to me, to determine, is, "What is to be the ultimate aim of our institution and instruction?" However moderately we may begin, and however slowly we may prosecute our plan, it should be directed to a well-considered result. The question with me of most concern is, "What is the good of the country and our fellow-citizens surrounding us—what does it require most—an Institution which shall be devoted to the highest teaching, or an institution which shall be devoted to the spread of its benefits more widely?" The two ultimate ends seem to pose a different course in the beginning. If we propose to have a large, populous Institution, where a great number will get an education, it will be different from that intended to cultivate only high scholars. Very few look to very high teaching. If the country must have such Institutions, and they exist elsewhere [i.e., Europe], with a fund perfectly untrammelled, as ours is, it would be very wise to determine what is the best thing for us to do. [4]

This statement is very important because, despite its hard-headed practicality, it clearly shows that when Gilman did decide to follow the course of "high teaching" and the cultivation of "high scholars," he found sympathy in his trustees. White's early suggestion of fellowships for graduate students may have been further stimulated and encouraged when some of the trustees visited President White at Cornell University. [5]

In one particular, Messieurs Eliot, White, and Angell unanimously agreed. They all recommended Daniel Coit Gilman for the presidency of the Johns Hopkins University. In a letter to Gilman, White assured him that the trustees had decided to ask him [Gilman] to be president

---

[1] "Remarks of President Angell, of the University of Michigan, before the Board of Trustees of the Johns Hopkins University, Baltimore, July 3, 1874." Lanier Room, Johns Hopkins University.

[2] Storr, *op. cit.*, pp. 112-117.

[3] Hawkins, *op. cit.*, p. 95.

[4] "Remarks of President Angell . . . , July 3, 1874," *loc. cit.* Quoted also in Hawkins, *op. cit.*, pp. 92-93.

[5] See Andrew D. White to D.C. Gilman, October 30, 1874. *Gilman Papers*, Lanier Room, *loc. cit.*

of Hopkins, and further that he had been already recommended for the post not only by President Eliot of Harvard, but by President Noah Porter as well. [1] With the typical dispatch of men of affairs, the trustees directed Trustee Johnson to offer the presidency of the new university to Gilman. [2] Johnson wrote to Gilman on October 23, 1874:

> I believe you are apprised of the existence and character of the Institution which I represent. It is the recipient of a fund of some three and a half millions of dollars—with no shakles of state or political influence, and with no restriction but the wisdom and sound judgment of the Board of Trustees. Not denominational—freed from all sectional bias, and entirely plastic in the hands of those to whom its founder has entrusted its organization and development. ... In casting around for a suitable individual to whom to entrust the development of the Institution, your name has been most prominent, coming with the fullest endorsement from the heads of leading universities, East and West; and I have been instructed by the board to open correspondence with you looking to your acceptance of the presidency. [3]

Gilman answered Trustee Johnson on November 10, 1874. Observing that "I do not know how the Regents [University of California] will feel and think in respect to my withdrawal," Gilman made it clear that he would accept:

> Your communication in behalf of the authorities of the Johns Hopkins University reached me on the fourth instant and has engaged my most serious consideration. The guidance of such a trust as you represent seems to me one of the most important educational responsibilities in our country ... I am deeply sensible of the honor and usefulness of the post to which your letter refers and am grateful to you and your associates for the confidence which has led them to communicate with me. My personal inclinations would lead me to resign my position here at once irrespective of any call elsewhere, on the ground that however well we may build up the University of California, its foundations are unstable because dependent on legislative control and popular clamor. ... But as I look at the opening sentences of your letter and read that this munificent gift is free from any phase of political and ecclesiastical interference, and is to be administered according to the judgment of a wise and judicious body of Trustees; when I think of the immense fund at your control; and when I think of the relations of Baltimore to the other great cities of the East, and especially of the relations which this University should have to the recovering states

---

[1] *Ibid.* White says in this letter that the trustees made a very close inspection of Yale, and from there went on to visit the University of Michigan.

[2] *Trustee Minutes*, October 15, 1874.

[3] Reverdy Johnson to D.C. Gilman, October 23, 1874. *Gilman Papers*, Lanier Room, *loc. cit.*

of the South, I am already [sic] to say that my services are at your disposal.
... The sum of this long letter then is this:—that the overtures of your
Committee are favorably entertained and that I shall immediately propose
to the regents to release me from their service. I shall then be free to accept
the position to which you refer. But I hope that a formal and final decision
will not be required of me, on your part, until we have met face to face. [1]

Johnson immediately wrote back to Gilman asking that Gilman come
to Baltimore during the winter. [2] To this Gilman agreed, stating that he
would come East in December. [3] When Gilman arrived in Baltimore
in late December 1874, the trustees were ready to confer with him as they
had with Presidents Eliot, White, and Angell, and their unanswered
question was: What shall the new institution be? In Gilman they found
a ready answer. What Gilman said exactly has not been recorded, but he
repeated what he said a few days later to his friend, E. L. Godkin of the
New York *Nation*, who published it. [4]

He [Gilman] said to them [the Trustees] in substance, that he would make
it [the Johns Hopkins University] the means of promoting scholarship
of the first order, and this by offering the kind of instruction to advanced
students which other universities offer in their post-graduate courses, and
leaving the kind of work now done by undergraduates to be done elsewhere.
For this purpose he would select as professors men now standing in the
front rank in their own fields; he would pay them well enough to leave
them at their ease as regards the commoner and coarser cares; would
give them only students who were far enough advanced to keep them
constantly stimulated to the highest point; and he would exact from them
yearly proof of the diligent and fruitful cultivation of their specialties
by compelling them to print somewhere the results of their researches.
Now, what this means, and how great a contribution it would be to the
intellectual progress and fame of the United States, may be inferred when
we say that we could at this moment name twenty men, employed at small
salaries in existing colleges, whose work in certain fields of research would
be of inestimable value to the science and literature of the world, but who
are compelled, in order to earn their livelihood, to pass most of their time
teaching the rudiments to boys, or preparing school-books; and that
American graduates who would like to pursue certain lines of culture
to their latest limits are compelled every year either to go abroad or content themselves with the necessarily imperfect aid which they can get in

---

[1] D.C. Gilman to Reverdy Johnson, November 10, 1874. *Gilman Papers*, Lanier
Room, *loc. cit.* Hawkins, *op. cit.*, p. 98, suggests that Gilman may have known of
the Hopkins foundation some years earlier but for this there appears to be no evidence.

[2] *Trustee Minutes*, November 24, 1874.

[3] *Executive Committee Minutes*, December 17, 1874.

[4] Franklin, *Life of Daniel Coit Gilman*, p. 188.

the post-graduate courses from overworked and halfpaid professors who are doing the work of schoolmasters. [1]

Gilman, thus, at once answered the question of "high teaching" and "high scholars" put by Trustee Dobbin to President Angell. The *Nation* article went further. In supporting Gilman's view, it continued:

> One of the results of the present state of affairs—and none see it more clearly than those who, like ourselves, are called on every week to compare the results of the intellectual activity of Europe with our own—is that our intellectual progress bears no sort of proportion to our progress in the accumulation of wealth and in the mechanical arts. To the higher thought of the world we contribute shamefully little. The books that rouse and stimulate men in the various great fields of speculation to-day are almost invariably European, and it shows what a mental condition some of us have fallen into, that [sic] it has been seriously proposed, within a few years, to remedy this state of things by putting a heavy customs duty on the product of the European mind—a proposal worthy of the year 1000. We are glad to say that the Hopkins Trustees fell in cordially with Mr. Gilman's terms, and offered him the presidency of the new institution, and that he will probably accept it. It is a great opportunity, and we hope and believe it will be rightly used. [2]

Gilman, many years later, noted that the trustees "responded heartily and promptly to this advanced view," and he further "[remembered] saying to them that if their purpose was to establish merely a city university, such as could be found in several other American cities, I should not be interested in the problem; but if they would take up the idea of founding an institution which should not only be of local importance, but should also become national in its scope, I should be very glad to aid them in the solution of the problem." [3] Although a formality, the trustees voted him the presidency on December 30, 1874. [4] Gilman seems to have completely won over the trustees, and to have "[given] my impressions with respect to the situation." [5] How far Gilman influenced the trustees in their educational thinking, or how far they had gone, before meeting with Gilman, in their determination to found a new type of university, remains conjectural. Hawkins believes that "They did not choose him

---

[1] New York *Nation*, XX (January 28, 1875), p. 60. Edwin L. Godkin (1831-1902) founded the New York *Nation*, a weekly critical journal, in 1865. See R. Ogden, *Edwin Lawrence Godkin.*

[2] *Ibid.*

[3] Gilman left *disjecta membra* of an autobiography, a typescript of which is in *The Johns Hopkins University Papers*, Lanier Room, Johns Hopkins University Library.

[4] *Trustee Minutes*, December 30, 1874.

[5] Autobiographical fragments, *loc. cit.* Also noted in Franklin, *op. cit.*, p. 188.

[Gilman] and then acquiesce in his ideas; they formed their ideas and then sought a man who shared them and could bring them to fruition." [1] One thing is clear. After his experiences at the University of California, Gilman was anxious not to undergo a similar experience. His conference with the trustees assured him that it could not happen at the Johns Hopkins University. In formally accepting the presidency of the new university, Gilman emphasized "the liberal views which you [the Trustees] hold in respect to advanced culture both in literature and science, [and] your corporate freedom from political and ecclesiastical alliances . . ." [2] Thus, Gilman became president of the Johns Hopkins University with his formal acceptance on January 30, 1875, and on the same day he wrote enthusiastically to his friend, Professor George Brush of the Sheffield Scientific School:

> I incline more and more to the belief that what is wanted in Baltimore is not a scientific school, nor a classical college, nor both combined; but a faculty of medicine, and a faculty of philosophy; that the usual college machinery of classes, commencements, etc. may be dispensed with; that each head of a great department, with his associates in that department,— say of Mathematics, or of Language or of Chemistry or of History, etc., —shall be as far as possible free from the interference of other heads of departments, and shall determine what scholars he will receive, and how he will teach them; that advanced students be first provided for; that degrees be given when scholars are ready to be graduated; in one year or in ten after their admission. [3]

How completely Gilman had imbibed the spirit of *Lernfreiheit* and *Lehrfreiheit*, as understood by the German academicians, is clearly illustrated in what Hawkins has called, "the most forthright and eloquent pronouncement Gilman ever made on the subject of intellectual freedom." [4]

> The Institution we are about to organize would not be worthy the name of a University, if it were to be devoted to any other purpose than the discovery and promulgation of the truth; and it would be ignoble in the extreme if the resources would have been given by the Founder without

---

[1] Hawkins, *op. cit.*, pp. 103-104. French observes: "It is pretty clear that the trustees named by Mr. Hopkins were feeling their way toward a radically different concept of university education." *Op. cit.*, p. 25.

[2] D.C. Gilman to Reverdy Johnson, January 30, 1875. *Gilman Papers*, Lanier Room, *loc. cit.*

[3] D.C. Gilman to George Brush, January 30, 1875. *Ibid.*

[4] Hawkins, *op. cit.*, p. 106. It seems strange that this passage has not been noted in the writings on academic freedom.

restrictions were limited to the maintenance of ecclesiastical differences or perverted to the promotion of political strife.

As the spirit of the University should be that of intellectual freedom in the pursuit of truth and of the broadest charity toward those from whom we differ in opinion it is certain that sectarian and partisan preferences should have no control in the selection of teachers, and should not be apparent in their official work.

Permit me to add that in a life devoted chiefly to the advancement of education I have found some of the best cooperators among those from whom I differed on ecclesiastical & political questions; and that I shall find it easy to work in Maryland with all the enlightened advocates and promoters of science and culture. To those who will labor for "The Johns Hopkins University," my grateful and cordial appreciation will go forth. We should hope that the Faculty soon to be chosen will be so catholic in spirit; so learned as to what has been discovered and so keen to explore new fields of research; so skillful as teachers; so cooperative as builders; and so comprehensive in the specialties to which they are devoted, —that pupils will flock to their instruction, first from Maryland and the states near to it,—but soon also from the remotest parts of the land. In seeking this result the board may rely on my most zealous coöperation. [1]

GILMAN'S SEARCH FOR TALENT

Gilman returned to Baltimore in May 1875, ready to assume his new duties. One immediate problem was the organization of a general plan for the university, and for this the trustees had awaited Gilman's arrival. [2] The plan which Gilman proposed served as the constitutional basis of the university in its earliest years, and it was speedily approved by the trustees on May 27, 1875. [3] This plan was later published in Gilman's *Second Annual Report* (1877), and its provisions made clear that a graduate school, among other things, was being established. The following provisions cogently outlined the basis on which the university was to grow, and like all Gillman's efforts, these provisions showed the eclectic spirit of compromise. They included:

1 The organization of the departments of medicine and law shall be postponed; and the first attention of the President and of the Committee [on organization] shall be directed to the departments of literature and science.

2 The Executive Committee shall forthwith direct the President to make

---

[1] D.C. Gilman to Reverdy Johnson, January 30, 1875. *Gilman Papers*, Lanier Room, *loc. cit.*

[2] *Trustee Minutes*, May 11, 1875.

[3] *Ibid.*, May 27, 1875. The full board of trustees approved the plan.

inquiries in respect to the selection of professors and Instructors, and this committee shall report to the Board, next autumn, the result of these inquiries, with the names of such persons as they recommend for appointment. An interval of two weeks shall pass after such a report is made before the Board proceeds to the election of any permanent professor. [1]

3 The committee shall have in mind the appointment of three classes of teachers:

Class I, the permanent Professors, on whom shall rest the chief responsibility of instruction and government, and who will be expected to give to the University their time and strength. The effort shall be made to secure the services of men of acknowledged ability and reputation, who are distinguished in special departments of study and who are capable of advancing these departments and of inciting young men to study and research. Among the number should be some who can be especially helpful in the organization of the University, and in influencing the character of young men. [2]

Class II will include Professors and Lecturers, resident or non-resident in Baltimore, who will give but a limited time and service to this University, and who will not be expected to take part in the administrative work. These instructors should be men of attainments in specialties which do not at present require full professorships, and men whose marked ability will be of service to the University. Professors in other colleges may thus be called to the Johns Hopkins University for a portion of the year, and possibly men from other lands. [3]

Class III will include Adjuncts and Assistants, who will usually be appointed for periods varying from one to five years. Their work will be chiefly subordinate to and in connection with the work of the permanent professors, who should be consulted in respect to their selection. The effort should be made to secure young men of ability and promise from whom the staff of permanent teachers may be in time reinforced.

4 The examinations for degrees shall be strict and comprehensive. The degree of A.B. shall be given for proficiency in classical studies, and

---

[1] The university did not officially open until February 22, 1876. From the approval of this preliminary plan, May 27, 1875, until the formal beginning, Gilman was occupied in the search for talent.

[2] How bold and revolutionary Gilman's action was can be discerned by a reading of Storr, *op. cit.*, pp. 129-134.

[3] This enabled Gilman to keep his permanent staff relatively small. In a sense, it was totally novel. See Storr, *op. cit.*, pp. 82-94.

that of B. Ph. for proficiency in scientific studies; but these degrees shall represent an equal amount of work pursued in different directions, and shall be coordinate in rank; and the candidates for these degrees shall have equal consideration in all the plans of the University. The second degree of Master of Arts and of Doctor of Philosophy [1] shall be given on examination only, at an interval of at least two years subsequent to the first degree.

5 Special facilities and encouragement shall be given to the graduates of colleges to come and profit by the instructions here provided, with or without reference to professional work or to the taking of a second degree. The effort shall thus be made to extend the benefit of the University to distant parts of the land, though it is also thought that many residents of Baltimore will be glad to avail themselves of such opportunities.

6 In the appointment of the Faculty care shall be taken to avoid sectarian and political influences, and the effort shall be made to bring together a staff of teachers who are known and esteemed in different parts of the country. [2]

Although the emphasis in this preliminary plan is on graduate education, it is apparent that Gilman did not found "a university in the authentic German tradition." [3] That provisions for an undergraduate school were from the first provided is clear. That Gilman's educational experience exerted tremendous influence and shaped the character of the preliminary organization is equally clear, for the dual undergraduate degrees at once suggest the Sheffield Scientific School and their proposed equality at the Johns Hopkins University resolved one of the problems which had plagued the new science at Yale. [4] Yet, even in the graduate emphasis,

---

[1] At first the M.A. and Ph.D. were united in one degree. See the *Johns Hopkins University Circular*, No. 7 (February 1877), p. 76.

[2] Johns Hopkins University. *Second Annual Report* (1877), pp. 25-29. With the exception of special departmental reports and other ancillary matters, the authorship of the reports was totally Gilman's. With these annual reports Gilman began a new kind of service to the public. "I hope that you [the Trustees] will deem it wise to communicate these reports annually to the public,—for although this is a private corporation, it is founded for public purposes . . . ." *First Annual Report* (1876), pp. 7-8.

[3] John S. Brubacher and Willis Rudy, *Higher Education in Transition*, p. 176.

[4] Gilman wrote to Professor Dana at Yale: "How often in these days I think of our talks 20 yrs. ago, exactly when the 'Prospectus of a School of Science,' was on the carpet. If this enterprize succeeds like that, it will be because of that." Gilman to J.D. Dana, April 4, 1876. *Gilman Papers*, Lanier Room, *loc. cit.*

Gilman had left the door wide open with his "special facilities [for] the graduates of colleges to come and profit by the instructions here provided, with or without reference to professional work or to the taking of a second degree." [1] Perhaps, most noteworthy in the preliminary plan was its elasticity. "The foundation at Baltimore began without formulas and rules, without decrees of the faculty or trustees, without regulations, and yet with that which was more binding than any code, the unanimous recognition of certain clear and definite principles in respect to the methods, the duties and the possibilities of a new university." [2]

With the preliminary plan for organization out of the way, the trustees suggested that Gilman travel to fill the university's first need—its faculty. Although the autobiographical notes Gilman left are sketchy, a study of these notes shows that he visited the Smithsonian Institute and Columbian (later George Washington) University in Washington. [3] He also visited New Haven, and the military academy at West Point, where he addressed the graduating class. [4] In the company of Trustee Johnson Gilman visited the University of Virginia, [5] and again he visited Yale, briefly stopped at Amherst, and at Harvard where he conferred with President Eliot, the journalist, E. L. Godkin, and Josiah D. Whitney, professor of geology. [6] Out of this tour of American colleges and universities, came one faculty appointment. While at West Point, Gilman conferred with Peter S. Michie, professor of Physics, about the scientific departments at Johns Hopkins. Obviously, Gilman asked Michie about any likely candidates for the departments and Michie at once suggested Henry A. Rowland, a young instructor at Rensselaer Polytechnic Institute. Gilman tells the story:

> "What has he done?" I said.
>
> "He has lately published an article in the *Philosophical Magazine*," was his reply, "which shows great ability. If you want a young man you had better talk with him."
>
> "Why did he publish it in London," said I, "and not in the *American Journal*?" [7]

---

[1] *Second Annual Report* (1877), p. 29

[2] Daniel C. Gilman, "The Johns Hopkins University," *Cosmopolitan*, XI (August 1891), p. 463.

[3] *Autobiographical Fragments*, Lanier Room, *loc. cit.*

[4] June 16, 1875. *Ibid.*

[5] June 22 and 23, 1875. *Ibid.*

[6] June 26 to July 1, 1875. *Ibid.*

[7] Professor Benjamin Silliman's *American Journal of Science and the Arts* to which Gilman had made many contributions while at Yale.

"Because it was turned down by the American editors," he said, "and the writer at onc forwarded it to Professor Clerk Maxwell, who sent it to the English perodical."

This at once arrested my attention and we telegraphed to Mr. Rowland to come from Troy, where he was an assistant instructor in the Rensselaer Polytechnic Institute. He came at once and we walked up and down Kosciusko's Garden, talking over his plan and ours. He told me in detail of his correspondence with Maxwell, and I think he showed me the letters received from him. At any rate, it was obvious that I was in confidential relations with a young man of rare intellectual powers and of uncommon aptitude for experimental science. When I reported the facts to the trustees in Baltimore they said at once, "Engage that young man and take him with you to Europe, where he may follow the leaders in his science and be ready for a professorship." And this was done. [1]

Gilman, with the trustees, recognized that the selection of the faculty for the Johns Hopkins University would be particularly delicate and difficult. "The selection of professors and teachers upon whom will devolve the instruction of youth, the chief work of the University, is peculiarly difficult because there are here [at Hopkins] no traditions for guidance, no usages in respect to the distribution of subjects, and none in respect to the kind of instruction to be given; and also because the plans of the Trustees must depend very much upon the character of the teachers whom they bring together." [2] In the search for "usages" and "traditions" and the kind of instruction to be offered, Gilman "was authorized to visit some of the principal institutions in Great Britain and on the Continent, in order that he might confer with European scholars and bring home fresh impressions of the progress of foreign Universities, as well as the plans, programmes, reports and other educational documents." [3]

Gilman sailed for Europe on July 7, 1875. [4] For his traveling companion he had young Henry Rowland whom the trustees had urged to go abroad. [5] In Dublin he visited Trinity College, conferring with Professor

---

[1] *The Launching of a University*, pp. 14-15. For Henry A. Rowland, see J. S. Ames, "Henry Augustus Rowland," *Johns Hopkins Alumni Magazine*, January, 1916. Rowland was twenty-five when appointed professor of Physics by the trustees. The editors of *The American Journal of Science* rejected his papers three times because they thought he was too young to publish. See Franklin, *op. cit.*, p. 199.

[2] *First Annual Report* (1876), pp. 19-20.

[3] *Ibid.*, pp. 8-9.

[4] *Autobiographical Fragments*, Lanier Room, *loc. cit.*

[5] Gilman had asked President White of Cornell to accompany him, but White declined. See White to Gilman, June 25, 1875. *Gilman Papers*, Lanier Room, *loc. cit.*

John P. Mahaffy and Professor John R. Leslie. [1] He also inspected most of the scientific institutions of the city with Professor William Fletcher Barrett of the Royal College of Science. [2] In London Gilman had long talks with Charles Appleton, the distinguished editor of the *Academy*; with James Bryce, who was later to be an astute observer of the American scene; [3] and Joseph D. Hooker, president of the Royal Society. [4] Gilman spent ten days in Paris where the International Geographic Congress particularly interested him. He visited most of the institutions of higher learning and ". . . did what [he] could to collect the recent reports and discussions on Instruction in France, and by the aid of a very intelligent bookseller made a valuable collection of volumes and pamphlets." [5] In Strassburg, he "saw to advantage the new library which has been brought together in the few years which have passed since the war (1870-71) and which numbers the incredible amount of over 350,000 volumes!" [6] At Freiburg Gilman conferred with the historian, Hermann von Holst, with whom he was already acquainted.

> The University [Freiburg] here is one of the oldest in Germany and one of the smallest, but it has some excellent professors, and a very interesting history. The attraction to me was the Professor of History, Von Holst, with whom I was already acquainted, and who was spending his vacation here at work upon the continuation of a History of the United States. He has given me most of his time for two days, and through his valuable suggestions I have obtained an insight into some of the tendencies of German university discussion. He assures me that the best thinkers, both scientific men and literary men, think that too great freedom has been allowed to students to chose their own work, so that special education, in distinction from general culture, has been disproportionally encouraged. [7]

After visiting Heidelberg and Frankfort, Gilman arrived in Berlin where he spent some ten days. [8] In Berlin he talked with Rudolph Gneist, professor of law; Albert Friedrich Weber, professor of Sanskrit; Ferdinand von Richtofen, geologist and president of the Berlin Geographical Society; and George Neumayer, government hydrographer.

---

[1] July 18 to 20, 1875. *Autobiographical Fragments*.

[2] *Ibid.*

[3] Bryce paid Hopkins great praise in his *The American Commonwealth*, II, pp. 728-729.

[4] July 28 to 30, 1875. *Autobiographical Fragments*.

[5] Gilman to the trustees, August 23, 1875. Franklin, *op. cit.*, p. 203. The letters to the trustees are lost but most were published by Franklin, *op. cit.*, pp. 199-218.

[6] *Ibid.* In Franklin, *op. cit.*, p. 204.

[7] Gilman to the trustees, August 30, 1875. Franklin, *op. cit.*, pp. 204-205.

[8] Gilman to the trustees, September 13, 1875. Franklin, *op. cit.*, pp. 205-207.

With them all I discussed educational problems as they now present themselves in Germany. It is interesting to observe how alive the best men are
to the importance not only of maintaining but of improving their High
Schools and Universities, and how clear are their convictions that a thorough general education is essential as the foundation for special acquisitions. No part of my visit has been more profitable than this German
experience, and if I cannot reproduce the conversations, I can carry with
me to America a number of important pamphlets and magazine articles
in which these and other writers have expressed their views. [1]

In Vienna Gilman was "impressed . . . more than [by] any city I have
seen [for] the magnificence of its projects for the encouragement of
education and science." [2] By mid-September, 1875, Gilman was back
in England where he spent a month before returning home. [3] He visited
Owens College in Manchester "which was founded by a wealthy man
whose name it bears, about a quarter of a century ago, and from a
modest beginning it has attained great prominence among the literary
and scientific institutions of Great Britain." [4] In Glasgow he discerned
what he felt was a special warning to himself and the trustees:

> Glasgow is distinguished among all the cities which I have visited by
> having recently built a great structure, Gothic, quadrangular, and very
> costly,—(a million and a half of dollars already) for all departments of
> the University . . . The site is admirable, and the buildings very im-
> pressive . . . but it is worth a visit to Glasgow to hear from the lips of the
> professors their statements as to how ill adapted it is to their requirements.
> Mr. [Reverdy] Johnson will remember the Gothic quadrangular plans
> which we went to Hartford to see. Here is a structure in stone like that we
> saw on paper, and the very difficulties which we foresaw are realized in
> fact. . . . It is enough to say that in a splendid building given by the munifi-
> cence of Glasgow gentlemen, the architects, and not the people for whom
> the college is designed, have had their way. [5]

Gilman visited Oxford and Cambridge, and at Cambridge conferred
with the mathematicians, Arthur Cayley, Isaac Todhunter, and Norman
Ferrers. [6] At Oxford, he had many talks with Benjamin Jowett, the
eminent Greek scholar, [7] and possibly with Jowett drew up "an outline

---

[1] *Ibid.* In Franklin, *op. cit.*, p. 206.

[2] Gilman to the trustees, September 4, 1875. Franklin, *op. cit.*, p. 207.

[3] Franklin, *op. cit.*, p. 209.

[4] Gilman to the trustees, October 3, 1875. Franklin, *op. cit.*, p. 209. This is the only
letter extant for Gilman's stay in England.

[5] *Ibid.* In Franklin, *op. cit.*, pp. 210-11.

[6] *Ibid.* See also *The Launching of a University*, pp. 11-13.

[7] Franklin, *op. cit.*, p. 211.

of the possible organization of our work in Baltimore," [1] which has been lost. Gilman described the plan as brief but comprehensive. [2] His work in Europe over, Gilman prepared to return to America in mid-October, 1875. [3]

Some very difinite ideas formed in Gilman's mind during his European sojourn; perhaps, none of these owed their origin to the European trip, itself, but represented the sharpening of ideas long held by Gilman. His description of the architectural fiasco in Glasgow firmly registers his opposition to the monstrous university buildings of his era, and his determination to emphasize "men, not buildings." [4] In the Owens College of Manchester he saw good argument for the gradualism which he was to successfully inaugurate at the Johns Hopkins. [5] His meeting with James Bryce, "who holds a non-resident professorship of International Law in the University [Oxford], which requires him to give an annual course of twenty lectures," [6] no doubt, more clearly formed the idea of the "visiting lecturer" which he was to develop at Hopkins. But, as Hawkins observes, "if Gilman imbibed relatively few new ideas [in Europe] himself, he had an excellent opportunity to send home constructive suggestions to the trustees—to educate them to his way of thinking." [7] In essence, Gilman's own statement, taken at face value, has historical corroboration:

> So we did not undertake to establish a German university, nor an English university, but an American university, based upon and applied to the existing institutions of this country. Not only did we have no model to be followed; we did not even draw up a scheme or programme of ourselves, our associates and successors. For a long time our proceedings were "tentative," and this term was used so often that it became a byword for merriment. [8]

The preliminary plan of the Hopkins, [9] in its wedding of undergraduate

---

[1] *The Launching of a University*, p. 11.   [2] *Ibid.*

[3] *Autobiographical Fragments*, Lanier Room, *loc. cit.*

[4] Nicholas Murray Butler saw this as one of Gilman's great achievements. "President Gilman's Administration at the Johns Hopkins University," *American Monthly Review of Reviews*, 23 (January 1901), pp. 23-49.

[5] See *The Launching of a University*, p. 49.

[6] Quoted in Franklin, *op. cit.*, p. 200.

[7] Hawkins, *op. cit.*, p. 199. "Though Gilman often in later years cited European precedents for activities at Hopkins, he seems to have done so more out of a wish to gain respect for his program than out of any real sense of historical obligation." *Ibid.*

[8] *The Launching of a University*, p. 49.

[9] See pp. 65-67, *supra.*

and graduate education, in its practical emphasis, and in its adaptation of German ideals of graduate study demonstrated how, "under intelligently controlled conditions, one variant of the German graduate school could be established in the United States quickly." [1] It came as an inexorable sequel to what Storr has called, "The early traditions of graduate education," [2] and its wellsprings were as much in the Sheffield Scientific School as they were in the German precept. [3]

THE ORIGINAL FACULTY

In the *First Annual Report* (1876), Gilman noted that the selection of a faculty presented to him and the trustees "One of the most difficult and delicate tasks." [4] Above all, Gilman and the trustees had resolved,

> to consider especially the devotion of the candidate to some particular line of study and the certainty of his eminence in that speciality; the power to pursue independent and original investigation, and to inspire the young with enthusiasm for study and research; the willingness to co-operate in building up a new institution; and the freedom from tendencies toward ecclesiastical or sectional controversies. [5]

Only Henry A. Rowland had been engaged as Professor of Physics, [6] at the time the *First Annual Report* (January 1, 1876) appeared and Gilman now turned his complete attention to the matter of faculty appointments. In December (?) 1875, Gilman had written a brief essay for the trustees on "The Selection of Professors." [7] In it he had made the following observations:

1 the greatness of the University would depend on its able scholars.
2 the professors appointed must be men of "distinguished reputations.
3 the University must hire specialists since "the day has passed for *a* professor of sciences or *a* professor of languages or *a* professor of history . . . those gentlemen willing to teach anything or take any chair are not those we most require." [8]

---

[1] Ernest V. Hollis, *Toward Improving Ph.D. Programs*, p. 13.

[2] Storr, *op. cit.*, pp. 129-134.

[3] It is this historical continuity not only in the development of Gilman's educational thought, but also in the evolution of graduate study, which has not been completely discerned. Cf. Abraham Flexner, "The Graduate School in the United States," *Proceedings of the Association of American Universities* (1931), pp. 114-115.

[4] *First Annual Report*, 1876, p. 19.

[5] *Ibid.*, p. 21.

[6] *Ibid.*, p. 22. Rowland was not actually appointed professor of Physics until April, 1876. See *Trustee Minutes*, April 3, 17, 1876.

[7] A typescript is deposited in the *Johns Hopkins University Papers*, Lanier Room. It is mentioned in the Trustee Minutes, December 6, 1875.

[8] *Ibid.*

By April 1, 1876, the number of applications for teaching positions had reached 198. [1] "I will not recall the overtures received from men of no mark, or the overtures made to men of mark. Nor can I say whether it was harder to eliminate from the list candidates . . . second best, or to secure the best.'. [2] The high standards which Gilman set for prospective faculty members were not easy to meet, and Gilman met with little success in attempting to raid other established faculties. Typical of his efforts to obtain established scholars was his invitation to Professor Francis J. Child, the great Anglo-Saxon and Chaucerian expert of Harvard University. Although Child lacked opportunities for advanced instruction at Harvard, he declined "for domestic reasons but [told] Gilman that it had helped him as well as pleased him because it had led to his being wholly relieved at last from the burden of correcting undergraduate compositions." [3] President Eliot of Harvard recognized, in Gilman's effort to lure away a luminary like Child, that research was an important part of higher education. [4] In the effort to secure a faculty which would be given opportunity for research and one which would be expected to advance knowledge, Gilman forced the older universities to examine and redefine their aims. [5] As Flexner put it, "Research was not recognized as one of the dominant concerns of higher education until the flag was nailed to the mast on the opening of Johns Hopkins University." [6]

Gilman's first success in obtaining an American professor of established reputation came in Basil Lanneau Gildersleeve (1831-1924), the classical scholar. [7] Gildersleeve had graduated from Princeton in 1849, and had then studied in Germany at the Universities of Berlin, Bonn, and Göttingen, taking his Ph.D. at Göttingen in 1853. At the University of Virginia, where he had been appointed in 1866, he was Professor of Greek and Latin. Gildersleeve is an excellent example of what Hopkins

---

[1] *Executive Committee Minutes*, April 1, 1876.

[2] Gilman, *The Launching of a University*, p. 14.

[3] Henry James, *op. cit.*, II, pp. 14-15.

[4] *Ibid.*, pp. 15-20.

[5] See the exchange of letters between Gilman and Eliot in Willis Rudy, "Eliot and Gilman: the History of an Academic Friendship," *Teachers College Record*, 54 (March 1953), pp. 307-318.

[6] Abraham Flexner, "Graduate Study," *Atlantic Monthly*, 136 (March 1925), p. 530.

[7] There are some 6000 letters, documents, etc. of Gildersleeve in the Johns Hopkins University Library which have been relatively untouched. For Gildersleeve, see Francis G. Allinson, "Basil Gildersleeve," *Dictionary of American Biography*, VII, pp. 278-282. Some notices are in the Festschrift, *Studies in Honor of Basil L. Gildersleeve* (1902).

offered the serious research scholar. He wrote to Gilman of the "relief from the drudgery of elementary instruction and consequent opportunity for work on a higher plan" as reasons for coming to the Johns Hopkins University. [1] Gildersleeve accepted Gilman's invitation as early as December 11, 1875, [2] and his formal appointment as Professor of Greek came on January 17, 1876. [3] "It was of him [Gilman] that Professor Gildersleeve, when asked how he liked his transfer from the quiet shades of the University of Virginia to the city of Baltimore, replied that President Gilman's idea of a university was the same as the Presbyterian's idea of heaven, namely, a place where meetings ne'er break up and congregations have no end." [4]

While in England, Gilman had been introduced to the mathematician, James Joseph Sylvester (1814-1897) [5] who was recommended for the professorship of mathematics at the Johns Hopkins University by Sir Joseph D. Hooker, the President of the Royal Society. Sylvester, the most brilliant geometrician of his time, [6] had graduated from St. John's College, Cambridge, in 1837, but had been denied his degree because he was a Jew until the repeal of the Tests Act in 1872. He had been professor of mathematics in the University College of London from 1837 to 1841, and had taught at the University of Virginia between 1841-1845. From 1855 to 1870, he was professor of mathematics at the Woolwich Military Academy, but at the time of his recommendation to Gilman he was without position. Independent of Professor Hooker's recommendation of Sylvester, Gilman received a letter in Sylvester's behalf by one of the most distinguished mathematicians in America, Professor Benjamin Peirce of Harvard. This letter is well quoted in full, for apart from its recommendation of Sylvester, its philosophy of graduate education shows graphically the dissatisfaction with the American college of the 1870's. [7]

---

[1] Gildersleeve to Gilman, February 29, 1876. *Gilman Papers*, Lanier Room, *loc. cit.*

[2] Gildersleeve to Gilman, December 11, 1875. *Ibid.*

[3] *Trustee Minutes*, January 17, 1876.

[4] Quoted in Nicholas Murray Butler, *Across the Busy Years*, I, p. 9.

[5] For Sylvester see G.B. Halsted, "Sylvester at Hopkins," *The Johns Hopkins Alumni Magazine* (March 1916); R.C. Archibald, "Unpublished letters of James Joseph Sylvester and Other New Information Concerning his life and work," *Osiris*, I (1936), pp. 93-126; Fabian Franklin, *An Address Commemorative of Professor James Joseph Sylvester* (1897).

[6] Fabian Franklin, *An Address Commemorative of Professor James Joseph Sylvester*, p. 6.

[7] Peirce had written as early as 1856 a pamphlet, *Working Plan for the Foundation*

Hearing that you are in England I take the liberty to write you concerning an appointment in your new university, which I think it [sic] would be greatly to the benefit of our country and of American science if you could make. It is that of one of the two greatest geometers of England, J. J. Sylvester. If you enquire about him you will hear his genius universally recognized, but his power of teaching will probably be said to be quite deficient. Now there is no man living who is more luminous in his language, to those who have the capacity to comprehend him than Sylvester, provided the hearer is in a lucid interval. But as the barn-door fowl cannot understand the flight of the eagle, so it is the eaglet only who will be nourished by his instruction. But as the greatness of a university must depend upon its few able scholars, you cannot have a great university without such great men as Sylvester in your corps of teachers. Among your pupils, sooner or later, there must be one who has a genius for geometry. He will be Sylvester's special pupil, the one pupil who will derive from his master knowledge and enthusiasm—and that one pupil will give more reputation to your institution than the ten thousand who will complain of the obscurity of Sylvester, and for whom you will provide another class of teachers. Some men regard this peculiarity of the masters of geometry, to be obscure to ordinary scholars, as a geometric peculiarity. But is it not the same in all departments to him who looks into the depths of the human understanding? Can every dunce read Shakespeare and Goethe and Demosthenes and Aeschylus? Is it not true reading of the princes of thought a royal attribute—which only princes possess in their lucid intervals? I hope you will find it in your heart to do for Sylvester what his own countrymen have failed to do—place him where he belongs, and the time will come when all the world will applaud the wisdom of your selection. [1]

Gilman took the suggestion, and after an extensive correspondence, Sylvester accepted the appointment as Professor of Mathematics in March 1876. [2]

Originally, Gilman had planned a sole appointment as professor of chemistry and physics, but he was dissuaded in this by Professor Woolcott

---

of a University. He had observed: "The best plan for founding a university is that which concentrates the interests of the largest community, and combines the greatest variety of intellect, with the smallest pecuniary outlay and the least provocation of opposition. . . . . Its professors must be the ablest men in their respective departments; it must be connected with a fine library, a well equipped observatory, and complete collections and laboratories for the elucidation . . . of every species of knowledge." Quoted in Storr, *op. cit.*, p. 89.

[1] Benjamin Peirce to D.C. Gilman, October 4, 1875. Peirce's prediction came true. Fabian Franklin, the biographer of Gilman, was Sylvester's star pupil at Hopkins and became as celebrated a mathematician as his master. See Halsted, "Sylvester at Hopkins," *loc. cit., passim.*

[2] See Gilman to Sylvester, November 29, 1875. Sylvester to Gilman, December 17, 1875; February 10, 1876; April 22, 1876; March 23, 1876. *Gilman Papers,* Lanier Room, *loc. cit.*

Gibbs of Harvard University, [1] and began enquiries for a suitable appointment in chemistry. He finally fixed upon Ira Remsen (1846-1927) as the most suitable candidate. [2] Remsen had been educated at the College of the City of New York, and had graduated at the College of Physicians and Surgeons (Columbia) in 1867. He had been resident in Germany for some years and had taken a doctorate in chemistry at Göttingen in 1870. Remsen had actually taught at the University of Tübingen, and in this respect, he offered the closest connections with German teaching methods. [3] Gilman had found Remsen at Williams College where he had been appointed professor of physics and chemistry in 1872, and where Remsen had been denied the research facilities he had known at Tübingen as the great Fittig's assistant. [4] Remsen accepted the Hopkins offer with alacrity. [5]

Gilman's last two appointments to the original faculty were Englishmen. The English biologist, Thomas Huxley, wrote to Gilman recommending his young assistant and collaborator, Henry Newall Martin. [6] Martin had attended the University of London; and by 1874, when he was only twenty-six, he was already a fellow of University College, London, and recognized for the value of his research. In the appointment of Charles D'Urban Morris as collegiate professor of Greek and Latin, Gilman demonstrated once again his interest in the undergraduate college. Rowland, Gildersleeve, Remsen, Martin, and Sylvester were the nucleus of a great research faculty, but Morris represented the dying classicism of an undergraduate world. Morris was a graduate of Lincoln College, Oxford and was an M.A. and fellow of Oriel College, and, at the time of Gilman's invitation, he was professor of classics at the University of the City of New York (New York University). [7]

---

[1] Gilman to Gibbs, January 4, 15, 18, 25, 1876. *Ibid.* Gibbs had been appointed Rumford Professor of Science at Harvard in 1863. See Henry James, *op. cit.*, I, pp. 102-112.

[2] See Frederick H. Getman, *The Life of Ira Remsen*; and W. A. Noyes and J. F. Norris, *Biographical Memoir of Ira Remsen.*

[3] Getman, *op. cit.*, pp. 46-48.

[4] *Ibid.*, pp. 131-137.

[5] See Remsen to Gilman, June 29, August 25, 1876. *Gilman Papers*, Lanier Room, *loc. cit.*

[6] Thomas Huxley to Gilman, February 20, 1876. *Gilman Papers*, Lanier Room, *loc. cit.* For Martin see W. H. Howell, "Henry Newell Martin," Johns Hopkins University *Circular*, n.s., 1908, p. 55; Russell H. Chittenden, "Henry Newell Martin," *Dictionary of American Biography*, XII, pp. 337-338. See also Martin to Gilman, June 21, 1876. *Gilman Papers.*

[7] Posterity has been very unkind to Morris. There is no notice of him in the *Diction-*

If Gilman complained to the historian Bancroft, "We can't have a great university without great scholars; & great teachers won't come to us till we have a great university," [1] he unwittingly had indicated his course of action in December, 1875, when he wrote to President James B. Angell of the University of Michigan that he "saw the answer [to the problem of a faculty] in young men who have won their spurs, and are now ready for a career." [2] Rowland, Martin, and Remsen were his young men ready for a career; Sylvester and Gildersleeve were established scholars who had been denied opportunity for research and the advancement of knowledge; and Morris was Gilman's connection with the collegiate world which assured its continuation. [3]

GILMAN'S INAUGURAL ADDRESS: A STATEMENT OF POLICY

When Daniel Coit Gilman invited President Charles W. Eliot of Harvard University to deliver a congratulatory address at the inaugural exercises of the Johns Hopkins University on February 22, 1876, he further strengthened a friendship founded on university reform. [4] It is inconceivable that Gilman should have invited President McCosh of Princeton, or his old colleague, President Porter of Yale. "Eliot and Gilman were in loyal and close alliance in pursuing their aims. Each clearly influenced the other. . . . They exchanged ideas, information, even professors. They became in every sense of the word indispensable to each other." [5] Gilman wrote to Eliot: "Historically, it would be a grand thing to have the oldest college in the land greet the youngest, especially as the counsels of the senior were sought so early and have been followed in so many important measures by the junior." [6] True

---

ary of American Biography. Even the redoubtable Dictionary of National Biography fails to include him. Franklin says of him: "In this appointment the college idea was explicitly recognized; and [he] represented . . . an element quite distinctive." Op. cit., pp. 217-218.

[1] Gilman to C.F.B. Bancroft, February 7, 1876. Gilman Papers, Lanier Room, loc. cit.

[2] Gilman to Angell, December 10, 1875. Ibid.

[3] Abraham Flexner seems to have completely missed Morris and the provision for collegiate instruction at Hopkins in his heavy insistence on the German model for Gilman's university. See his Universities, American, English, German, passim.

[4] See Henry James, op. cit., II, pp. 13-18.

[5] Willis Rudy, "Eliot and Gilman: the History of an Academic Friendship," loc. cit., p. 315. Rudy is stretching the point when he sees the basis of the friendship as originating in "Darwinian evolution, scientific empiricism, and pragmatism." Ibid.

[6] Gilman to Eliot, January 25, 1876. Gilman Papers, Lanier Room, loc. cit.

to form, Eliot did more than deliver a congratulatory address. He took the occasion to make a major pronouncement:

> There is a too common opinion that a college or university which is not denominational must therefore be irreligious; but the absence of sectarian control should not be confounded with lack of piety. A university whose officers and students are divided among many sects need no more be irreverant and irreligious than the community which in respect to diversity of creeds it resembles. . . . A university can not be built upon a sect, unless, indeed, it be a sect which includes the whole of the educated portion of the nation. [1]

In introducing Gilman, Reverdy Johnson remarked: "The University now stands forth baptized with ancient Harvard as its sponsor." [2]

In his inaugural address as President of Johns Hopkins University, Gilman made public the policy that the new university would pursue. He noted at once that, "The almoners of his [Johns Hopkins'] bounty are restrained by no shackles bequeathed by a departed benefactor, as they enter upon their course bearing in the one hand the ointment of charity and in the other the lamp of science." [3] Above all, the foundation of the Johns Hopkins University came after "numerous experiments, some with oil in the lamps and some without; after costly ventures of which we reap the lessons, while others bear the loss; after Jefferson, Nott, Wayland, Quincy, Agassiz, Tappan, Mark Hopkins, Woolsey, have completed their official services and have given us their supreme decisions; while the strong successors of these strong men, Eliot, Porter, Barnard, White, Angell and McCosh, are still upon the controversial platform." [4] And he cautioned, in the ubiquitous impression of the German *Wissenschaft*, that "At a distance, Germany seems the one country where educational problems are determined; not so, on a nearer look. The thoroughness of the German mind, its desire for perfection in every detail, and its philosophical aptitudes are well illustrated by the controversies now in vogue in the land of universities. In following, as we are prone to do in educational matters, the example of Germany, we must

---

[1] *Addresses at the Inauguration of Daniel C. Gilman* . . . , p. 8.

[2] *Ibid.*, p. 4.

[3] *Ibid.*, p. 23.

[4] *Ibid.*, p. 27. Gilman had voiced the same sentiments some years earlier in "Four College Inaugurals: White, McCosh, Eliot, Porter," *Christian Union*, II (January 31, 1872), pp. 119-120. Gilman was magnanimous, to say the least, to include McCosh and Porter among the reformers. Yet, it was typical of Gilman's effort to unite the old and the new.

beware lest we accept what is there cast off; lest we introduce faults as well as virtues, defects with excellence." [1]

Then, what must the Johns Hopkins aspire to be? First, it must be a "university" and not a "college" alone. "The University [Gilman continued] is a place for the advanced special education of youth who have been prepared for its freedom by the discipline of a lower school." [2] It is unlike the college, for the college "implies, as a general rule, restriction rather than freedom; tutorial rather than professional guidance; residence within appointed bounds; the chapel, the dining hall, and the daily inspection. The college theoretically stands *in loco parentis*; it does not afford a very wide scope; it gives a liberal and substantial foundation on which the university instruction may be wisely built." [3] But, in his review of the historical antecedents of the Hopkins, Gilman introduced the following cogently made observations which clearly show that Thwing's statement is in error when he says: "The keynote of the German system was also the keynote of Mr. Gilman's conception of the University that was to be." [4]

> The earliest foundations in our country were colleges, not universities. Scholars were often graduated early in this century at the age when they now enter. Earnest efforts are now making to establish universities. Harvard, with a boldness which is remarkable, has essentially given up its collegiate restrictions and introduced the benefits of university freedom; Yale preserves its college course intact, but has added a school of science and developed a strong graduate department; the University of Michigan and Cornell University quite early adopted the discipline of universities, and already equal or surpass not a few of their elder sisters; the University of Virginia from its foundation has upheld the university in distinction from the college idea. *The cry all over the land is for university advantages, not as superseding but as supplementing collegiate discipline.* [5]

And the eclectic note sounded at the University of California is again made clear. "Most institutions are not free to build anew; they can only re-adjust. It has been playfully said that 'traditions and conditions' impede their progress. But whatever may be the concrete difficulties,

---

[1] *Ibid.*, pp. 28-29.

[2] *Ibid.*, p. 31.

[3] *Ibid.*, p. 32.

[4] Charles F. Thwing, *The American and the German University*, pp. 108-109. Taking her cue from Thwing, Mary Pierson repeats the same statement in her *Graduate Work in the South*, p. 18. It is made, in another way, by Abraham Flexner, *The American College*, pp. 177-179.

[5] *Ibid.*, pp. 34-35. Gilman had developed this thesis in his article, "Education in America, 1776-1876," *North American Review*, 122 (January 1876), pp. 193-196.

on many abstract principles there is little need of controversy. Our effort will be to accept that which is determined,—to avoid that which is obsolescent, to study that which is doubtful,—'slowly making haste'." [1]

Thus, for Gilman, the American university was essentially an indigenous phenomenon and its success, in 1876, lay in seizing and welding together the *disjecta membra* of the earlier reformers, seizing what Pierson has called "their zeal for professional schools, their faith in the scientific method applied to learning, their desire for Ph.D.'s, their knowledge of so many techniques—in short, the way they built around and on top of and inside of or in place of the old fashioned college." [2] How was this to be done? Gilman suggested that a statement be drawn up enumerating what had been agreed upon in university education, and that this statement be a point of departure. [3] In this wise, he listed twelve points which he felt must be the blueprint for the success or failure of the Hopkins experiment.

1 All sciences are worthy of promotion; or in other words, it is useless to dispute whether literature or science should receive most attention, or whether there is any essential difference between the old and the new education.

2 Religion has nothing to fear from science, and science need not be afraid of religion. Religion claims to interpret the word of God, and science to reveal the laws of God. The interpreters may blunder, but truths are immutable, eternal and never in conflict. [4]

3 Remote utility is quite as worthy to be thought of as immediate advantage. These ventures are not always most sagacious that expect a return on the morrow. It sometimes pays to send our argosies across the seas; to make investments with an eye to slow but sure returns. So it is always in the promotion of science. [5]

4 As it is impossible for any university to encourage with equal freedom all branches of learning, a selection must be made by enlightened governors, and that selection must depend on the requirements and deficiencies of a given people, in a given period. These is no absolute standard of preference. What is more important at one time or in one place may be less needed elsewhere and otherwise. [6]

---

[1] *Ibid.*, p. 35.

[2] George W. Pierson, "American Universities in the Nineteenth Century: The Formative Period," in *The Modern University*, ed. by Margaret Clapp, pp. 89-90.

[3] *Addresses at the Inauguration of Daniel C. Gilman . . . ,* p. 36.

[4] For a modern discussion of the problem, see Sir Walter Moberly, *The Crisis in the University*, Chapter V.

[5] Cf. Gilman, *The Launching of the University*, pp. 237-251.

[6] This is an oft repeated theme with Gilman. In his inaugural speech at the University of California, he had observed: "It is not the University of Berlin nor of New Haven

5 Individual students cannot pursue all branches of learning, and must be allowed to select, under the guidance of those who are appointed to counsel them. Nor can able professors be governed by routine. Teachers and pupils must be allowed great freedom in their method of work. Recitations, lectures, examinations, laboratories, libraries, field exercises, travels, are all legitimate means of culture. [1]

6 The best scholars will almost invariably be those who make special attainments on the foundation of a broad and liberal culture.

7 The best teachers are usually those who are free, competent and willing to make original researches in the library and the laboratory. [2]

8 The best investigators are usually those who have also the responsibilities of instruction, gaining thus the incitement of colleagues, the encouragement of pupils, the observation of the public.

9 Universities should bestow their honors with a sparing hand; their benefits most freely. [3]

10 A university cannot be created in a day; it is a slow growth. The University of Berlin has been quoted as a proof of the contrary. That was indeed a quick success, but in an old, compact country, crowded with learned men eager to assemble at the Prussian court. It was a change of base rather than a sudden development.

11 The object of the university is to develop character—to make men. It misses its aim if it produces pedants, or simple artisans, or cunning sophists, or pretentious practitioners. Its purport is not so much to impart knowledge to the pupils, as to whet the appetite, exhibit methods, develop powers, strengthen judgment, and invigorate the intellectual and moral forces. It should prepare for the service of society a class of students who will be wise, thoughtful, progressive guides in whatever department of work or thought they may be engaged.

12 Universities easily fall into ruts. Almost every epoch requires a fresh start. [4]

For Gilman, then, the university, to justify its existence, must serve actively the basic needs of American society. [5] The twelve points he

---

which we are to copy; it is not the University of Oakland nor of San Francisco which we are to create; but it is the university of this state." *University Problems in the United States*, p. 157

[1] Gilman is referring to the fexibility of the undergraduate curriculum at the Sheffield Scientific School.

[2] Points 6 and 7 are modifications of the German concepts of *Lernfreiheit* and *Lehrfreiheit*.

[3] An obvious reference to the free bestowal of honorary degrees. See S.E. Epler, *Honorary Degrees: A Survey of their Use and Abuse*. In its first ten years, Hopkins conferred only two honorary degrees. See the *Eleventh Annual Report*, 1886, p. 67.

[4] *Addresses at the Inauguration of Daniel C. Gilman . . .* , pp. 36-38.

[5] See, in this connection, Josiah Royce, "Present Ideals of American University Life," *Scribner's Magazine*, 10 (September 1891), p. 383. "The real mind which the university has to train is the mind of the nation." *Ibid.*

enumerated caught up most of the directions which had evolved from the efforts of the earlier reformers of higher education. If the "achievement of the prewar reformers was to establish a tradition of aspiration and experimentation," [1] Gilman's contribution lay in the implementation of the earlier ideas. Eloquently, Gilman observed that universities are born in social crises and give birth to those *qui genus humanum ingenio superavit.* [2] Two other points are worthy of note in Gilman's inaugural address. The first of these was Gilman's concern with obtaining young men of promise who would furnish not only his graduate student body but assure the reservoir from which future faculty members would be drawn. [3] In this matter, he observed:

> We shall hope to secure a strong staff of young men, appointing them because they have twenty years before them; selecting them on evidence of their ability; increasing constantly their emoluments, and promoting them because of their merit to successive posts, as scholars, fellows, assistants, adjuncts, professors and university professors. This plan will give us an opportunity to introduce some of the features of the English fellowship and the German system of privat-docents; or in other words, to furnish positions where young men desirous of a university career may have a chance to begin, sure at least of a support while waiting for promotion. [4]

In establishing the fellowship at the Johns Hopkins University, Gilman was not original, [5] but his use of the fellowship as the adjunct of graduate study proved the most imaginative and fruitful use made up to that time.[6] In the second matter, Gilman was not successful. From the very first Gilman was concerned with the higher education of women. At the University of California, he had favored and provided for the admission of women to all departments. [7] At Hopkins he reiterated his earlier statement: "Of this I am certain, that they are not among the wise, who depreciate the intellectual capacity of women, and they are not among the prudent, who would deny to women the best opportunities for education

---

[1] Storr, *op. cit.*, p. 129.

[2] D.C. Gilman, *The Benefits which Society Derives from Universities*, p. 11.

[3] This led to Pierson to observe: "In a word Gilman closed the gap between need and demand for advanced studies by first 'hiring his students.'" George W. Pierson, "American Universities in the Nineteenth Century," *loc. cit.*, p. 75.

[4] *Addresses at the Inauguration of Daniel C. Gilman . . .* , p. 49.

[5] See Frederick P. Keppel, "Fellowship," *Cyclopedia of Education*, ed. by Paul Monroe, II, pp. 591-596.

[6] See *infra*, pp. 85-89.

[7] *Statement of the Progress and Condition of the University of California*, p. 47.

and culture." [1] But he did not go on to recommend the free admission of women; instead, he suggested a separate college for women allied with the Johns Hopkins University and closely modeled on the plan of Girton College at the University of Cambridge. [2] As it was, women were not admitted to the graduate courses until 1907, and then only because of the insistence of a female benefactor. [3]

THE PH.D. PROGRAM AND THE GRADUATE FELLOWSHIP

It becomes apparent from a study of Gilman's annual reports that the Hopkins Ph.D. was not clearly defined at first but rather developed in terms of the experience of the university in the first two years. That Gilman struck out boldly to establish the Ph.D. as the chief reward for graduate study is in itself significant. [4] He was not totally without model, [5] for he had personally assisted in the institution of the doctorate at the Sheffield Scientific School and his letters show that he was in frequent communication with Professors George Brush and James D. Dana of the Sheffield Scientific School during 1875 and 1876. [6] But the Hopkins was a new foundation, and Gilman literally implemented his definition of "the university freedom." "If we would maintain a university, great freedom must be allowed both to the teachers and scholars. This involves freedom of methods to be employed by the instructors on the one hand, and on the other, freedom of courses to be selected by the students." [7] Accordingly, the plan which Gilman proposed as the original constitutional basis of the university contented itself with the simple statement, "The second degree of Master of Arts and of Doctor of Philosophy shall be given on examination only, at an interval of at least two years subsequent to the first degree." [8] No notice was made as to

---

[1] *Adresses at the Inauguration of Daniel C. Gilman* . . . , p. 53.

[2] A reading of the *Trustee Minutes* in 1876, 1877, and 1879 shows that Trustee Reverdy Johnson was unalterably opposed to the admission of women, and Hawkins, *op. cit.*, p. 97, suggests that Johnson finally withdrew in protest against the admission of women to the special classes in physiology for teachers.

[3] See French, *op. cit.*, p. 147.

[4] "The early reformers had not agreed to make the Ph.D. degree the chief reward for graduate study. The seminary had hardly begun its career. Even research, although frequently mentioned and highly valued, had yet to receive the concentrated attention which later became a distinguishing mark of graduate studies." Storr, *op. cit.*, p. 134.

[5] *Addresses at the Inauguration of Daniel C. Gilman* . . . , p. 38.

[6] See, e.g., Gilman to Brush, January 30, 1875; to Dana, April 4, 1876. *Gilman Papers*, Lanier Room, loc. cit.

[7] *Addresses at the Inauguration of Daniel C. Gilman* . . . , p. 54.

[8] *Second Annual Report* (1877), p. 28.

class attendance, credit hours or grades in courses. [1] As to the departments of instruction, provision was made for:

1 Ancient Languages, including Greek, Latin, Comparative Philology.
2 Modern Languages, including English, French, German, Spanish, Italian.
3 Mathematics, including Pure and Applied.
4 Physical Sciences, including Chemistry and Physics.
5 Natural Sciences, including Geology, Mineralogy, Zoology and Botany.
6 Moral and Historical Sciences, including Ethics, Political Economy, History, International and Public Law. [2]

As an integral part of the Ph.D. program, Gilman instituted the graduate fellowship. The graduate fellowship was somewhat tenuously announced in the *First Annual Report*, [3] but within a year the conditions of appointment were carefully defined.

The graduate fellowship was nothing new but "the real beginning of the fellowship system came in 1876, when twenty university fellowships were established at Johns Hopkins, each bearing a stipend of $ 500, less tuition." [4] As finally defined the fellowship program "offered twenty fellowships or graduate scholarships, yielding $ 500 a year and renewable, to be bestowed for excellence in any one of the following subjects:

Philology	Mathematics
Literature	Engineering
History	Physics
Ethics and Metaphysics	Chemistry.
Political Science	Natural History." [5]

The object of the program was "to give to scholars of promise the opportunity to prosecute further studies, under favorable circumstances, and likewise to open a career for those who propose to follow the pursuit of literature or science." [6] Each candidate was expected to give evidence of a liberal education, and of "decided proclivity toward a special line of study." [7] He was expected "to devote his time to the prosecution of

---

[1] *Johns Hopkins University Circular*, No. 7, (February 1877), p. 80.

[2] *Second Annual Report* (1877), p. 27.

[3] *First Annual Report* (1876), p. 32. "Ten fellowships, each yielding $ 500, are offered to college graduates, who exhibit special acquisitions in some branch of science or literature . . . ."

[4] *Second Annual Report* (1877), p. 12.

[5] *Ibid.*

[6] *Ibid.*, pp. 12-13.

[7] *Ibid.* "The University expects to be benefitted by their presence and influence, and by their occasional services; form among the number it hopes to secure some of its permanent teachers." *Idem.*

special study (not professional) with the approval of the President, and before the close of the year, to give evidence of progress by the preparation of a thesis, the completion of a research, the delivery of a lecture, or by some other method." [1] A total of 152 applications were received, and out of these, 107 were deemed eligible. Their applications were referred "to specialists in each department, who examined carefully the claims of the candidates and reported to the Trustees the persons whom they deemed worthy of receiving the appointment." [2] Thus, Gilman solved one of the problems which plagued the early educational reformers. As Storr as observed, there was a "vast difference between *need* as felt by a few academic reformers and *demand* as evidenced by actual appearance of students. It was one thing for a few far-sighted men to sense a need in this country for highly trained men; it was another thing for immature B.A.'s to give up the opportunity for quick fortunes in order to become specially trained for anything." [3] But there is another side to the coin; unerringly, Gilman sensed in the imaginative use of the fellowship program the means whereby a quick corps of graduate students could be assembled, and the number of initial applications which he received, demonstrates that a far greater demand for graduate study existed than has been indicated by the earlier investigators. [4] In point of fact, the enrollment of graduate students in 1876-1877 numbered 54 students; in 1877-1878, it numbered 58 students; and in 1878-1879, it numbered 55 students. [5] In the first three years of instruction the nucleus of graduate students had as its core the twenty graduate fellowships. [6]

Of the first twenty fellows, two already had received the Ph.D. at other institutions which further illustrates Gilman's imaginative use of the fellowship to bring talent to the new university. Herbert Baxter Adams (1850-1901), who was given a fellowship in history, was a graduate

---

[1] *Ibid.* p. 13.

[2] *Ibid.*, pp. 13-14.

[3] As quoted in George W. Pierson, "American Universities in the Nineteenth Century," *loc. cit.*, pp. 74-75. It is in this context that Pierson makes the observation: "In a word Gilman closed the gap between need and demand for advanced studies by first hiring his students." *Idem.*

[4] There is no notice of the fellowships in Thwing, *op. cit.* or in Mary B. Pierson, *op. cit.* Ryan, *op. cit.*, mentions the fellowship *en passant*. Flexner, *Daniel Coit Gilman*, pp. 76-78, in a brief discussion, fails to relate the fellowship to the Ph.D. program.

[5] *Third Annual Report* (1878), p. 42.

[6] See Gilman's statement. *Ibid.*

of Amherst College and had taken his Ph.D. at Heidelberg in 1876. [1]
It was Adams who introduced the German *Verfassungsgeschichte*
tradition into American graduate instruction, [2] and who fulfilled Gilman's expectations by becoming, in due course, an associate and finally
professor of history in 1880 at the new university. [3] The second Ph.D.
among the original fellows was Charles R. Lanman (1850-1941), who
following his graduation at Yale in 1871, had spent several years in
Germany and had taken his Ph.D. at Leipsic in 1875. [4] Lanman was
appointed fellow in philology; the following year he was made assistant
professor of Sanskrit, and in a short stay at the Hopkins he had as one
of his students, Maurice Bloomfield, whose career marked "the end of
an epoch in philological scholarship." [5] The philosopher, Josiah Royce
(1855-1916), was also one of the original twenty and after leaving the
Hopkins in 1878 went on to a distinguished career at Harvard University. [6] Of the original twenty, "thirteen later held professorships in
American colleges, two were scientists in the government service, three
more were well-recognized scholars and consultants, and two became
successful lawyers." [7]

By 1878, four of the holders of fellowships were ready to be admitted
to the Ph.D., and the requirements for the degree became set and fixed. [8]
In the long tenure of Gilman's presidency the requirements for the degree
were only slightly modified, and to a great measure the Hopkins Ph.D.,
as it evolved in its first two years, became the standard for the American
graduate school. [9] The requirements were fixed as follows:

---

[1] There are over 6000 separate documents of Adams in the Lanier Room of the
Johns Hopkins University Library, largely unworked.

[2] See W. Stull Holt, ed., *Historical Scholarship in the United States, 1876-1901 as
revealed in the Correspondence of Herbert Baxter Adams*, p. 131.

[3] *Fifth Annual Report* (1880), p. 31.

[4] Lanman regarded the fellowship program as Gilman's greatest contribution to
American graduate education. See his "Daniel Coit Gilman (1831-1908)," *Proceedings
of the American Academy of Arts and Sciences*, 52 (1917), p. 838.

[5] Franklin Edgerton, "Maurice Bloomfield," *Johns Hopkins Alumni Magazine*,
17 (March 1929), p. 115.

[6] Royce wrote of his Hopkins experience: "The beginning of the Johns Hopkins
University was a dawn wherein 'twas a bliss to be alive'." "Present Ideals of American
University Life," *Scribner's Magazine*, 10 (September 1891), p. 383.

[7] French, *op. cit.*, p. 44.

[8] The M.A. was awarded with the Ph.D. in 1878 and 1879. *Third Annual Report*
(1878), p. 37; *Fourth Annual Report* (1879), p. 25. It was thereafter discontinued and
not reinstituted as a separate degree until 1909. French, *op. cit.*, p. 344. French seems
unaware of the M.A. 's earlier existence.

[9] See Ernest V. Hollis, *Toward Improving Ph. D. Programs*, p. 21. If one is disposed

1 The candidates must already have been admitted, two years or more previously, to the first or Baccalaureate degree in a respectable institution of recognized standing.

2 Each candidate devotes his attention to one main subject and to one subsidiary subject. It is required that these subjects shall be sufficiently broad to require prolonged and arduous study, and that the secondary subject shall be pertinent to the principal theme. [1]

3 A residence of not less than one year in this University is now required of all candidates for this degree. [2]

4 The examination for this degree is threefold. In every case the candidate presents an elaborate thesis, on a topic approved by his chief adviser in the Faculty. The preparation of this thesis requires labor for the greater part of an academic year, and the completed paper is supposed to show the candidate's mastery of his subject, his powers of independent thought as well as of careful research, and his ability to express, in a clear and systematic order, and in appropriate language, the results of his study.

5 Every thesis is submitted by the Faculty to one of their own number, or to some other competent examiner who certifies whether or not, in his opinion, it is sufficiently good to be accepted. In case of its approval, the personal examination of the candidate goes forward, and this varies in form at the convenience of the examiner and in accordance with the requirements of the subject. As a part of the examination, the candidate appears before the professors collectively, or before some of their number, and submits to an oral questioning; at another time prepared questions are set before him for careful answers in writing.

6 An acquaintance with Latin, French, and German, so far at least that writings in these languages may be easily read, is in all cases expected. [3]

7 Evidence of acquaintance with the methods of modern scientific research, in at least one branch of science, is also expected in the case of those whose principal studies are in such departments as language, history, philosophy, etc.

8 In addition to the resident professors, scholars of distinction are from time to time invited to participate in the examinations, and examine the theses of the candidates. [4]

---

to argue a qualitative difference, it must be admitted that, quantitatively, the American Ph.D. requirements remain essentially those which Gilman instituted. Cf. the requirements of present day American faculties in Frederic W. Ness, ed., *A Guide to Graduate Study*.

[1] Later extended to two subsidiary subjects. See *Eleventh Annual Report* (1886), p. 11.

[2] Gilman at first entertained the examination scheme for degrees used by the University of London as a possible method but never adopted it. See *Third Annual Report* (1878), pp. 37-38.

[3] The requirement of Latin was later dropped. See French, *op. cit.*, p. 342.

[4] *Third Annual Report* (1878), pp. 37-38. The requirements for the Ph.D., as outlined by Gilman, essentially answer some of the criticisms of the Ph.D. made by the Com-

It was under these conditions that Henry C. Adams, Thomas Craig, Josiah Royce, and Ernest G. Sihler were the first candidates admitted to the Ph.D. on June 13, 1878. [1] Each had held a fellowship, and each had earned his degree under the principles outlined above. Josiah Royce's candidacy was typical:

> Josiah Royce, of California, A Bachelor of Arts of the University of California [1875], presented a thesis on the *Interdependence of the Principles of Human Knowledge*, which was referred to Professor Porter of Yale College.
> His main subject was the History of Philosophy, ancient and modern, upon which he was examined by Professor G. S. Morris, of the University of Michigan, by written questions. His subsidiary examination was on the history of German literature of the eighteenth and nineteenth centuries, which was conducted by Assistant Professor Brandt, partly in the presence of the Faculty. [2]

Gilman's use of the outsider for examination of doctoral candidates was typical of his flexible approach to the problem of graduate study. In the absence of a large resident staff, he chose to use the entire backyard of American education to give his institution and his graduates an immediate academic respectability. The invitation to the outside examiner continued through all of Gilman's tenure; it was dropped only after Ira Remsen became the second president of the Johns Hopkins University in 1901. [3] Only slight modifications of the Ph.D. requirement were made during Gilman's long tenure. In 1883 a Board of University Examiners was constituted consisting of the President, professors and associate professors of the philosophical faculty which was given charge

---

mittee on Policies of the Association of Graduate Schools. The Committee's recommendations for shorter time limits, stricter admission to candidacy, and more stringent examination on the thesis, are all met in Gilman's proposals. See Jacques Barzun, "Doctors and Masters—Good and Bad," *Journal of Proceedings and Addresses*, Ninth Annual Conference of the Association of Graduate Schools (1957), pp. 1-7. Certainly, Gilman and the Hopkins were not responsible for what William James later characterized "The Ph.D. Octopus." See William James, "The Ph.D. Octopus," *The Harvard Monthly*, March, 1903. Gilman's aim was never the creation of a *gelehrtes Publikum*.

[1] *Third Annual Report* (1878), pp. 38-39. Henry C. Adams (1851-1921), the economist, is often confused with Herbert B. Adams, the historian. Henry C. Adams taught at Cornell and in 1887 became professor of political economy at the University of Michigan. See R. M. Wenley, et al., "Henry C. Adams," *Journal of Political Economy*, 30 (April 1922), pp. 201-11.

[2] *Third Annual Report* (1878), p. 39. The annual reports contain full notices of all graduates, theses, and some notices of examiners. For a list of the Ph.D.'s and theses, 1878-1886, see Appendix II.

[3] See French, *op. cit.*, p. 341.

of the general arrangements for the instruction of graduate students and the examination of candidates for the degree of Doctor of Philosophy. [1] The two year interval between the first degree and the doctorate was extended to three. [2] In 1887 a further revision was made in requiring that theses be printed in whole, or in part, and that one hundred and fifty copies be given to the University for use by the library for exchange purposes. [3]

Although much has been made of Gilman's introduction of the graduate seminar at Hopkins, [4] it is difficult to speak of the seminaries (so they were first called)[5] with any fixed definition or plan. Gilman, himself, defined the seminar as "associations of advanced students guided by a director in the prosecution of special researches." [6] Only two seminars were originally organized, by Professor Gildersleeve in Greek and by Associate Herbert B. Adams in History. [7] In the sciences the seminar was never very successful; the instructors seemed to prefer to work with the students in individual conferences. [8] But, above all, the seminar was very much something which was fashioned by the individual instructor. Perhaps, nearest to the German *seminarium* method was Herbert Baxter Adams who brought the *Historische Gesellschaft* with him fresh from Heidelberg. [9] By 1892, Adams had graduated thirty eight students in history from his seminar in "institutional history" and the early theses done under his direction clearly show the preoccupation with the German *Verfassungsgeschichte* then so popular in Germany. [10] It has suggested that when thesis topics began to run out, Adams advised his students to turn from American to European history and that the youthful Frederick Jackson Turner took such patriotic umbrage at

---

[1] *Eleventh Annual Report* (1886), pp. 11-14.

[2] *Ibid.*, p. 11.

[3] French, *op. cit.*, p. 343. Prior to this, the theses were returned to the candidates. For example John Dewey's thesis (1884) on *The Psychology of Kant* (as noted in the *Ninth Annual Report*, 1884, p. 75) is not extant.

[4] Byrne J. Horton, *The Graduate School . . .* , Chapter II.

[5] See *Fourth Annual Report* (1879), pp. 51-56.

[6] "Remarks of President Gilman at the Second Anniversary Meeting, February 22, 1878," typescript in *Gilman Papers*, Lanier Room.

[7] *Fourth Annual Report*, (1879), pp. 54-55.

[8] *Ibid.*, pp. 52-53.

[9] See Herbert B. Adams, "Special Methods of Historical Study," in Andrew D. White, Charles K. Adams, *et al.*, *Methods of Teaching History*.

[10] See W. Stull Holt, ed., *Historical Scholarship in the United States, 1876-1901, as revealed in the Correspondence of Herbert Baxter Adams*. For a description of the history seminar at Hopkins in 1896, see Appendix I.

this attitude that he turned to the epoch-making studies of the frontier which marked the beginning of the successful broadening of the study of American history. [1] The description of Professor Gildersleeve's seminar in Greek, as held in 1883-84, is representative:

> Under the direction of Professor Gildersleeve, the advanced students of Greek have been organized into a Greek Seminary. According to the plan of the Seminary the work of each year is concentrated on some leading author or some special department of literature. During the past year the work has been in the Greek historians.
>
> In the seminary proper, which met twice a week during the academic year, select portions of Thucydides were interpreted in turn by the different members of the seminary, with lectures and illustrative papers by the Director and the students. [2]

G. Stanley Hall, while at Hopkins, found the seminar "a vigorous feature . . . and I, of course, had my own in which alternate weeks were devoted to the field of the history of philosophy and experimental psychology." [3]

It was characteristic of Gilman that he allowed the faculty members to develop the seminar as they saw fit, keeping only in mind that the seminar serve as an adjunct to teaching, "where the professor, by personal example and inspiration, guides the reading and study of a select class, seated around a reading table. The seminary work [must] be supplemented by lectures and examinations, on the one hand; and on the other, by the meetings of associations devoted to science, to philology, to history, etc., in which many persons, both teachers and students, are brought together, sometimes for informal conferences, oftener for the purpose of listening to carefully prepared papers." [4]

Gilman had planned very carefully; as the first decade came to an end, he had established a Philosophical Faculty, had recruited the nucleus of a staff of able teachers, and had carefully instituted an American doctorate "based upon the notion that the students who enter upon it have already pursued such disciplinary courses as fit them for the

---

[1] *Ibid.*, pp. 78-81. See also Ernest V. Hollis, *op. cit.*, p. 18.

[2] *Ninth Annual Report* (1884), pp. 24-25.

[3] G. Stanley Hall, *Life and Confessions of a Psychologist*, p. 327. Hall came first to Hopkins as a visiting lecturer in 1881, was made lecturer in 1882, and professor of psychology in 1884. *Ninth Annual Report* (1884), p. 61. Hall also, at Gilman's invitation, taught pedagogy but tells us that Gilman objected to a proposed course in the history of education. See Hall, *op. cit.*, p. 251. His course in "pedagogics" is described in the *Eleventh Annual Report* (1886), p. 47.

[4] *Eleventh Annual Report* (1886), pp. 12-13.

freer methods of study encouraged in lecture-rooms and seminaries, in laboratories and libraries, under the guidance of the various professors." [1] He was ready to admit that "much of the success of the institution is due to the system of fellowships." [2] But his achievement went far beyond the success that he so keenly felt in the foundation of a new and dynamic graduate university. He developed conjointly with the graduate school an undergraduate college of some new force and direction; and in the institution of the visiting lectureship and the scholarly journal (which were to particularly thrive at Hopkins in the 1880's and 1890's), he stimulated American intellectual life at all levels.

---

[1] *Ibid.*, p. 11. Despite the heavy scientific orientation and the philological study of the *litterae humaniores*, Gilman did not neglect the *belles-lettres*. He brought Sidney Lanier, the poet, to the university as a lecturer in English Literature. He wrote to Lanier: "I Think your scheme may be admirably worked out not only ... in English, but with all other literary courses, French, German, Latin and Greek. The teachers of these subjects study ... for linguistic and philological more than literary reasons. We need ... someone like you, loving literature and poetry." Gilman to Lanier, July 16, 1879. *Gilman Papers, Lanier Room, loc. cit.*

[2] *Eleventh Annual Report* (1886), p. 15.

CHAPTER FIVE

DANIEL COIT GILMAN AT HOPKINS (1886-1902)

In 1886, Daniel Coit Gilman delivered an address at the opening of the Johns Hopkins Hospital in which he observed:

> To the attainment of these noble ends, "the relief of suffering and the advancement of knowledge," the foundations of Johns Hopkins are forever set apart. On the one hand stands the university, where education in the liberal arts and sciences is provided, and where research is liberally encouraged; on the other hand stands the hospital where all that art and science can contribute to the relief of sickness and pain is bountifully provided. [1]

Above all, Gilman "believed in the direct application of university teaching and research to the needs of everyday community life." [2] If Thorstein Veblen decried the practical emphasis and orientation of the Johns Hopkins University, he only reaffirmed in his observation Gilman's intentions. [3] In his inaugural address Gilman had asked, "What is the significance of all this activity?" His answer was immediate and clear:

> It is a reaching out for a better state of society than now exists; it is a dim but an indelible impression of the value of learning; it is a craving for intellectual and moral growth; it is a longing to interpret the laws of creation; it means a wish for less misery among the poor, less ignorance in schools, less bigotry in the temple, less suffering in the hospital, less fraud in business, less folly in politics; it means more study of nature, more love of art, more lessons from history, more security in property, more health in cities, more virtue in the country, more wisdom in legislation, more intelligence, more happiness, more religion. [4]

In poetic language Gilman described the university in society as "a hill not very high [from which] we have looked upon a broad area, distinguish-

---

[1] *Charity and Knowledge: An Address Delivered at the Opening of the Johns Hopkins Hospital*, pp. 25-26. The influence of the Hopkins on medical education is outside the purview of this report. See Richard H. Shryock, *The Unique Influence of Johns Hopkins University on American Medicine*; Abraham Flexner, *Medical Education in the United States and Canada*.

[2] W. Carson Ryan, *Studies in Early Graduate Education*, p. 30.

[3] Thorstein Veblen, *The Higher Learning in America*, pp. 85-92. See also for Veblen's criticisms, Joseph Dorfman, *Thorstein Veblen and his America*, *passim*.

[4] *Addresses at the Inauguration of Daniel C. Gilman ...* , p. 30

ing only the chief features of the landscape,—but we have seen the mountains and the sea." [1]

How committed to the service of contemporary need Gilman was is clearly shown in the fact that in its first decade the Johns Hopkins University graduated eighty-four Ph.D.'s, but along with them it graduated one hundred and nineteen A.B.'s. [2] Along with the graduate school, its Ph.D., seminaries and fellowships, Gilman established an undergraduate college "holding to the fundamental notion, that collegiate instruction is essentially the training of the mind and character to habits of fidelity, attention, perseverance, memory and judgment." [3] If in distant parts of the country "the advanced work of our students attracts the most attention; at home, the collegiate work finds its chief recognition." [4] From the very first, undergraduate scholarships were awarded, [5] and Gilman "endeavored to give a liberal education to every one who was in training for the degree of Bachelor of Arts, and to encourage all over whom [he] had any influence, to take this degree before proceeding to professional or technical studies." [6] Gilman not only "tolerated a college." [7] He recognized that an undergraduate college was a basic foundation for any university which serves a community's needs; further he perceived that only a college could guarantee a reservoir of trained students for the higher faculties and, in a sense, assure the success of a graduate school. [8] For Gilman this was not totally new, for the university in New Haven was thought to consist of an undergraduate college "to which were added distinct graduate courses or graduate schools, probably with facilities for unmatriculated students." [9] And Gilman's work at the Sheffield Scientific School had largely been the application of such a philosophy of higher-education. In essence,

---

[1] *The Benefits which Society Derives from Universities*, p. 40.

[2] *Eleventh Annual Report* (1886), p. 14. This report includes a complete review of the years 1876 to 1886.

[3] *Ibid.*, p. 10.

[4] *Ibid.*, pp. 9-10.

[5] *Twenty-First Annual Report* (1896), pp. 8-9. See also the *Second Annual Report* (1877), pp. 15-16.

[6] *Twenty-First Annual Report* (1896), p. 10.

[7] George W. Pierson, "American Universities in the Nineteenth Century: The Formative Period," in *The Modern University*, ed. by Margaret Clapp, p. 71. Similarly, Brubacher and Rudy observe: "The whole emphasis [at Hopkins] was on productive research." *Higher Education in Transition*, p. 177.

[8] *Tenth Annual Report* (1885), pp. 3-7.

[9] Richard J. Storr, *The Beginnings of Graduate Education in America*, p. 131.

the situation at the Hopkins was turned around; if at Yale the graduate departments evolved out of an existing and somewhat inflexible liberal arts college, at Hopkins graduate and undergraduate departments were simultaneously instituted and at once complimented each other's efforts. [1] It is this important facet of the Hopkins foundations which seems to have been missed by the students of American graduate education. [2]

The Undergraduate College and the Group System of Studies

Since Gilman was enjoined to provide an undergraduate college by the terms of the Hopkins bequest, it was only natural that he should turn to his experiences at the Sheffield Scientific School for example and precept. [3] Gilman had assisted in the institution of a "group system of studies" at the Sheffield Scientific School and the lessons learned there were turned to good account when the problem of undergraduate instruction presented itself at the Hopkins. [4] The group system could not flourish at Yale because of the inherently irresolvable conflict between old Yale College and the new Scientific School, [5] but at Hopkins Gilman faced no such problem. He was able, in a sense, to begin where he had left off in the development of what he regarded as "a good collegiate system." [6]

Within two years of the opening of the new university a definite pattern of undergraduate work was apparent. [7] Beyond certain required subjects —English, French and German, history, philosophy, and a laboratory science—the student was free to select one of "seven combinations of collegiate study . . . either of which will lead to a baccalaureate degree." [8]

---

[1] John C. French, *A History of the University Founded by Johns Hopkins*, pp. 64-71.

[2] Although outside the chronological purview of Storr, *op. cit.*, the observation may have well been made by him. The matter is not dealt with by Willis Rudy, "The Revolution in American Higher Education," *Harvard Educational Review*, 21 (Summer 1951), pp. 155-174; or in W. Carson Ryan, *op. cit.*

[3] A clear acknowledgement is in Gilman's *University Problems in the United States*, pp. 146-147.

[4] For the group system at the Sheffield Scientific School see pp. 30-32, *supra*.

[5] See George W. Pierson, *Yale College*, pp. 57-63; R. H. Chittenden, *History of the Sheffield Scientific School*, I, Chapter III.

[6] Daniel C. Gilman, "The Group System of College Courses in the Johns Hopkins University," *Andover Review*, 37 (June 1886), p. 22.

[7] There are only brief notices of undergraduate work in Gilman's *First Annual Report* (1876) and *Second Annual Report* (1877). The *Third Annual Report* (1878), pp. 21-24, is specific and detailed.

[8] *Third Annual Report* (1878), p. 22.

There was nothing arbitrary about the institution of the group system. [1] At the Sheffield Scientific School the group system had evolved to meet the problem of the new scientific studies and with the institution of the Ph.D. in the Scientific School, it had palpably attempted to meet the needs of the students who were planning advanced work in the sciences.[2] It is not odd, then, that Gilman profited from the lessons of the Sheffield; the group system, as he instituted it at the Hopkins, was essentially practical. [3] Specialization on the graduate level demanded earlier and more intense specialization on the undergraduate level, and the undergraduate student had to be better prepared to take up without loss of time the advanced work of graduate studies. [4] Gilman felt that the group system of studies alone could assure the best results; but the group system was a system of "freedom under control." [5] Gilman was careful not to let go the traditional college training in classical subjects. He observed:

> The permission of eclectic courses enables us to give simultaneously to different sets of pupils, the traditional college training in classical subjects or the fundamental studies of the modern scientific schools. At the same time there is no marked subdivision between those who follow the old paths and those who choose the new. The same standard of matriculation is established, the same firmness and persistence of application are expected, the same severity of examinations is maintained for all students, and care will be given that everyone who receives the Baccalaureate degree shall be liberally trained in language, mathematics and some branch of science, the proportions of different studies being left to the choice of the student under the regulations of the Faculty. [6]

Gilman was determined that contemptuous rejection and derision given the Ph.B. and the new curriculum of the Sheffield Scientific School at

---

[1] Gilman gave wide publicity to his carefully formulated plans for the group system of studies. See, "The Group System of College Courses in the Johns Hopkins University," *Andover Review*, 37 (June 1886), pp. 13-26; "Present Aspects of College Training," *The North American Review*, 136 (June 1883), 327-336; "The Shortening of the College Curriculum," *Educational Review*, 1 (January 1891), pp. 1-7.

[2] Chittenden, *op. cit.*, I, Chapter III.

[3] Gilman, "Present Aspects of College Training," *loc. cit.*, p. 331.

[4] Gilman, "The Group System of College Courses in the Johns Hopkins University," *loc. cit.*, pp. 13-15.

[5] Gilman used the phrase in the semi-centennial address which he delivered at the Sheffield Scientific School in 1897. See his *University Problems in the United States*, p. 133.

[6] *Third Annual Report* (1878), p. 22. A contemporary echoing of Gilman's wedding of the old humanism and the new science is made by the director of the Max Planck Institute at the University of Göttingen. Werner Heisenberg, "A Scientist's Case for the Classics," *Harper's Magazine*, 216 (May 1958), pp. 25-29.

Yale College would not be repeated at the Hopkins. [1] Eclectically, Gilman wed the old and the new curricula both at the undergraduate and graduate levels; neither level of instruction was totally distinct, and both flourished simultaneously. [2] "A university cannot thrive unless it is based upon a good collegiate system; and it may rightly encourage or establish a college, if needed, as an important development of its activity." [3]

The group system included seven combinations of undergraduate study, any one of which led to the B.A. The courses were arranged as follows:

1 For one who wishes a good Classical training:
Marked proficiency in Greek and Latin.
In addition—Modern Languages, Philosophy, and any one scientific subject.

2 For one who looks towards a course in Medicine:
Marked proficiency in Biology, and either Chemistry or Physics.
In addition—Either Chemistry or Physics, Modern Languages and Philosophy.

3 For one who prefers Mathematical studies, with reference to Engineering, Astronomy, Teaching:
Marked proficiency in Mathematics and Physics.
In addition—Modern Languages, Philosophy and Chemistry.

4 For one who wishes an education in Scientific subjects, not having chosen his specialty:
Marked proficiency in Mathematics, and one of the following subjects: Chemistry, Physics, or Biology.
In addition—Modern Languages, Philosophy.

5 For one who expects to pursue a course in Theology:
Marked proficiency in Greek and Hebrew.
In addition—Philosophy and two scientific subjects.

6 For one who proposes to study Law:
The same as No. 1, with the substitution of Philosophy and History for Greek, and two (instead of one) scientific subjects.

---

[1] See George W. Pierson, *Yale College*, pp. 62-67. See Gilman to Andrew D. White, May 5, 1871, *Gilman Family Papers*, Yale University Archive.

[2] It is that this point be better made that the discussion of the group system has been delayed in the present study. With the Hopkins Ph.D. and graduate instruction in perspective, the group system's integral connections with Gilman's university are better understood. Butts's discussion which suggests that the group system was part of the elective struggle, and that the Hopkins undergraduate college was totally subordinate, is in error. R. Freeman Butts, *The College Charts its Course*, pp. 94-98.

[3] *Seventh Annual Report* (1882), p. 87. This report includes Appendix E, "The Johns Hopkins University as a place for College Students," pp. 86-93.

7 For one who wishes a Literary training not rigidly Classical:
Marked proficiency in Modern Languages and Philosophy.
In addition—Latin, and two other subjects. [1]

Obviously, the groups were designed with two purposes in mind: to prepare for one or another of the learned professions or to prepare the student to go on to a higher degree in a graduate department. In his *Annual Report* for 1886, noting that it was essential that "each institution explain its own vocabulary." [2] Gilman explained the purpose of his group system as follows;

> We have not required these courses to be identical, but in recognition of the wants of most of those who have come to us, we have marked our several parallel plans of study,—which have come to be called "Groups," —and have offered them to the choice of matriculated students. Each of these courses has been so arranged as to make it certain that the student who completes it will have a good mathematical discipline, a knowledge of Latin, French and German, at least one year of instruction in science, besides an introduction to logic, ethics, and psychology and to history, physical geography, and English. In addition, during two years of his college course he must give steady attention to two dominant subjects, such as the classics, mathematics, physical, chemical or biological science, history and politics, or the modern languages. In this way we have endeavored to provide a liberal education which should have a tendency toward some future occupation. [3]

No fixed time was required to complete any of these courses. It "may be three or four years; or it may be less if the student comes with attainments beyond what are demanded for matriculation, or if he is favored by the possession of unusual ability. He is not kept backward by the ordinary class system. He proceeds at a slower or more rapid rate according to circumstances." [4] With an eye to the shadowing graduate department, Gilman noted: "The presence of a company of older and more advanced students in the university exerts a strong influence upon undergraduates. The whole establishment becomes a laboratory where everybody is busy, and where enthusiasm in study is the predominant characteristic. Minute regulations are not often called for, because the interest awakened in pursuits which the scholar himself has chosen, secures application and industry on the part of nearly all; and the few who are indifferent to the advantages afforded them soon drop out

---

[1] *Third Annual Report* (1878), pp. 22-23.
[2] *Eleventh Annual Report* (1886), p. 10.
[3] *Ibid.*, pp. 10-11.
[4] *Seventh Annual Report* (1882), p. 88.

of the ranks." [1] In 1886-1887 more than one half of 108 undergraduates chose Groups III and IV; some eighteen chose Group I which showed the strength of the traditional classical course; and only three chose Group VII. [2]

In his last annual report Gilman reported that the group system had been eminently successful at the Hopkins. Out of 1,499 men who had entered the university as undergraduate students, 383 students had continued as graduate students and a goodly number of these had taken the Ph.D.[3] Throughout all of Gilman's presidency the group system remained essentially unchanged,[4] but with the remove of the main university site from Baltimore to suburban Homewood in 1911 the group system was only skeletally retained.[5] For the first forty years of the Johns Hopkins University the group system had adequately solved two problems which faced the new university, problems not exclusively those of Gilman or the Hopkins. It had provided a ready reservoir of undergraduate talent for the graduate departments, and it had allowed "an intelligent compromise between a liberal education and vocational training and between prescription and undirected election."[6] Only Gilman's "broadly sympathetic"[7] attitude to collegiate work during his administration made this feasible.

Where the group system of Hopkins has been discussed it has generally been confused with the elective struggle.[8] Gilman's phrase, "freedom under control," clearly differentiates it from Charles W. Eliot's elective system. Eliot himself disavowed the group system when he wrote, rather stringently, to Gilman and characterised Gilman's group system as "the arbitrary devise of a few minds."[9] And if Eliot's elective system

---

[1] *Ibid.*, pp. 88-89. Scarcely one of Gilman's annual reports fails to report on some aspect of the group system. Gilman is constantly reiterating the distinction between collegiate and university instruction and their interdependence. *Cf.* the *Twenty-First Annual Report* (1896), "Retrospect of Twenty Years," pp. 7-9.

[2] *Johns Hopkins University Register* 1886-87, p. 8.

[3] *Twenty Sixth Annual Report* (1901), p. 27.

[4] In 1889 Dr. Edward H. Griffin of Williams College was made dean of the college faculty. Griffin was a Presbyterian minister and had studied theology at Princeton. See *Fourteenth Annual Report* (1889), p. 13.

[5] See French, *op. cit.*, pp. 69-70.

[6] *Ibid.*, p. 71.

[7] The phrase is French's. *Ibid.*, p. 71.

[8] See Butts, *op. cit.*, pp. 94-98. See also John A. Sexson and John W. Harbeson, *The New American College*, pp. 12-13. French, *op. cit.*, pp. 64-71, is more prescient but does not relate the group system to any other type of collegiate reform.

[9] Eliot to Gilman, December 8, 1885. *Gilman Papers*, Lanier Room, Johns Hopkins University Library. See also Henry James, *Charles W. Eliot*, II, pp. 42-50.

invoked the ire of parents (*I would rather send my son to Hell than to Harvard*),[1] Gilman's group system was proposed to parents as "favorable, it is believed, not only to the preservation of good order, but to the formation of good habits." [2] Pierson has remarked of the elective system: "Now Eliot did not invent this system, nor first use it. On the contrary, Jefferson, Ticknor, Nott and Wayland had all preceded him. And in his own time the Sheffield Scientific School, Cornell, and Johns Hopkins (and later Stanford) all used it. But they used it as a device for letting students with different interests choose *on entering* between specialist programs, each of which was required and drawn up by the professors in advance. Eliot, on the other hand, encouraged college men to choose *after entering* and to keep on electing—even when a few chose entirely one-sided programs, and the majority elected programs so scattered and capricious, or so elementary and easy, that neither discipline nor mastery were obtained." [3] Of course Pierson's statements are too sweeping, but they graphically differentiate Gilman's efforts from those of Eliot. The basic difference between Gilman's group system and Eliot's elective plan, David Starr Jordan's major-minor plan at Stanford University,[4] and William Rainey Harper's junior college plan at the University of Chicago,[5] lies in Gilman's purposely cultivated *liaison* between undergraduate and graduate departments and their simultaneous development.[6] In this connection Gilman even further recommended a central authority to confer *all* degrees and that all modifications of the B.A., except in Law and theology, be given up.[7]

How successful this close wedding of graduate and undergraduate school was from the very experience of students is, perhaps, best seen in the testimony of Abraham Flexner who was a Hopkins undergraduate from 1884-86. Flexner reminisced:

> There was little oversight on the part of the university as to how the student used his time, whether he was a graduate or an undergraduate. It was assumed that a student who attended the university was serious enough

---

[1] Henry James, *op. cit.*, II, p. 48.

[2] *Seventh Annual Report* (1882), p. 92.

[3] George W. Pierson, "American Universities in the Nineteenth Century: the Formative Period," *loc. cit.*, pp. 86-87.

[4] For the major-minor plan see David S. Jordan, *The Days of A Man*, I, pp. 323-325.

[5] See William Rainey Harper, *The Trend in Higher Education*, pp. 1-34.

[6] Gilman, "The Shortening of the College Curriculum," *Educational Review*, 1 (January 1891), pp. 1-7.

[7] Gilman, "The Use and Abuse of Titles," *North American Review*, 140 (March 1885), pp. 267-268.

to be left to his own devices. . . . The studies at the Hopkins were organized on the "group system," allowing scope for choice, but preserving continuity. I selected the classical group; others followed the scientific group or the history and political science group. The studies were all solid, and the classes were conducted by able and scholarly men. There was no froth in the Johns Hopkins University of my time—no special schools for the things that cannot be taught anyway, such as journalism, business education etc. . . . There is, I think, no question that with all the enrichment of our laboratories and libraries and other facilities the quality of American collegiate and university education as a whole has deteriorated precisely in the degree in which it has departed from the simple and severe ideals that Mr. Gilman introduced. [1]

Flexner, as an undergraduate, saw much of Professors Morris, Fabian Franklin, Gildersleeve, Rowland, Remsen, Herbert Adams and Martin.[2] He was able to freely consult even President Gilman whom he characterizes as epitomising Erlich's motto: *Viel arbeiten, wenig publizieren*.[3] Wilson, the future president of Princeton University, had pretty much the same experience,[4] and a correspondent who went to the new university to see for himself reported to the public:

There is no rigid theory to which students must be broken in; but like an organic life, development goes on in response to the demands made upon it, and subordinated to the surrounding conditions. Thus, the professors and associates are free from routine work, and are free from the danger of falling into ruts in their modes of thinking and instruction while the students are free to live an individual life, untrammeled by the restrictions of the class. They are permitted and directed how to grow, not molded and hammered and chiseled into form. [5]

Gilman's "freedom under control" and his admonition that the mind of the student "[be] kept fixed on certain definites to be attained by [the] course of study, while at the same time he is prevented from becoming narrow,"[6] has not a little in common with the Thomist, Robert M. Hutchings, who has observed: "What we want is specialized institutions and unspecialized men."[7]

---

[1] Abraham Flexner, *I Remember*, p. 57.

[2] *Ibid.*, p. 59.

[3] *Ibid.*, p. 51.

[4] See Ray Stannard Baker, *Woodrow Wilson: Life and Letters*, I, pp. 172-173.

[5] S.B. Herrick, "Hopkins," *Scribner's Monthly*, 19 (December 1879).

[6] Gilman, "Retrospect of Twenty Years, 1876-1896," in *Twenty-First Annual Report* (1896), p. 9.

[7] Robert M. Hutchins, *The University of Utopia*, p. 46.

THE VISITING LECTURER PLAN

In his *Annual Report* for 1886, reviewing the work of the first decade of the Hopkins, Gilman called attention to the visiting lectureship: "In addition to the systematic courses of study here prescribed, many lectures have been given in Hopkins Hall to which the public have been admitted on easy conditions and to which students have likewise been invited, though their attendance has been voluntary."[1] At first Gilman felt that a new university like the Hopkins had to turn to a company of non-resident professors and lecturers to supplement the small permanent staff;[2] but he soon recognized that he had inadvertently begun the development of a new idea in higher education which was to add immeasurably to the influence, prestige and rapid growth of the Johns Hopkins University. Ryan has said that Gilman developed the visiting lectureship "with a thoroughness that has probably never been equalled,"[3] and a reading of Gilman's annual reports, *seriatim*, certainly underscores the truth of the observation.

Where Gilman found the idea of the visiting lecturer cannot be definitely fixed; Ryan suggests that he got the idea from a reading of Benjamin Peirce's *Working Plan for the Foundation of a University* (1856).[4] Gilman does not speak of the plan's origin in any of his usually detailed annual reports, or in *The Launching of a University* where he speaks of some of the nonresident lecturers.[5] However, it appears that the idea was largely born of necessity, and if its origin must be traced somewhere it probably lies in Gilman's observations and study of the English universities where the non-resident lecturer was quite common. His meeting with James Bryce, "who holds a non-resident professorship of International Law in the University [Oxford], which requires him to give an annual course of twenty lectures,"[6] no doubt, clearly suggested the "visiting lecturer" to Gilman. When he did formulate the plan of the visiting lectureship it took the form of a series of twenty lectures with the lecturer spending as much time as he was able at the Hopkins during the academic year. Each lecturer's situation was different, some

---

[1] *Eleventh Annual Report* (1886), p. 23.
[2] *Third Annual Report* (1878), pp. 25-26.
[3] Ryan, *op. cit.*, p. 40.
[4] *Ibid.*
[5] *The Launching of a University*, pp. 61-66.
[6] Gilman to the Hopkins Trustees, quoted in Fabian Franklin, *The Life of Daniel Coit Gilman*, p. 200.

giving but a single lecture, others staying for long terms, and in a true sense, being resident members of the staff even though not designated as such.[1] The following letter from Gilman to Professor Francis J. Child, the distinguished Chaucerian of Harvard University, inviting Child to lecture at the Hopkins presents the lecture plan in capsule:

> The arrangement to continue three years, to be then renewed if agreeable to both parties. The service to be one month,—& the compensation $ 1000.—annually. A course of daily lectures to be given (say twenty in all) on any subject the lecturer may choose in his own department of study; the theme to be determined not later than June in order that an announcement of the course may be made in our Prospectus. These lectures to be "college lectures" and not designed for large miscellaneous audiences. It is fair to expect from 50 to 100 educated hearers. The lectures to present some subject in its fullness—e.g. Chaucer or the Early Ballads; rather than to cover a wide range on English Literature in general. The hearers to be encouraged to read and study in connection with the lectures. The lecturer to be accessible for an hour daily, aside from his lecture, to guide the inquiries or studies of those who may wish to consult him,—in his own way. The lecturer to coöperate with the Trustees & the Faculty in the development of this department of the university. [2]

Where Gilman was unable to secure a distinguished scholar for permanent staff membership at Hopkins, he was usually able to arrange a lectureship which brought the scholar to Baltimore and made him available to the graduate students in the scholar's speciality.[3]

Thus, Gilman closed the graduate circle. His fellowships provided a nucleus of advanced students; his undergraduate college supplied a potentially continuing source of graduate students; his permanent faculty was picked with an eye to productive research, and visiting lecturers

---

[1] Cf. the varying "residencies" of some of the lecturers in the *Tenth Annual Report* (1885), pp. 26-27.

[2] Gilman to Child, December 21, 1875. Houghton Library, Harvard University. Photostat of letter furnished by Professor William Jackson of Harvard University. Child did give lectures at the Hopkins in 1877-78. *Tenth Annual Report* (1885), p. 26. For Gilman efforts to lure Child away from Harvard permanently, see James, *op. cit.*, II, pp. 14, 15, 25.

[3] A good example is William James of Harvard. Although Gilman failed to get James as a permanent faculty member, he did bring James to Baltimore to lecture. See *Tenth Annual Report* (1885), p. 27. See also Jackson I. Cope, "William James's Correspondence with D.C. Gilman," *Journal of the History of Ideas*, 12 (October 1951), pp. 609-627. He did fail completely, however, in the case of Henry Adams. See W.S. Holt, "Henry Adams and the Johns Hopkins University," *New England Quarterly*, 2 (September 1938), pp. 632-8.

furnished the best minds available in Gilman's America.[1] That Gilman realized the importance of his lectureship plan is evident in his statement made in 1906:

> This was [the opening of the Hopkins] an auspicious beginning, never to be forgotten. The world was expectant, everybody was inquisitive, not a few were sceptical—some may have been distrustful, none were hostile. In order to illustrate the activities of other universities, and to secure the counsel of eminent scholars in respect to our development, the decision had been reached already that academic lectures on various important and attractive themes should be opened to the public, and that the professors should come from institutions of acknowledged merit established in the North, South and West. The usages of the *College de France* were [2] in mind. Thus the instructions of a small faculty were to be supplemented by courses which should be profitable to the enrolled students, and entertaining, if not serviceable, to the educated public. [3] Gildersleeve and Mallet, the Grecian and the Chemist, were representatives of the inimitable methods of the University of Virginia. Judge Cooley, the constitutional lawyer, the distinguished jurist, came from the great state University of Michigan; and Allen, the classical-historian, from a kindred institution in Wisconsin. Harvard loaned to us its two leading men of letters, Child and Lowell. Whitney, then at the height of his renown, came from Yale, and likewise Francis A. Walker. Hilgard and Billings represented the scientific activities of Washington—the former chosen because of his experience in Geodesy, and because of our desire at that early date, to initiate surveys in the State of Maryland; and the latter, because of his acknowledged distinction in medicine which was soon to be a leading department of study among us. Simon Newcomb, the illustrious astronomer, was another man of science in the service of the government. [4]

Professor Leonce Rabillon, from the University of France, was a lecturer from 1876 to 1886.[5] George S. Morris, who had as a student John Dewey, gave lectures between 1878 and 1885.[6] Charles S. Peirce, the father of philosophical pragmatism, lectured on Logic from 1879 to 1884.[7] G. Stanley Hall began his Hopkins connection as a lecturer in 1882 and

---

[1] The lecturers included English, French, German and Italian scholars with whom Gilman had personal acquaintance.

[2] Gilman never elaborated on this French influence. The visiting lectureship was, no doubt, largely European in its origin in Gilman's thinking.

[3] Some of the lectures are called "public" in the annual reports, but this remained a subsidiary function.

[4] *The Launching of a University*, pp. 61-62.

[5] *Tenth Annual Report* (1885), p. 26.

[6] *Ibid.*, p. 27.

[7] *Ibid.*, p. 27. See Max H. Fisch and Jackson I. Cope, "Peirce at Hopkins," in Philip P. Wiener and Frederick H. Young, eds., *Studies in the Philosophy of Charles S. Peirce*.

was appointed professor of psychology and pedagogics in 1884.[1] Hermann von Holst, the historian from the University of Freiburg, was a lecturer in 1883.[2] Rodolfo Lanciani, the Italian archaeologist, was guest lecturer from the University of Rome in 1887.[3] William T. Harris, the United States Commissioner of Education, gave the historical students a course of lectures on "educational influence of art and literature."[4] The English historians, James Bryce and Edward A. Freeman, gave lectures on Roman Law and history.[5] And the Rev. Schechter, Reader in the Talmud in the University of Cambridge, lectured to the students of the Oriental Seminary.[6] All in all, these are but a representative few; during all of Gilman's presidency a steady procession of the world's talent came to Baltimore and the annual reports are a record of the great academic reputations of the last quarter of the nineteenth century.[7]

Gilman estimated that some 300 guest lecturers had been invited to the Hopkins during his tenure:

> I have made no count of the lecturers and speakers who have spoken in Baltimore, but in the course of five and twenty years there must have been 300—some, indeed, giving but single addresses, like Huxley, [8] Moissan and Klein; others like Cayley and Kelvin, remaining a good while. Thus it has come to pass that I have met upon familiar terms a great many of the scholars of this generation, and have learned to estimate their services and admire their genius. [9]

As for the students, the opportunities were inestimable. Gilman, himself, notes that "sometimes bright students were spotted by these visiting professors, and afterward invited to positions of usefulness and distinction elsewhere." [10] Fabian Franklin, who took his Hopkins Ph.D. in 1880, [11] wrote:

---

[1] *Tenth Annual Report* (1885), p. 27.

[2] *Ibid.*

[3] *Twelfth Annual Report* (1887), p. 52.

[4] *Twentieth Annual Report* (1895), p. 12.

[5] *Tenth Annual Report* (1885), p. 27.

[6] *Twentieth Annual Report* (1895), p. 11.

[7] For a skeletal list of lecturers (114 names), see "Lecturers, 1876-1896" in *Statements Respecting the Johns Hopkins University of Baltimore Presented to the Public on the Twentieth Anniversary* [Johns Hopkins Press], 1896, pp. 35-38.

[8] Thomas Huxley delivered the opening address at the opening of the Hopkins to students in October, 1876. The text of the address is in his *American Addresses*, pp. 225-227. In a sense, he was not truly a non-resident lecturer.

[9] *The Launching of a University*, p. 63.

[10] *Ibid.*, p. 62.

[11] *Fifth Annual Report* (1880), p. 22.

Without the background of history, without the stimulus of comparison or rivalry with similar institutions, in an environment offering no sustenance to the peculiar and specialized activities being carried on by little groups of workers, it requires no great effort to imagine the danger that there might be something arid or anaemic about the life of the Johns Hopkins University in its beginning. As a matter of fact quite the opposite of all this actually characterized those early years, and it would be difficult to say in just what measure this happy result was brought about by that added touch of breadth and distinction which was given by the presence of men like Lowell and Child and Whitney and Newcomb and Cooley and Walker, and by the refreshing perspectives of great fields of thought which they and other non-resident and resident lecturers of the first two years placed before this little body of university pioneers and the cultivated public of Baltimore. [1]

Perhaps, one of the most profitable uses of the visiting lectureship in graduate education was Gilman's assembly of concentrated talent in one field and the institution of a lecture-symposium session at the university which would last for the greater part of a term. An excellent example was the symposium held in "pedagogical themes"[2] in February and March of 1891. The participants included:

Professor Nicholas Murray Butler of Columbia College, President of the New York College for the Training of teachers [who spoke] on The Use and Abuse of Examinations.

Hon. W. T. Harris, U.S. Commissioner of Education, [who spoke] on Books serviceable to Teachers of Colleges and High Schools at the beginning of their Career.

Hon. J. L. M. Curry, of Washington, General Agent of the Peabody Education Fund, [who spoke] on the study of Pedagogics in the University.[3]

The graduate student could not but profit from such association and he usually did.[4]

THE SCHOLARLY JOURNALS

When Professor Sylvester addressed a reception given in his honor by the university on the eve of his departure for the Savilian Professorship

---

[1] Fabian Franklin, *op. cit.*, pp. 233-234. For another student commentary on the non-resident lecturers, see Edward Ingle, "The First Ten Years at Johns Hopkins," *The Johns Hopkins Alumni Magazine*, 4 (November 1915), pp. 7-26.

[2] Gilman's interest in education as a subject for study has not been noted by the earlier investigators. G. Stanley Hall's appointment in 1882 allowed the start of a graduate program in education.

[3] *Sixteenth Annual Report* (1891), pp. 10-11.

[4] It was through the non-resident lecture plan that Thorstein Veblen came to know Charles Peirce, and recognized him to be "a creative intellectual force," whose thinking was a radical departure from the "method of authority." Joseph Dorfman, *op. cit.*, p. 41.

of Geometry at Oxford, he underscored one of Gilman's lasting contributions to American university education—the scholarly journal.[1]
Sylvester said:

> You have spoken about our *Mathematical Journal.* Who is the founder?
> Mr. Gilman is continually telling people that I founded it. That is one of my
> claims to recognition which I strenuously deny. I assert that he is the found-
> er. Almost the first day that I landed in Baltimore, when I dined with him
> in the presence of Reverdy Johnson and Judge Brown, I think, from the
> first moment he began to plague me to found a *Mathematical Journal*
> on this side of the water something similar to the *Quarterly Journal
> of Pure and Applied Mathematics* with which my name was connected as
> nominal editor. I said it was useless, there were no materials for it. Again
> and again he returned to the charge, and again and again I threw all the
> cold water I could on the scheme, and nothing but the most obstinate
> persistence and perseverance brought his views to prevail. To him and
> to him alone, therefore, is really due whatever importance attaches to the
> foundation of the *American Journal of Mathematics* . . . . [2]

That is was truly Gilman who spearheaded the drive for the scholarly
journals at the Hopkins is further affirmed by the early letter of the
astronomer, Simon Newcomb, who wrote to him:

> It is my duty to inform you herewith of the possible *faux pas* which I
> made last night, but which I hope will turn out the opposite. Supposing
> that the subject of the Mathematical Journal had been discussed by your
> executive committee, I asked Judge Brown what he thought of it. Having
> thus let the pussy out of the bag, I was taken aback by finding him dis-
> claiming all knowledge of her. However, he took so kindly to the project,
> which I now tried to paint in the most glowing terms, that I trust no harm
> will be done. [3]

In 1882 when G. Stanley Hall thought of starting the *American Journal
of Psychology,* he found that "President Gilman favored it, for the establishment of departmental journals was one of the prominent items in
the program of the Johns Hopkins."[4] And the absolute need for media for
scholarly publication was in Ira Remsen's mind when he wrote to Gilman:

---

[1] It is one of the ironies of academic history that Sylvester who was denied his
degree at Cambridge because of the Test Acts should ultimately hold one of the great
professorships of the English universities. Sylvester has been called one of the greatest
mathematicians of all time. See *Osiris,* I (1936), pp. 93-126, for estimate of his importance in the history of mathematical thought.

[2] Stenographic copy of address by J. J. Sylvester, December 20, 1883. *Gilman Papers,*
Lanier Room, *loc. cit.* Reprinted in part in Franklin, *op. cit.,* pp. 230-31.

[3] Simon Newcomb to Gilman, November 4, 1876. *Gilman Papers,* Lanier Room,
loc. cit.

[4] G. Stanley Hall, *Life and Confessions of a Psychologist,* p. 227.

> At the present juncture it is desirable to publish preliminary announce-
> ments describing what we have thus far done and what we intend to do.
> It is desirable mainly for two reasons; 1st, that we may be recognized
> as soon as possible as belonging to the working chemists of the country;
> 2nd, that the results of our labors may be insured to us, or, in other words,
> to establish our priority. [1]

Gilman acknowledged that the inspiration for the scholarly journals
had been his observations of European university practices. "While I
was on the continent of Europe, my attention was constantly called to
the importance of encouraging professors to engage in independent
investigations, and of providing means for the publication of such
results as they might reach."[2] Gilman had noted that "In Germany,
especially, it was regarded as essential to the life of a vigorous university
that it should make contributions to knowledge, through the members
of its staff."[3] Certainly, one of the great needs of American scholarship
in the 1870's was for adequate specialized journals for the publication
of research.[4] The trouble lay in the fact that no journal could hope to be
self-supporting from the beginning;[5] subsidy had to be provided from
some source. Gilman recognized both the challenge and the opportunity
for the new university, and from the very first he realized that any
journals published must aim at a national, not a local, audience.[6] Not
only were the Hopkins scholars given an outlet for publication; in many
ways, they were expected to publish. The early annual reports contain a
Bibliographia Hopkinsiensis which "include[d] books and articles published by members of the Johns Hopkins University, written during the
connection of the author with the university, or based on work carried
on while here."[7] Although these lists were discontinued, it is obvious
that a man's reputation was, in large part, based on his bibliography.[8]

It is noteworthy that of all the journals founded at the Hopkins

---

[1] Remsen to Gilman, May 7th, 1877. *Gilman Papers*, Lanier Room, *loc. cit.* Published
in part in French, *op. cit.*, p. 53.

[2] *The Launching of a University*, p. 115.

[3] *Ibid.*

[4] For the deficiencies, see Simon Newcomb, "Progress of Abstract Science in
America," *North American Review*, 122 (January 1876), 123-156.

[5] *Cf.* G. Stanley Hall's initial difficulties with the *American Journal of Psychology*.
Hall, *op. cit.*, pp. 227-228.

[6] *The Launching of a University*, p. 116.

[7] *Seventh Annual Report* (1882), p. 100.

[8] See G. Stanley Hall, *op. cit.*, p. 252. "Gilman established, if he did not introduce,
the custom of printing in the Register the academic record of each professor and
graduate student." *Idem.*

during Gilman's presidency only one suspended publication. All others
have remained active to the present time. The first of the journals founded
was *The American Journal of Mathematics* (1878) with Professor Sylvester
as editor.[1] This was followed by *The American Chemical Journal* (1879),
edited for its first forty years by Ira Remsen.[2] For three years the university published the *Journal of Physiology* (1881-84), which was jointly
edited by Sir Michael Foster of the University of Cambridge and Professor
Martin of Johns Hopkins.[3] In 1880, largely with Gilman's encouragement,
Gildersleeve began the publication of the *American Journal of Philology*
which continued under his editorship for almost forty years.[4] Although
the *Johns Hopkins University Studies in Historical and Political Science*
was a monograph series, it represented one of the most voluminous out-
lets for scholarly research in its field. The series began in 1882 with Dr.
Herbert Baxter Adams as its editor until his death in 1901.[5] Thereafter,
it was edited by a committee of the Departments of Political Economy,
History, and Political Science.[6] Professor A. Marshall Elliott, who had
been appointed Professor of Romance Languages in 1884,[7] initiated
Modern Language Notes in 1886.[8] The outlet for research in the natural
and physical sciences and in the humanities which these journals afforded
was supplemented by the Johns Hopkins University *Circulars*, the biblio-
graphical maze of which remains yet to be mapped.[9] These *Circulars*
began publication in 1879 and continued to be issued irregularly until
1912, when they were supplanted by the *Johns Hopkins Alumni Magazine*.[10]
Gilman tells us that they were modeled on the *University Reporter* of
Cambridge and were designed "for spreading information in respect

---

[1] *Twenty-First Annual Report* (1896), p. 30. This report includes a brief history of
the scholarly journals at Hopkins.

[2] *Ibid.*, p. 31. See also French, *op. cit.*, pp. 53-54.

[3] *Sixth Annual Report* (1881), p. 19. It suspended publication in 1884, although no
reason is given in its last issue. It is last mentioned in the annual report for 1883.

[4] *Fifth Annual Report* (1880), p. 21. See also French, *op. cit.*, p. 55.

[5] *Seventh Annual Report* (1882), pp. 27-28. See also French, *op. cit.*, p. 55.

[6] See W. Stull Holt, ed., *Historical Scholarship in the United States*, 1876-1901,
. . . ., p. 138.

[7] *Tenth Annual Report* (1885), p. 25.

[8] *Eleventh Annual Report* (1886), p. 23.

[9] By 1896 the irregualrly issued *Circulars* numbered 127. See the "Retrospect of
Twenty Years," *Twenty-first Annual Report* (1896), p. 32.

[10] *Twenty-First Annual Report* (1896), p. 32. See also French, *op. cit.*, p. 396. They
included university announcements, class schedules, reports of research in progress
and much miscellanea. They are not completely catalogued in the Johns Hopkins
University Library.

to scientific and literary investigations which were here in progress."[1] Reaching out for international association and reputation, Gilman encouraged the publication of *Contributions to Assyriology and Comparative Semetic Philology*. This journal was begun in 1889 and published in Leipsic with Professor Paul Haupt of Hopkins[2] and Professor Delitzch of Breslau as co-editors.[3]

The journals became what Gilman had forecast they would—an attraction to "the best students, and serviceable to the intellectual growth of the land."[4] Out of them grew the first American university press called such by name.[5]

A Statistical Overview

Although statistics are not in themselves conclusive evidence, they can offer some perspective; and Gilman's observation (1904) that "the growth of American universities must arrest the attention of all who look back over the last half-century"[6] can be effectively translated into statistical terms. In 1876, the year the Johns Hopkins University opened, a total of 389 graduate students were reported in American colleges and universities; by 1900, this figure had increased to 5,831.[7] In 1871, a handful of 44 graduate students were reported.[8] In 1876 American colleges and universities granted 44 Ph.D.'s; in 1900, they granted 342 Ph.D.'s.[9] Whether one agrees or not with Rudy in attributing this remarkable growth to "the impact of the Johns Hopkins experiment."[10] one fact is clear. From its opening in 1876 to the end of the century, the Hopkins equalled or surpassed in any one year the number of doctorates granted at any other American university. Only Harvard University, whose dynamic president acknowledged the Hopkins's influence,[11]

---

[1] *Seventh Annual Report* (1882), pp. 68-69.

[2] Paul Haupt was appointed Professor of Semitic Languages in 1883. *Tenth Annual Report* (1885), p. 25.

[3] *Twenty-First Annual Report* (1896), p. 32.

[4] *First Annual Report* (1876), p. 21.

[5] See French, *op. cit.*, pp. 219-227.

[6] *The Launching of a University*, p. 152.

[7] Walton C. John, *Graduate Studies in Universities and Colleges in the United States*, pp. 12-13.

[8] *Ibid.*

[9] *Ibid.*, p. 19.

[10] S. Willis Rudy, "The Revolution in American Higher Education, 1865-1900," *loc. cit.*, p. 169.

[11] "I want to testify that the Graduate School of Harvard University ... did not thrive until the example of Johns Hopkins forced our Faculty to put their strength

was a close doctoral competitor, and ". . . although Eliot never did properly understand research, he showed his usual open-mindedness and readiness to learn by trying to further it more generously after Johns Hopkins had convinced him of the necessity."[1]

In the subjoined table the graduate student enrolment and the Ph.D.'s granted at Harvard University, and at the Johns Hopkins University are summarized for the years 1876 through 1902.

Year	Graduate Enrolment Harvard	Graduate Enrolment Hopkins	Ph.D.'s Harvard	Ph.D.'s Hopkins
1876-77	61	54	4	–
1877-78	67	58	7	4
1878-79	50	63	3	6
1879-80	52	79	5	5
1880-81	43	102	3	9
1881-82	50	99	1	9
1882-83	56	125	5	6
1883-84	80	159	6	15
1884-85	72	174	4	13
1885-86	71	184	6	17
1886-87	78	228	2	20
1887-88	97	220	7	27
1888-89	99	202	6	20
1889-90	111	209	8	33
1890-91	132	233	8	28
1891-92	200	298	6	37
1892-93	216	297	13	28
1893-94	259	261	18	34
1894-95	272	284	18	47
1895-96	299	253	18	36
1896-97	306	210	26	42
1897-98	293	215	26	36
1898-99	336	210	24	42
1899-1900	341	185	36	35
1900-1901	353	168	29	30
1901-1902	315	172	31	17 [2]

For the years summarized Harvard granted 320 Ph.D.'s while Hopkins

into the development of our instruction for graduates." Charles W. Eliot in *Johns Hopkins University. Celebration of the Twenty-Fifth Anniversary . . .*, p. 105.

[1] Henry James, *op. cit.*, II, p. 20.

[2] The Harvard figures are from James, *op. cit.*, II, p. 345. The Hopkins figures are from Gilman's *Twenty-Sixth Annual Report* (1901), p. 27, and from the *Johns Hopkins Catalogue* (1902), p. 11.

granted 596;[1] but another observation is more arresting. The graduate enrolment at Harvard surpassed that of the Hopkins for most of the listed years which graphically underscores the much greater doctoral productivity at the Hopkins and its presumptively better defined Ph.D. programs. Put another way, the figures show that Gilman was able to put more Ph.D.'s into the field because the Hopkins doctoral programs, with their seminars and fellowships and ready consultation of specialized lecturers, allowed candidates a quicker completion of research in progress. If one is willing to allow the high standard of the Hopkins Ph.D., the statistics clearly show that Gilman's success was both qualitative and quantitative measured alongside that of the oldest university in the country.

GILMAN'S ACHIEVEMENT AT THE JOHNS HOPKINS UNIVERSITY [2]

When the newly-formed Federation of Graduate Clubs met in 1896 at the University of Pennsylvania to set up graduate school standards, it defined the minimum requirements which were to be required for the Ph.D. These minimum requirements, which included a recognized bachelor's degree, two years of resident graduate study and a thesis, Gilman had accepted as minimum requirements for the Ph.D. at Hopkins which he had instituted twenty years earlier.[3] The doctoral standards adopted by the newly-formed Association of American Universities in 1900 were essentially those standards which had been instituted in 1876 at the Johns Hopkins University.[4] As early as 1886, James Bryce, the English historian, had decried what he saw in American education in "this enormous total [345] of degree granting bodies very few [of which] answer to the modern conception of a university."[5] But he had excepted the Hopkins from this criticism and had given it high praise.[6] Gilman's first contribution to American graduate education was the carefully

---

[1] No comparative figures have been cumulated. For some *total* figures see John, *op. cit.*, p. 19. For comparative Yale figures see *Yale College Registers* for years detailed.

[2] The probable influence of Gilman and the Hopkins on American graduate education is treated in Chapter VII of the present study.

[3] See Barclay W. Bradley, *The Graduate Handbook* (1899), p. 21. For the efforts to standardize the American Ph.D., see *A Handbook for Graduate Students* (1893-94); John, *op. cit.*, pp. 23-32; Ernest V. Hollis, *op. cit.*, pp. 12-21.

[4] *Journal* of the Proceedings and Addresses of the Association of American Universities, I (1900), p. 11.

[5] *The American Commonwealth*, II, pp. 715-716.

[6] *Ibid.*, p. 718.

defined Hopkins Ph.D., which definition lay almost inevitably in his differentiation between collegiate and university study.[1] The Hopkins doctorate became the model for the protean Ph.D.,; it was carefully defined where there had been no definition,[2] and its emphasis was on productive research. In Gilman's words:

> Investigation has thus been among us the duty of every leading professor, and he has been the guide and inspirer of fellows and pupils, whose work may not bear his name, but whose results are truly products of the inspiration and guidance which he has freely bestowed. [3]

Yet, even with the careful definition of the Ph.D. and the emphasis on research there was no assurance of the graduate experiment at the Hopkins realizing success. Storr's investigations into the history of pre-Civil War American graduate education show that careful definition of the Ph.D. and a research orientation, alone, could not assure success for an American graduate program.[4] There were ancillary problems which had to be solved. The most important of these problems was the relation of the proposed graduate school to the traditional classical curriculum of the American undergraduate college, with its heavy English leanings, and, correlatively, the impact of the German university where American students had found "an ineffaceable impression of what scholarship meant, of what a university was and of what a long road higher education in America had to travel before it could hope to reach a plane of equal elevation."[5] Gilman's solution of the "college problem" was essentially pragmatic. His "group system of studies" allowed the continuation of the classical undergraduate college with a minimum of change; a dynamic, essentially flexible college curriculum allowed the undergraduate college to complement, not impede, the graduate department. With the experiences of Yale and California behind him, Gilman was careful to avoid any rivalry between undergraduate and graduate programs but rather to promote a mutual interdependence which would make for simultaneous growth and development. If the undergraduate college at Hopkins

---

[1] Gilman constantly reiterated the differentiation. See his "The Johns Hopkins University (1876-1891)," *Johns Hopkins University Studies in Historical and Political Science*, Ninth Series, III-IV (March-April 1891), pp. 64-66.

[2] Storr, *op. cit.*, pp. 133-134. See also Hollis, *op. cit.*, pp. 1-10.

[3] *The Launching of a University*, p. 135.

[4] Storr, *op. cit.*, pp 129-134. "Even research, although frequently mentioned and highly valued, had yet to receive the concentrated attention which later became a distinguishing mark of graduate studies." *Ibid.*, p. 134.

[5] Nicholas Murray Butler, *Across the Busy Years*, I, p. 126.

receives in Gilman's *Annual Reports* equal solicitude and mention, it is because Gilman regarded it as vital to the success of his graduate program. And if Gilman is "the patron saint of the American graduate school,"[1] he has not been adequately recognized for his labors in the collegiate vineyards.

In his assemblage of the nucleus of a strong graduate faculty, supplemented by specialized non-resident lecturers, Gilman solved not only the problems of an infant university but struck out boldly as well at the problem of student migration.[2] The Hopkins graduate student found the talent he sought in Baltimore where research projects could be brought to completion and Gilman's encouragement of the scholarly journals and other publication adjuncts assured the dissemination of results. Nicholas Murray Butler regarded Gilman's fellowship program at Johns Hopkins as one of the outstanding innovations in early graduate education.[3] Certainly, the fellowship program solved what George W. Pierson has felicitously called "the need and demand for advanced studies." [4]

The formal celebration of the twenty-fifth anniversary of the Johns Hopkins University and of the inauguration of its second president, Ira Remsen, took place on February 22, 1902. It was also the occasion to pay homage to the achievement of Daniel Coit Gilman's twenty-five years of service. Speaking for the alumni, students, and faculty, Woodrow Wilson (Ph.D., 1886) said:

> If it be true that Thomas Jefferson first laid the broad foundation for American universities in his plans for the University of Virginia, it is no less true that you were the first to create and organize in America a university in which the discovery and dissemination of new truths were

---

[1] Ernest V. Hollis, *op. cit.*, p. 14.

[2] For the problem of student migration in search of teachers, see John, *op. cit.*, pp. 25-26; Hollis, *op. cit.*, pp. 19-20. "Many of the stipulations as to residence were enacted to control what was regarded as excessive migration." Hollis, *op. cit.*, p. 20.

[3] "Perhaps Mr. Gilman's most striking innovation was the foundation of twenty annual fellowships of a value of $ 500 each, open to the graduates of any college. The principle was not new; but in America, at all events, it was the custom to restrict appointments, where they existed, to graduates of the college supporting them. Mr. Gilman ... threw open the Johns Hopkins Fellowships to general competition; and it was this step ... which fixed the relation of the new university to the colleges of the country and which attracted to it at once the most promising of the younger scholars." Butler, "President Gilman's Administration at the Johns Hopkins University," *Review of Reviews*, 23 (January 1901), p. 54.

[4] George W. Pierson, "American Universities in the Nineteenth Century: The Formative Period," *loc. cit.* p. 75.

conceded a rank superior to mere instruction, and in which the efficiency and value of research as an educational instrument were exemplified in the training of many investigators. In this, your greatest achievement, you established in America a new and higher university ideal, whose essential feature was not stately edifices, nor yet the mere association of pupils with learned and eminent teachers, but rather the education of trained and vigorous young minds through the search for truth under the guidance and with the co-operation of master investigators—*societas magistrorum et discipulorum*. That your conception was intrinsically sound is attested not only by the fruitfullness of the institution in which it was embodied at Baltimore, but also by its influence upon the development of the university ideal throughout our country, and notably at our oldest and most distinguished seats of learning. [1]

And President William Rainey Harper of the University of Chicago, underscoring Wilson's remarks, observed: "We are celebrating the close of the first period of university education in these United States." [2]

---

[1] *Johns Hopkins University. Celebration of the Twenty-Fifth Anniversary of the Founding of the University* . . . , pp. 39-40.

[2] *Ibid.*, p. 58.

CHAPTER SIX

DANIEL COIT GILMAN AT THE CARNEGIE INSTITUTION (1902-1904)

In late May of 1896 a concerted effort got under way to appoint Daniel Coit Gilman to the superintendency of the public schools of New York City.[1] It was remarkable "that a man who had nearly completed his sixty-fifth year should be called away from the sphere of university work to which his whole life had been devoted, to undertake the reorganization of a vast system of popular education in a city presenting the extraordinary complexities that exist in the huge metropolis of our country." [2] The anxiety of the Hopkins faculty in the prospect of Gilman's loss to the university led to the presentation to Gilman of a faculty petition which implored him to remain at Hopkins. The faculty appeal noted, in part:

> The point which we wish chiefly to emphasize is the effect of your retirement upon the welfare of the University. As its first and only President, you occupy a relation to this university such as is rarely parallelled: its organization and the development of its distinctive features are mainly due to you. . . . The singular harmony and goodwill which have prevailed among all associated in the work of the University are eminently due to your influence. [3]

Gilman chose to remain at Hopkins. In his answer to the faculty, he said: "I could receive no greater reward than the assurance that those with whom I have lived and worked day by day for twenty years still wish me to remain with them." [4] In November, 1900, however, pleading the infirmity of age, Gilman formally notified the Hopkins Trustees that he would retire at the end of the academic year.[5] To all intents and purposes, Gilman's career of educational service was over. However,

---

[1] See Fabian Franklin, *The Life of Daniel Coit Gilman*, pp. 306-315. See Seth Low to Gilman, May 22, 1896, *Gilman Papers*, Lanier Room, Johns Hopkins University Library; W. L. Strong to Gilman, May 22, 1896, *Gilman Papers*, *loc. cit.* Low was president of Columbia University, and Strong was mayor of New York City at the time.

[2] Franklin, *op. cit.*, pp. 312-313.

[3] Ira Remsen, et al., to Gilman, May 23, 1896, *Gilman Papers*, Lanier Room, *loc. cit.*

[4] Gilman to Remsen, May 28, 1896, *Gilman Papers*, Lanier Room, *loc. cit.*

[5] Gilman's formal resignation is dated February 22, 1901. *Gilman Papers*, *loc. cit.* See also Franklin, *op. cit.*, pp. 385-386.

he found that he could not refuse a further service into which he was literally forced.

When Andrew Carnegie decided to make a benefaction to the city of Washington, he was not certain which form the benefaction should take.[1] He consulted with President Theodore Roosevelt, his secretary of state, John Hay, and finally with Andrew Dickson White in mid 1901.[2] White, who was United States Ambassador to Germany at the time, recommended that Carnegie confer with Gilman.[3] White may even have suggested that Gilman head whatever institution Carnegie intended to found since Gilman's resignation from the Hopkins was, by that time, common knowledge.[4] It is, however, apparent that White acted as intermediary in bringing Gilman and Carnegie together to discuss Carnegie's proposed benefaction.[5]

As originally proposed, Carnegie had in mind the creation of a great national university in Washington.[6] From the days of George Washington this issue had been cogently debated, and in the 1890's had again been prominently brought forward by its perennial champion, John Wesley Hoyt.[7] White seems to have encouraged Carnegie in this design;[8] but Carnegie abandoned the idea of a national university, and in one of his letters White observed:

> You suggest a National University at Washington, Washington's desire. Several have; but while this does, as you say, ensure immortality to the founder, it has hitherto seemed to me not needed, and this puts immortality under foot. [9]

Gilman first met with Andrew Carnegie in November, 1901 to discuss the Washington plans.[10] It appears that Carnegie had not formulated any definite plans as to the nature of the benefaction except to propose to Gilman and Johns S. Billings, whom he had summoned: "I am willing

---

[1] *Autobiography of Andrew Carnegie*, p. 260.

[2] *Autobiography of Andrew D. White*, II, pp. 205-206.

[3] *Ibid.*, II, p. 205.

[4] Burton J. Hendrick, *The Life of Andrew Carnegie*, II, pp. 228-230.

[5] See White to Gilman, May 20, 1901, *Gilman Papers*, Lanier Room, *loc. cit.*

[6] Hendrick, *op. cit.*, II, p. 227-228.

[7] See E. B. Wesley, *Proposed: The University of the United States*, Chapter I. The history of the national university movement in America remains to be written. Despite its excellent bibliography, Wesley's thin volume is a polemic in its behalf.

[8] Hendrick, *op. cit.*, II, p. 227.

[9] Quoted in Hendrick, *op. cit.*, II, p. 227.

[10] Gilman to Andrew D. White, December 7, 1901, *Gilman Papers*, Lanier Room, *loc. cit.* Also quoted in Franklin, *op. cit.*, p. 400.

to give ten millions for an institution the purpose of which shall be the advancement of knowledge." [1] Gilman has left a record of this initial interview:

> Mr Carnegie raised many hard questions. How is it that knowledge is increased? How can rare intellects be discovered in the undeveloped stages? Where is the exceptional man to be found? Would a new institution be regarded as an injury to Johns Hopkins, or to Harvard, Yale, Columbia, or any other university? What should the term "knowledge" comprise? Who should be the managers of the institution? How broad or how restricted should be the terms of the gift? [2]

It was at first meeting that Carnegie told Gilman: "You must be President." [3] The discussions continued through December, 1901. That some matters had not gone as Gilman anticipated is clear in a letter to Andrew D. White:

> I have kept you informed of the progress of events. On Friday last, 27th [November, 1901], I met at the house of Mr. Carnegie. . . . Suggestions and counter suggestions were made, —and finally the list of names of the Trustees, and a brief statement, for their information. Of course your name has been at the front since the beginning. I hope you will cable to Mr. Carnegie your acceptance. The present plan is to incorporate in the Dist. of Columbia, next Saturday, January 4, elect the Directors, and call a meeting of them at an early day for organization. Not everything has gone on as you would prefer, nor as others would prefer, but on the whole I am delighted with the plan. [4]

The Carnegie Institution of Washington was incorporated on January 28, 1902.[5] At the first meeting of the trustees, January 29, 1902, Gilman was elected President of the Institution.[6]

The Carnegie Institution "is not, as it has been called, a university or a place for the systematic education of youth, in advanced or professional departments of knowledge." [7] Gilman said that it was "unique in the history of civilisation," [8] and Abraham Flexner noted that it was not a foundation in the sense that that word is employed.[9] Perhaps, it is

---

[1] Gilman, *Launching of a University*, p. 107.

[2] *Ibid.*

[3] Franklin, *op. cit.*, p. 392.

[4] Gilman to White, December 29, 1901, *Gilman Papers*, Lanier Room, *loc. cit.*

[5] For the deed of trust see Robert M. Lester, *Forty Years of Carnegie Giving*, pp. 128-130.

[6] *Year Book of the Carnegie Institution of Washington* (1902), p. 3.

[7] Gilman, *Launching of a University*, p. 109.

[8] *Ibid.*, p. 111.

[9] *Funds and Foundations*, p. 106.

best described in Flexner's words as "an institution without teachers
or students, but with funds sufficient to maintain a group of scholars
and scientists engaged in penetrating the unknown without regard to
utility." [1] In many ways the Carnegie Institution of Washington was the
model of the Institute for Advanced Study at Princeton University
which Abraham Flexner was to head many years later, and of which
he has said: "In creating the Institute for Advanced Study and in selecting
its original staff, I adopted Gilman's procedure." [2] Gilman reported
Carnegie as stating the aim of the new institution in these words:

> It is proposed to found in the city of Washington an institution which
> with the coöperation of institutions now or hereafter established, there or
> elsewhere, shall in the broadest and most liberal manner encourage in-
> vestigation, research, and discovery; show the application of knowledge
> to the improvement of mankind; provide such buildings, laboratories,
> books, and apparatus, as may be needed; and afford instruction of an
> advanced character to students properly qualified to profit thereby. [3]

The aims were officially reduced to the following six points:

1 To promote original research, paying great attention thereto as one of
   the most important of all departments.
2 To discover the exceptional man in every department of study whenever
   and wherever found, inside or outside of schools, and enable him to
   make the work for which he seems specially designed his life-work.
3 To increase facilities for higher education.
4 To increase the efficiency of the universities and other institutions of
   learning throughout the country, by utilising and adding to their existing
   facilities and aiding teachers in the various institutions for experimental
   and other work, in these institutions as far as advisable.
5 To enable such students as may find Washington the best point for their
   special studies, to enjoy the advantages of the museums, libraries,
   laboratories, observatory, meteorological, piscicultural, and forestry
   schools, and kindred institutions of the special departments of the
   government.
6 To insure the prompt publication and distribution of the results of
   scientific investigation, a field considered highly important. [4]

In these broad outlines of aims and objectives, the Carnegie Institution
was planned as an institution whose work lay beyond the range of the
graduate school; and Gilman, in commenting on these aims, stressed

---

[1] *Ibid.*, p. 105.

[2] Abraham Flexner, *I Remember*, p. 48. The Institute for Advanced Study was
founded in 1930. See Flexner, *op. cit.*, pp. 356-397.

[3] *The Launching of a University*, p. 111.

[4] *Ibid.*, pp. 111-112. There is no statement in the first *Yearbook* (1902).

the logical connections between such an institution and the American graduate schools.[1] In a speech delivered at the convocation of the University of Chicago (June, 1903), Gilman noted that education and research were the distinct functions of civilised life, and that "they may be promoted by different corporations." [2] The two functions were mutual, and, in a sense, interdependent. "The two functions must [not] always be separated. They may be united." [3] The Carnegie Institution gave "emphasis to research." [4] Thus, Gilman saw the Carnegie Institution as a necessary culmination (without precursor and parallel)[5] in a scheme of education in which science "is accepted as synonymous with exact knowledge, [in which] truth takes the place of tradition, and the study of nature has usurped the throne of human authority." [6] It was a gigantic temple to the new god of research in which men "devote themselves, with the ardour of enthusiasm which has never been surpassed, to searching and researching, hoping and believing, almost knowing, that every step of progress contributes to the welfare of humanity, to the physical, intellectual, moral, and social improvement of the race." [7]

It is significant that Gilman, as the architect of a pure research endowment, found his greatest task in differentiating the research institute from the concept of the university which he had championed for over a quarter of a century. This was not an easy task, and Gilman saw its solution in his advocacy of the research institute as an indispensable adjunct to the university wherein "I cannot imagine anything like rivalry existing between this institution and any other which exists; but I can imagine a great many ways in which this institution can be of service to existing institutions, and I think the first note of our proceedings will be that of coöperation with what exists and welcoming other things that may be brought to our knowledge." [8] In common with Abraham Flexner's problem of some years later, Gilman had to promote the idea of an institute which would grow with and within, not outside the uni-

---

[1] Gilman, "The Carnegie Institution," *Science*, New Series, 15 (February 1902), pp. 201-203.
[2] *The Launching of a University*, p. 250.
[3] *Ibid.*
[4] *Ibid.* "A few objections are heard, *Vox et praeterea nihil." Ibid.*, p. 251.
[5] *Ibid.*, p. 250. The words are Gilman's.
[6] *Ibid.*, p. 251.
[7] *Ibid.*
[8] Stenographic copy of "Address to the Trustees of the Carnegie Institution," January 29, 1902. *Gilman Papers*, Lanier Room, *loc. cit.*

versities which it complemented.[1] Particularly difficult for Gilman was the problem of allaying the fears of those who had championed the idea of the national university in Washington.[2] From the very first he made clear that the national university idea was in no way adumbrated, and in his short tenure as President of the Carnegie Institution he found it necessary to reiterate this point.[3]

> In the first place, for a long period,—since 1873, certainly,—Governor Hoyt and others working with him, including a very large number of the universities of the Western states, had been urging upon Congress the establishment of a National University, and many of them were disappointed to see this, which they think might have gone to a national university, go instead to a separate institution. We shall probably hear that. But I beg you to bear in mind that such a university as they have projected, as people commonly understand and speak of when they speak of the National University, is still left untouched. If Congress should see fit to establish a National University, or . . . if others should see fit to do it, this does not interfere at all; it may even be helpful to his [Carnegie's] institution. That question is not touched at all by his gift. [4]

That Wesley was able to argue cogently for the establishment of a national university as late as 1936, graphically shows that the Carnegie Institution of Washington neither hindered nor helped the cause of the proposed University of the United States.[5]

Gilman's tenure as President of the Carnegie Institution extended only from January 29, 1902 to December 13, 1904.[6] The brevity of his tenure precludes any great achievement truly measurable; however, the original design of the Carnegie Institution appears to have been Gilman's [7] but this design was never carried out. The students spoken of in its original aims never materialized, and the Institution has been concerned only most meagerly with "facilities for higher education." [8] Primarily, the Institution has turned itself to scientific research with a

---

[1] See particularly Flexner, *I Remember*, pp. 378-379.

[2] See John W. Hoyt, "The Proposed National University," *Science*, New Series, 14 (October 1901), pp. 505-517.

[3] Particularly in "The Carnegie Institution," *Science*, New Series, 15 (February 1902), pp. 201-203.

[4] Stenographic copy of "Address to the Trustees of the Carnegie Institution," January 29, 1902. *Gilman Papers*, Lanier Room, *loc. cit.*

[5] E. B. Wesley, *Proposed: The University of the United States.*

[6] *Year Book of the Carnegie Institution of Washington* (1904), p. 6.

[7] This is concurred in by Hendrick, *op. cit.*, II, pp. 227-30 and by Franklin, *op. cit.*, pp. 390-392.

[8] See the *Year Books, seriatim*, 1902-1958.

heavy emphasis on "larger projects" and "the investigation of the more difficult problems in the better organized fields of knowledge." [1] In this sense, it never became the adjunct to the graduate school which Gilman visualized. Perhaps, the original aims had been defined with such looseness that no one could have predicted the development of the Institution. In substance Gilman's recommendation that the Institution advance knowledge, encourage talent, and publish results [2] had been achieved but not in the close association with graduate departments, and, certainly, not in close emulation of the advanced programs of study at the Johns Hopkins University. Gilman's last service to the Carnegie Institution was the modification of its by-laws to permit the President more power in the formulation of basic policy. [3]

---

[1] Ellwood P. Cubberley, "Carnegie Institution," *A Cyclopedia of Education*, ed. by Paul Monroe, I, pp. 539-540. This was apparent by 1911, the date of Cubberley's article.

[2] "Those are the three things to which attention has been directed;—the advancement of knowledge; the encouragement of talent; and the publication of results." Stenographic copy of "Address to the Trustees of the Carnegie Institution," January 29, 1902. *Gilman Papers*, Lanier Room, *loc. cit.*

[3] *Year Book of the Carnegie Institution of Washington* (1903), pp. 12-13. Franklin, *op. cit.*, p. 399, suggests that this dissatisfaction with the by-laws which gave the real policy power to the Executive Committee may have been Gilman's reason for retiring but there is no evidence given for the statement. It is repeated by Abraham Flexner, *Daniel Coit Gilman*, p. 160. At his retirement, Gilman was seventy-three and in poor health.

CHAPTER SEVEN

THE REPUTATION OF DANIEL COIT GILMAN

Only four years after his death, Daniel Coit Gilman was eulogized in Paul Monroe's *Cyclopedia of Education* as responsible for "the establishment of full-fledged graduate schools, the naturalization of research as a leading element in American universities, and the development of a great scale of scientific and scholarly publications [which] date from the foundation of Johns Hopkins University." [1] Gilman has been called "the patron saint of the American graduate school," [2] and Rudy has written that "the most significant effect of [Gilman's] Baltimore experiment was to speed up, by a process of emulation, the development of strong graduate schools at other important centers of learning." [3] In his long tenure as President of the Johns Hopkins University, Daniel Coit Gilman touched many of the leaders in American higher education. Although direct influence can only at best be presumptively argued in any of history's agencies, two factors in the history of American graduate education in the last quarter of the nineteenth century are indisputable. One factor is the tremendous growth of American graduate education in the period defined; [4] the second factor is the constantly reiterated acknowledgment of the influence of Gilman in the promotion of the growth of graduate studies in America. Clark University and the University of Chicago were founded in the historical shadow of the Hopkins and their first presidents acknowledged Gilman's model, but the influence extended beyond the new enterprises; it touched the older establishment whose leaders publicly declared their indebtedness to the Baltimore experiment. The English historian, James Bryce, suggested that Gilman's influence and achievement went beyond the

---

[1] Fabian Franklin, "Daniel Coit Gilman," *A Cyclopedia of Education*, ed. by Paul Monroe, III (1912), p. 112.

[2] Ernest V. Hollis, *Toward Improving Ph. D. Programs*, p. 14.

[3] S. Willis Rudy, "The Revolution in American Higher Education, 1865-1900," *Harvard Educational Review*, 21 (Summer 1951), p. 168.

[4] See Walton C. John, *Graduate Study in Universities and Colleges in the United States*, pp. 1-23; W. Carson Ryan, *Studies in Early Graduate Education*, pp. 139-147; Richard Hofstadter and C. DeWitt Hardy, *The Development and Scope of Higher Education in the United States*, pp. 57-100.

American academic scene and, at base, touched university organization in general:

> He had a true and just perception of the relation that ought to exist in the plans and organization of a university to secure due attention to each of the two branches of its work, viz., to research and to instruction. Appreciating the importance of both of these, he made due provision for each; nor has anything more contributed to the progress of the university. We in England have been much perplexed by this problem, which his wide and just view of the history and functions of a university enabled him to solve effectively. As the creation of Johns Hopkins has been a very important factor in the recent growth and change in the character of the higher education in this country, his sound appreciation of the conditions of this problem deserves the fullest recognition. [1]

At Harvard University graduate studies began very feebly in the 1870's;[2] primarily, the graduate impulse came from its Lawrence Scientific School [3] very much as Yale College first developed a graduate school in its Sheffield Scientific School.[4] That Charles William Eliot, who became President of Harvard in 1869, was not fully aware of the need for graduate studies in the 1870's has been established by Henry James.[5] And Eliot had shown his lack of sympathy with a true graduate program when he had conferred with the Hopkins trustees in 1874 as to the direction their proposed university should take:

> A university is not built in the air, so to speak. It is a growth, and I should doubt very much whether any institution, old or young, could cut loose from the educational foundations of the community in which it is placed— taking that word community in a large sense. We are as well off at Harvard as at any place in the country for carrying on education of a high order; but we could not deliberately undertake to give only a high degree of education for a few. We could not deliberately undertake that, not even if we were starting anew. [6]

Of course, Eliot's anxiety was pretty much that which the *ante-bellum*

---

[1] James Bryce, "Address," in *Daniel Coit Gilman, First President of the Johns Hopkins University*, 1876-1901, p. 29. Bryce was British ambassador to the United States at the time (1908).

[2] See Charles H. Haskins, "The Graduate School of Arts and Sciences," *The Development of Harvard University*, 1869-1929, ed. by Samuel E. Morison, pp. 451-455.

[3] *Ibid.*, p. 453.

[4] See George W. Pierson, *Yale College*, pp. 49-63.

[5] Henry James, *Charles W. Eliot*, II, pp. 9-15.

[6] "Stenographic copy of the remarks of Charles William Eliot at a meeting with the Johns Hopkins University Trustees, June 4, 1874." *Trustee Minutes*, June 4, 1874. President's Office, Johns Hopkins University.

educational reformers had encountered,[1] and his situation at Harvard was very much unlike that of Gilman at Hopkins. As James has remarked, "The Johns Hopkins was a pot-started plant that had no initial root-attachments in anything near it and that depended for a number of years upon the skill of the gardener who fed and tended it." [2] Eliot, on the other hand, faced a Harvard where he was "compelled to devote a large portion of [his] energies to undergraduate instruction and college business." [3] If Eliot was "relatively deficient in certain qualities which, in Gilman, contributed to Johns Hopkins's success," [4] he was ready to declare that it was Gilman and the Hopkins which gave him example and precept for graduate education.

At the twenty-fifth anniversary of the foundation of the Johns Hopkins University, President Eliot declared:

> President Gilman, your first achievement here, with the help of your colleagues, your students, and your trustees, has been, to my thinking —and I have had good means of observation—the creation of a graduate school, which not only has been in itself a strong and potent school, but which has lifted every other university in the country in its departments of arts and sciences. I want to testify that the graduate school of Harvard University, started feebly in 1870 and 1871, did not thrive, until the example of Johns Hopkins forced our faculty to put their strength into the development of our instruction for graduates. And what was true of Harvard was true of every other university in the land which aspired to create an advanced school of arts and sciences. [5]

And that Eliot now understood that research was the distinguishing feature of any graduate program was also attributed to the example of Gilman: [6]

> And, sir, I wish to mention as an achievement of this university under your leadership, that it has promoted, and taught others to promote, research, scientific investigation, the careful probing of external nature and man's nature in the hope of discovering some new thing which may

---

[1] Richard J. Storr, *The Beginnings of Graduate Education* . . . , pp. 129-134.

[2] Henry James, *op. cit.*, II, pp. 7-8.

[3] *Ibid.*, II, p. 15.

[4] *Ibid.*, II, p. 16.

[5] *Johns Hopkins University. Celebration of the Twenty-Fifth Anniversary of the Founding of the University* . . . , pp. 105-106.

[6] "But until Gilman's invitation [to Francis J. Child to leave Harvard for Hopkins] providentially brought both men to a just apprehension of the situation, Child had been compelled to let his Chaucerian studies and his researches in ballad literature suffer the interference of what [undergraduate instruction] he chafed against as a loathsome chore." Henry James, *op. cit.*, II, p. 15.

lead on to another new thing. This a very genuine, substantial and durable achievement of this young university, and I desire here to congratulate you all upon it, and to recognize the full scope and meaning of the policy which led to this great issue. [1]

Even more conclusive evidence of the influence of the Hopkins on Harvard is the history of the Harvard Ph.D. At first nebulously defined (as it was at most of the older endowments),[2] it began in the 1880's to take definite shape and form.[3] The residence requirement, as at Hopkins, was minimally defined as one year, a thesis was required, and the candidate was required to work in a disciplined area, with some subsidiary related interest.[4] Unlike Gilman at Hopkins, Eliot at Harvard faced the problem of "the superimposition of a graduate school upon the college." [5] But it was almost historically axiomatic that Eliot and the older foundations had to approach the problem of graduate studies through a college corridor.[6] "So, while Johns Hopkins began as a pot-plant tended by Gilman's skill, the Harvard Graduate Department came up like a patch of vegetation on open ground. Eliot, the bigger man with less delicate fingers, did not often touch its foliage; but with his spade, the elective system, he kept loosening and deepening the soil. He had no doubt that this labor was well applied." [7] As late as the 1890's, Gilman was furnishing Eliot with detailed information on the successful "group system" of Hopkins undergraduate studies as the key adjunct to a graduate program.[8] Eliot's "elective system" may have revolutionized the American undergraduate curriculum but "[its] shallowness has been undergoing a fundamental re-examination during the past few years, though not as much criticism has been levelled at Gilman's relatively more conservative 'group system'." [9] What the other adjuncts of a successful Ph.D. program were, Eliot learned slowly from Gilman's

---

[1] *Johns Hopkins University. Celebration of the Twenty-Fifth Anniversary of the Founding of the University* . . . , p. 106.

[2] Ernest V. Hollis, *op. cit.*, pp. 10-12.

[3] Charles H. Haskins, "The Graduate School of Arts and Sciences," *The Development of Harvard University*, 1869-1929, ed. by Samuel E. Morison, p. 451.

[4] *Ibid.*, pp. 451-455.

[5] Henry James, *op. cit.*, II, p. 11.

[6] Richard J. Storr, *op. cit.*, pp. 129-134.

[7] Henry James, *op. cit.*, II, p. 27.

[8] Gilman to Eliot, November 30, 1890; December 8, 1890; October 9, 1894. Harvard College Archive, Houghton Library.

[9] Willis Rudy, "Eliot and Gilman: The History of an Academic Friendship," *Teachers College Record*, 54 (March 1953), p. 317.

example. He never widely employed Gilman's visiting lectureship,[1] but he early saw the advantage and the need for the publication of scholarly monographs. In 1880 he wrote to Gilman:

> Your methods, being in some respects novel, need to be made known. Dignified silence, or mere lists of lectures, are not for you just yet. Indeed the methods of Oxford and Berlin are not for any of us in this generation. We are compelled by the rawness of the country to proclaim in set terms the advantages which we offer. [2]

In one respect Eliot outdid his master. Although Gilman had hoped to see equal facilities at the Hopkins for women students,[3] this was not achieved during his presidential tenure.[4] At Harvard, on the other hand, "The Society for the Collegiate Instruction of Women" was founded in 1879; in 1891 it became Radcliffe College and in 1902 it conferred its first Ph.D.'s. [5] "Harvard granted it a privilege of inestimable value: it agreed to admit Radcliffe students, with such limitations as might be agreed upon by the officers of both institutions, to courses which the University designated as primarily for graduate students." [6] In still another way Gilman's Hopkins kept Eliot and Harvard alert. Gilman entered the academic market looking for a staff and he kept recruiting offering, if necessary, better salary. Although he had little success luring men away from Harvard, the threat to Eliot was always there and Eliot was forced to act, if only to retain his key professors.[7] "When Gilman began to organize his staff at Johns Hopkins, this difficulty was in a measure increased for Eliot. Until that time—that is, since Eliot assumed the Presidency, raised salaries, and began to liberalize the curriculum— teaching positions at Harvard had enjoyed a power of attraction that was unique; but Johns Hopkins offered better remuneration and Gilman fished in all waters, casting his lures where-ever he saw the man he wanted." [8] Thus, Gilman directly and indirectly forced Harvard to act. In

---

[1] See Henry James, *op. cit.*, II, pp. 13-14.

[2] Charles W. Eliot to Gilman, April 6, 1880. *Gilman Papers*, Lanier Room, Johns Hopkins University Library. See also Eliot to Gilman, May 7, 1886, *Gilman Papers*, *loc. cit.*

[3] "They are not among the prudent who would deny to women the best opportunities for education and culture." *Addresses at the Inauguration of Daniel C. Gilman . . ,* p. 53.

[4] John C. French, *A History of the University Founded by Johns Hopkins*, pp. 71-75.

[5] *Graduate Education For Women: The Radcliffe Ph. D.*, pp. 7-8.

[6] *Ibid.*, p. 8.

[7] See Henry James, op. cit., II, pp. 12-16.

[8] *Ibid.*, II, p. 13.

a sense, he furnished both the model and the stimulus, and the pattern was not much different at the other old establishments.[1]

As at Yale College and Harvard University, graduate instruction at Columbia College began in a scientific school. Graduate work began in its Columbia School of Mines which had been organized in 1864,[2] and its first Ph.D. was granted in 1875.[3] The real impetus to graduate work at Columbia, however, came in 1876 when John W. Burgess accepted a call as professor of history, political science, and international law.[4] Within four years Burgess and his associates had established a School of Political Science based on the example of the *École Libres des Sciences Politiques* at Paris.[5] A Faculty of Philosophy was added in 1890, and two years later a Faculty of Pure Science was organized.[6] These three faculties constituted the graduate school at Columbia, and since 1909 have been administered by a single dean.[7] It is, then, in the late 1890's that the fruits of a graduate program at Columbia are to sought, by which time the Hopkins had become fully established as "literally a German university in America." [8]

In his pioneering graduate work, Burgess acknowledges the inspiration of Gilman and the Hopkins.[9] Although he does not specifically relate certain features of the School of Political Science to the Hopkins example, the similarity is too marked to be dismissed:

> [We] set up a program of studies in history, economics, public law, and political philosophy, extending over a period of three years, with a degree of Ph.B. or A.B. to be conferred upon students completing the first year

---

[1] Yale College is an exception. Gilman had participated in the institution of the Ph. D. at Yale's Sheffield Scientific School and its first earned doctorate was granted in 1861 but the administration of Noah Porter had seriously arrested the progress of graduate studies at Yale. Gilman's pioneering work at Yale furnished the impulse which fructified many years later. See pp. 17-34, *supra*. See also George W. Pierson, *Yale College*, pp. 53-64, and Russell H. Chittenden, *History of the Sheffield Scientific School*, I, Chapter III.

[2] Frederick P. Keppel, *Columbia*, pp. 20-21.

[3] J. H. Van Amringe, "The School of Mines," *School of Mines Quarterly*, 10 (January 1890), pp. 339-351.

[4] Munroe Smith, "The Graduate Schools," in *History of Columbia University*, 1754-1904, p. 269.

[5] *Ibid.*, pp. 268-269.

[6] John Herman Randall, "Introduction," *A History of the Faculty of Philosophy. Columbia University*, p. 3.

[7] *Ibid.*

[8] *Ibid.*, p. 6. In 1890, the combined Columbia graduate faculties granted 10 Ph.D.'s. *Ibid.*, p. 18.

[9] *Reminiscences of an American Scholar*, p. 243, and *passim*.

and of Ph.D. to be conferred upon students completing the curricula of the three years and presenting an approved thesis. Other elements in the plan conceived at the outset and ultimately were a system of graduate fellowships, a journal of the political sciences edited by the faculty (*The Political Science Quarterly*), and a series of treatises, textbooks, and monographs in the field of the social sciences. [1]

The plan contained the elements of Gilman's success: it included graduate fellowships, a definite time scheme, and the scholarly journal and the monograph.[2] Burgess further noted that, "The decade from 1890 to 1900 was the period of bloom in the faculty and school of political science. It became firmly established as the leading graduate faculty and school in the university union and as the model for such faculties and schools throughout the country." [3] Burgess stood "equally with Gilman for intellect and scholarship—for the training of specialists in critical methods, and the fostering of research that would advance the frontiers of human knowledge." [4]

Nicholas Murray Butler arrived on the Columbia scene in 1885, and by 1887 he was teaching five graduate courses in the Department of Philosophy.[5] Butler's German sojourn [6] had imbued him with the new *Geisteswissenschaften* and, like Burgess, he felt that the professors of the graduate faculties "were always to present original material, the fruit of their own thought and research. Their seminars were to work with young apprentices in the furtherance of knowledge. They were, as Butler used to put it, a company of scholars, thinkers, and investigators rather than teachers, who would rather incidentally reproduce their own kind of specialists." [7] It is not strange that Butler reacted warmly and sympathetically to the Hopkins experiment and widely proclaimed his respect and admiration for Gilman. Over the years Butler conferred many times with Gilman about the selection of Columbia faculty members,[8] and he early perceived the value and correctness of Gilman's methods:

---

[1] Quoted in W. Carson Ryan, *op. cit.*, p. 12.

[2] For further development of the program, see R. Gordon Hoxie, *et al.*, *A History of the Faculty of Political Science*, Chapters I-III.

[3] Burgess, *op. cit.*, p. 244.

[4] John Herman Randall, "The Department of Philosophy," *A History of the Faculty of Philosophy. Columbia University*, p. 110.

[5] *Ibid.*, p. 109.

[6] See his autobiography, *Across the Busy Years*, I, pp. 69-103. See also his "The Department of Philosophy at Columbia," *Columbia University Quarterly*, 3 (1901), p. 143.

[7] John Herman Randall, "The Department of Philosophy," *loc. cit.*, p. 111.

[8] *Across the Busy Years*, I, 162.

> For here, still young and still taking form, was the promise of a real university. Here had been brought together by the genius of President Gilman a company of really advanced scholars and a small group of really inspired and productive university teachers. Everything was being subordinated to the university ideals of inquiry, of productive scholarship and of publication. [1]

And when Butler founded the *Educational Review* in 1891, he invited Gilman to be one of the first contributors.[2] Like Gilman, "Butler's forte was the organization of knowledge rather than its advancement," [3] and he found ready support in Gilman for what was later to become Teachers College.[4] Gilman had early emphasized that education should be included as a field of graduate study:

> I can hardly doubt that such arrangements as we are maturing will cause this institution to be a place for the training of professors and teachers for the highest academic posts; and I hope in time to see arrangements made for unfolding the philosophy, principles, and methods of education in a way which will be of service to those who mean to devote their lives to the highest departments of instruction. [5]

With these sentiments Butler was in complete agreement, and his early work at Columbia had been in behalf of teacher education and the university's acceptance of a teachers' college.[6]

In an analysis of the Hopkins experiment, Butler concluded that Gilman "has held up new ideals, suggested new methods, enforced new and high standards of excellence and achievement." [7] Butler saw many elements in the success of the Johns Hopkins University. Foremost of these was the guidance and organization provided by Gilman. From the very first, Butler observed, Gilman understood what a "university" really was, and had been determined to create one; the emphasis upon men, rather than buildings; the annual fellowships, open to graduates

---

[1] *Ibid.*, I, p. 112.

[2] *Ibid.*, I, p. 202. Gilman's contribution was "The Shortening of the College Curriculum," *Educational Review*, 1 (January 1891), pp. 1-7.

[3] John Herman Randall, "The Department of Philosophy," *loc. cit.*, p. 111.

[4] Of Teachers College Gilman said: "Normal schools have long been maintained in this country; professorships of pedagogy have recently been established. But there is nowhere such a training school for teachers as here exists." *University Problems in the United States*, p. 269.

[5] *Addresses at the Inauguration of Daniel Coit Gilman* ..., p. 7.

[6] See *Across the Busy Years*, I, Chapters 1-3.

[7] Nicholas Murray Butler, "President Gilman's Administration at the Johns Hopkins University," *American Monthly Review of Reviews*, 23 (January 1901), p. 53.

of any college;[1] the opportunities for research and publication—all these elements assured the success of the Baltimore experiment. Whether Butler emulated each of these elements at Columbia as a result of his study of Hopkins and his association with Gilman is beside the point: significantly, he was headed in Gilman's direction. In 1911 Butler could boast of Columbia "as the American university in which graduate and research work are most emphasized and that in which there is much the largest attendance of graduate students." [2]

Harvard and Columbia Universities are, perhaps, the best examples of the older institutions at which Gilman's influence and the impression of the Hopkins are distinctly measurable. Although no direct connections can be discerned between Gilman and some of the other representative old universities, still it can be presumptively argued that the graduate program of the Hopkins influenced them. Thus, James Burrill Angell of the University of Michigan where graduate education had gained an early foothold in the work of Henry Tappan, acknowledges Gilman's importance in American graduate education [3] and further observed in a letter to Gilman: "No one of us has done so much as you to make an epoch in graduate work in America. I have always been proud that I had a part, however humble, in persuading your Trustees to bring you from California to Baltimore." [4] Andrew D. White, who became president of Cornell University in 1867, drew many of his ideas on graduate education directly from his life-long friendship with Gilman,[5] and many of the Hopkins elements were introduced at Cornell by White with varying success.[6] In the Hopkins fellowship White saw a plan he had long wished to carry out: "Johns Hopkins has carried into practice a policy I have so often recommended to this board and which has been held in abeyance only on account of our lack of means, i.e., the policy of establishing a number of Fellowships for Post Graduate study." [7]

---

[1] Of the fellowships, Butler remarked: "And it was this step as much as any other single one, which fixed the relation of the new university to the colleges of the country and which attracted to it at once the most promising of the younger scholars." *Ibid.*, p. 54.

[2] *Report of the President* (1911), p. 30.

[3] James B. Angell, *Reminiscences, passim.* See also, Shirley W. Smith, *James B. Angell*, 79.

[4] James B. Angell to Gilman, November 22, 1900. *Gilman Papers*, Lanier Room, *loc. cit.*

[5] See his *Autobiography*, I, pp. 34, 447; II, pp. 119, 122, 206.

[6] Walter P. Rogers, *Andrew D. White and the Modern University*, pp. 197-200.

[7] Quoted in *Ibid.*, p. 199.

Like Gilman, White was unalterably opposed "to the conferring of honorary degrees . . . and his influence in directing Cornell's policy away from the granting of honorary degrees was a most salutary one." [1] In retrospect White regarded "[Gilman's] work at Johns Hopkins as peculiarly original and valuable. He rendered a great service by it to every other institution of advanced learning throughout the whole country." [2]

Hollis has observed that "During the quarter-century following the founding of Johns Hopkins University, a dozen other institutions were sufficiently influenced by the standard it set to try, each in its own way, to give acceptable shape to its own rather formless graduate school." [3] Where acknowledgement is not made directly of the Hopkins's influence, the progress of the graduate program at other universities presumptively suggests the influence. The development can be discerned at the University of Pennsylvania,[4] at Princeton University,[5] and at the University of Virginia. [6] In the American South, graduate work developed slowly but its development was largely stimulated by the men who had been trained in the new graduate faculties, of which the Johns Hopkins was the best known.[7] Perhaps, the greatest measure of influence exerted by Gilman in American graduate education was on the new universities which were formed in the shadow of the Johns Hopkins University. Both at Clark University, and at the University of Chicago, there was ready acknowledgement of the model furnished by Gilman's Hopkins.

Ryan has noted that "When G. Stanley Hall left Johns Hopkins in 1888 to head the newly created Clark University at Worcester, Massachusetts, it was with the expectation of developing a purely graduate institution that would carry out the original Johns Hopkins purposes even more substantially than had been done at Baltimore." [8] Hall saw the

---

[1] *Ibid.*, p. 201. Gilman had written: "Honorary degrees are bestowed in extravagant profuseness without any respect to the academic study of the recipient." "The Use and Abuse of Titles," *North American Review*, 140 (March 1885), p. 262.

[2] Quoted in Franklin, *Life of Daniel Coit Gilman*, p. 326.

[3] Ernest V. Hollis, *op. cit.*, p. 12.

[4] See Edward P. Cheyney, *History of the University of Pennsylvania*, Chapter VIII.

[5] See Thomas J. Wertenbaker, *Princeton University*, Chapter IX.

[6] See Philip A. Bruce, *History of the University of Virginia*, III, 37-42.

[7] Mary B. Pierson, *Graduate Work in the South*, pp. 30-31.

[8] W. Carson Ryan, *op. cit.*, p. 47. For the history of Clark University see, Edmund C. Sanford, "A Sketch of the History of Clark University," *Publications of the Clark University Library*, 7 (January 1923), pp. 1-23, which pays considerable attention to the early period.

true seed of the Clark University experiment in Hopkins, and he envisaged Clark as the logical continuation of the Gilman plan.

> The epoch-making work of the Johns Hopkins University had leavened the colleges and roused them from the life of monotony and routine which then prevailed, and kindled a strong and widespread desire for better things. But financial clouds had already begun to threaten this great Southern luminary, and there were indications that, if the great work it had begun was to be carried on, parts of it, at least, must be transplanted to new fields. [1]

Hall reasoned that, with a dozen colleges within a radius of a hundred miles of Worcester, Clark University should take the "inevitable next step" beyond Hopkins, eliminating "college work" altogether, waiving the test of numbers, "selecting vigorously the best students, seeking to train leaders only, educating professors, and advancing science by new discoveries." [2] The genesis of Clark University, as Hall admits, was in the Hopkins experiment even though Hall tended to judge Gilman's policies somewhat negatively. But the first few years of Hall's presidency of Clark University show—with the exception of Gilman's undergraduate "group system"—that Hall transferred, virtually without change, most of the salient features of the Hopkins graduate program.

When Clark University opened its doors in late 1889, it offered fellowship and scholarship aid; it opened, like Hopkins, with a carefully selected faculty and student body; and it was "to the need of [Ph.D.] students that the lectures, seminaries, laboratories and collections of books and apparatus will be especially shaped, and no pains will be spared to afford them every needed stimulus and opportunity." [3] The fellowships, the seminar, and the Ph.D. emphasis were all clearly from the Hopkins experiment in which Hall had shared, but the academic connection was even greater in the recognition that everything in the early Clark University, as at Hopkins, was firmly grounded in the "resolute determination to meet what were felt to be urgent contemporary needs that were not being met in the higher institutions of the day." [4] In this sense, Clark University was not truly different from Hopkins but, rather, more decisively oriented to the aims of Gilman which the first decade of the Hopkins had proven

---

[1] *Clark University*, 1889-1899: *Decennial Celebration*, p. 48.

[2] Quoted in Ryan, *op. cit.*, p. 47. "Whatever questions were to arise later as to the function of the University, President Hall did his best to make clear at the outset the specialized graduate opportunity he visioned for Clark." *Idem.*

[3] G. Stanley Hall quoted in Ryan, *op. cit.*, pp. 55-56.

[4] Ryan, *op. cit.*, p. 68.

practicable. One might argue that Hall's difficulties at Clark lay in his inflexible academic idealism and in his refusal to deal eclectically, as had Gilman, with the collegiate problem.[1] Certainly, the hegira of his faculty, following the raid of William Rainey Harper, to "[the] richer financial soil" [2] of the University of Chicago does not, in itself, explain the decline of Hall's expectations at Worcester.[3] The explanation, perhaps, lies in the fact that Hall, without the long educational experience of Gilman, failed to perceive the inevitable relationship that any program of graduate education had to have to what preceded it in the American historical framework. [4]

Hall characterised Gilman as "the most creative mind in the field of the higher education that this country has yet produced," [5] and he ascribed this distinction to Gilman's new policies:

> First of all, he realized that as civilization advanced, all critical decisions and new steps must be made by experts who could command all the available knowledge in their field and perhaps add something new to the sum of the world's knowledge. To have made a contribution to this, however small, marks the real attainment of majority in our world. Scholarship is a prime condition but erudition is not enough; each must have the unique experience of having contributed some tiny brick, however small, to the Temple of Science, the construction of which is the sublimest achievement of man. . . . Anything and everything must be subordinated to this, and Gilman must have had great satisfaction in realizing that in this kind of productivity the Hopkins University, at least for a decade or two, was the leader and pioneer in this land. [6]

Strangely, Hall remarked that the undergraduate college at Hopkins "grew in favor and recognition slowly but surely, until it became not only a very important bond between the city and the university but gave the unique kind of training that real university work needed and presupposed and without which it would have been an air plant." [7] Evidently,

---

[1] For the difficulties between Hall and Jonas Gilman Clark, see Ryan, *op. cit.*, pp. 59-63; and Wallace W. Atwood, *The First Fifty Years* [of Clark University] pp. 40-58.

[2] G. Stanley Hall, *Life and Confessions of a Psychologist*, p. 297. Hall regarded Harper's action as "the assassination of an institution." *Ibid.*, pp. 296-297.

[3] See Hall's account in his *Life and Confessions of a Psychologist*, pp. 295-298.

[4] When Jonas Gilman Clark died in 1900 it was found that he had carried out his plan of providing for an undergraduate college. The college was to use the same facilities of the existent University. See Ryan, *op. cit.*, p. 66.

[5] Hall, *op. cit.*, p. 248.

[6] *Ibid.*, pp. 248-249.

[7] *Ibid.*, p. 250.

he had not entertained such an opinion of undergraduate education in his early days at Clark University.[1] Excepting the undergraduate curriculum, Hall noted that "Clark University is, in a sense, an offshoot of the Johns Hopkins, for here, small as it has been so far, the inevitable next step of attempting university work was first tried although there was no undergraduate section." [2]

Hall had singular success with the seminar and the scholarly journal as the adjuncts of graduate instruction at Clark University; [3] like Gilman, he maintained high standards at Clark and exercised great restraint in the granting of the Ph.D.[4] He brought to Clark, too, some of the personal traits he had discerned in Gilman:

> Gilman was essentially an *inside* president. His interest in the work of the individual members of his faculty did not end when they were engaged, but began. He loved to know something of their every new investigation, however remote from his own specialty, and every scientific or scholarly success felt the stimulus of his sympathy. His unerring judgment of men was triumphantly justified in the achievements of those he appointed; and although in selecting young men he had to walk by faith, he nowhere showed more sagacity than in applying individual stimuli and checks, so that in this sense and to this extent he was a spiritual father of many of his faculty, the author of their careers, and for many years made the institution the paradise and seminarium of young specialists. This made stagnation impossible, and the growth of professors there in their work was, I believe, without precedent. [5]

Generously, Hall observed that the model of graduate education furnished by Gilman "found the warmest response in every able and original mind in all academic America, as is abundantly witnessed by the fact that the Hopkins fashions have been so generally cultivated in later years by all our higher institutions. ... The leadership of this institution is now relatively less pronounced only because its ideals have been so infectious in so many other centers." [6]

---

[1] See Ryan, *op. cit.*, pp. 59-61. See also Louis N. Wilson, "Some Recollections of our Founder," *Publications of the Clark University Library*, 8 (February 1927), pp. 8-11.

[2] *Op. cit.*, p. 247.

[3] Ryan, *op. cit.*, pp. 77-80; 89-90.

[4] Clark granted only 90 Ph.D.'s in its first fifteen years. See Louis N. Wilson, "List of Degrees Granted at Clark University, 1889-1920," *Publications of the Clark University Library*, 6 (December 1920), pp. 6-13.

[5] Hall, *op. cit.*, pp. 246-247. For a similar estimate of Hall, see Sara C. Fisher, "The Psychological and educational work of Granville Stanley Hall," *American Journal of Psychology*, 36 (January 1925), pp. 1-52.

[6] Hall, *op. cit.*, p. 249. "True history in the field of higher education was perhaps

At the celebration of the twenty-fifth anniversary of the Johns Hopkins University, President William Rainey Harper of the University of Chicago congratulated Gilman and the Hopkins in these words:

> In the changes which have come about in thirty years, the Johns Hopkins University has been the principal factor. The ideals of its founders, the contributions of his professors, and the work of its alumni have constituted the principal agency in bringing about this wonderful growth. During this first period the Johns Hopkins University has been the most conspicuous figure in the American university world, and to its achievements we are largely indebted for the fact that we may now enter upon a higher mission. I desire to present upon this occasion the greetings and the congratulations of the scores of institutions in the West and Far West which have been strengthened by the presence in their faculties of Johns Hopkins men, and have been encouraged and stimulated to higher work by the influence of Johns Hopkins ideals. [1]

At the very opening of this congratulatory address he had observed: "But within thirty years institutions have come into existence possessing, not only the name, but the character of universities; and old institutions have changed, not only their character, but their names. In other words, the university idea has beyond question established itself upon a strong foundation." [2] And he did not except from this characterization his own University of Chicago.

The University of Chicago was begun in 1890, largely through the benefaction of John D. Rockefeller.[3] In one of his early letters to Rockefeller concerning the proposed university, Harper wrote: "Naturally we ought to be willing to begin small and grow, but in these days when things are done so rapidly, and with the example of Johns Hopkins before our eyes, it seems a great pity to wait for growth when we might be born full-fledged." [4] In a sense, Harper's letter discerns the only difference between Hopkins and the University of Chicago in the matter

---

never so hard to write as in this country, pervaded as it is with insidious biases for competing institutions, and the day of impartiality and competency of judgment will dawn late; but just in proportion as love of the highest learning and research prevails, Dr. Gilman's qualities will become the ideals of leaders in our American system." *Ibid.*, p. 246.

[1] *Johns Hopkins University. Celebration of the Twenty-Fifth Anniversary of the Founding of the University* . . . , p. 62. The address is also in Harper's *The Trend in Higher Education*, pp. 151-155.

[2] *Ibid.*, p. 58; *The Trend in Higher Education*, p. 151.

[3] For the beginnings of the University of Chicago, see Ryan, *op. cit.*, pp. 91-138; Thomas W. Goodspeed, *The Story of the University of Chicago*; and the latter's *William Rainey Harper*.

[4] Quoted in Ryan, *op. cit.*, p. 107.

of graduate education.[1] All of the elements of the Hopkins were present in the Chicago graduate program, but at Chicago these elements took on gargantuan form. Harper contemplated graduate work in no less than twenty-one fields; in fourteen of these fields advanced work was immediately offered upon the opening of the university. [2] He assembled a faculty of 120 persons—more faculty members than the Hopkins had students in its early years,[3] and forthwith made provisions for sixty fellowships, thrice the number at Hopkins. And what had been the scholarly journal at Hopkins became at Chicago a separate division of the university.[4] When the university formally opened for instruction it had enrolled some 594 students, more than half of whom were to do graduate work.[5] Harper's faculty numbered many individuals who were recruited by G. Stanley Hall for the graduate program at Clark University,[6] and as Ryan observes: "This migration from Clark provided the new university with a group of the best-equipped men to be had anywhere in America, already selected and trained to do, in graduate work especially, the very things Harper wanted the University of Chicago to undertake." [7]

Thus, dedicated to research and a graduate program, in essence that of Hopkins, William Rainey Harper continued the work of Gilman. Like Gilman, he was alive to contemporary needs and provided undergraduate work; very much like his predecessor he attempted the modification of the undergraduate curriculum.[8] The Chicago Ph.D. assumed the pattern established at the Hopkins, and Harper put the same emphasis on the relation of research and teaching held by Gilman. [9] In

---

[1] The sectarian basis of the University of Chicago's foundation remains a fundamental difference. In its origins the University of Chicago was a Baptist enterprise. Ryan, *op. cit.*, pp. 95-99.

[2] Thomas W. Goodspeed, *A History of the University of Chicago: the First Quarter Century*, p. 142.

[3] *Ibid.* p. 247.

[4] Called in Harper's ambitious scheme, "The University Publication Work." Thomas W. Goodspeed, *The Story of the University of Chicago*, p. 51, pp. 142-143.

[5] Ryan, *op. cit.*, p. 124. See also *The University of Chicago: Its Future* (1925) for much statistical information on the early period.

[6] See Thomas W. Goodspeed, *A History of the University of Chicago*, p. 247 for Harper's side of the story.

[7] Ryan, *op. cit.*, p. 119.

[8] For discussion of Harper's junior college plan, see John A. Sexson and John W. Harbeson, *The New American College*, pp. 15-17. See also Harper, *The Trend in Higher Education*, pp. 338-348.

[9] Thomas W. Goodspeed, *A History of the University of Chicago*, p. 372. See also Harper's *President's Reports*, *seriatim*, for notices of research underway.

a speech on research at the University of Chicago in June, 1903, Gilman was able to characterize the new university as "the most suggestive, the most comprehensive, the most successful, and the most hopeful of many new foundations among us for the advancement of higher education." [1]

In a perceptive article, Edwin E. Slosson speaks of the Johns Hopkins University and the University of Chicago as universities "raised from seed." [2] The characterization is not inept for the seeds of university reform in America had been planted in the social and cultural forces which influenced the development of higher education in America before the founding of the Johns Hopkins University in 1876.[3] Gilman and the Hopkins were catalysts which hastened the graduate impulse and their influence has been acknowledged by graduate agencies as antithetic as the pontifical Catholic University of America[4] and the Stanford University of David Starr Jordan.[5] And although there is some exaggeration in the unrestrained eulogium of Abraham Flexner, there is in it, too, a felicitously expressed elemental truth:

> One important aspect of Gilman's achievement is in danger of being forgotten. Educational processes and systems are usually of evolutionary origin. Three centuries of gradual development are responsible for present day elementary, secondary, and college systems. But the graduate school, research institutes, and medical schools now flourishing in the United States are not the slow outcome of evolution: they represent an unprecedented leap in the dark, with none of the gradual intervening stages characteristic of evolutionary change. Mr. Gilman took this leap. The Johns Hopkins University . . . was an outright innovation; the ground had not been prepared for it. Yet so complete and rapid was its success that within two decades its own graduates reproduced it, in a form more or less pure, in a considerable number of American institutions of learning. A single generation of scholars thus displaced evolutionary growth that might otherwise have required a century or more. [6]

---

[1] *The Launching of a University*, p. 237.

[2] Edwin E. Slosson, "The University of Chicago," *Independent*, January 6, 1910, p. 21.

[3] See Richard J. Storr, *op. cit.*, pp. 129-134. See also Carter V. Good, "History of Graduate Instruction in the United States," in Nelson B. Henry, ed., *Graduate Study in Education, Part I*, pp. 1-5.

[4] See John T. Ellis, *The Formative Years of the Catholic University of America*, pp. 20-38, 99-113, 398-399; Patrick H. Ahern, *The Catholic University of America, 1887-1896*, pp. 87-96.

[5] See Orrin L. Elliott, *Stanford University: The First Twenty-Five Years*, pp. 37-40; David Starr Jordan, "The New University," in *The Care and Culture of Men*, pp. 259-267.

[6] Abraham Flexner, *I Remember*, pp. 64-65.

In more restrained and objective form, Pierson has observed: "In 1876 D. C. Gilman boldly nailed the flag of research to the mast by organizing Johns Hopkins as primarily a graduate university. And this time the idea did succeed. But the idea succeeded, one cannot help noting, in part because of the eminence of the individuals Gilman imported to Baltimore, in part because of the spectacular salaries he was able to pay, in part because of the visiting lectureships he set up, in part because of the royal fellowships he was able to offer our brightest young men. In a word, Gilman closed the gap between need and demand for advanced studies by first hiring his students." [1]

---

[1] George W. Pierson, "American Universities in the 19th Century: The Formative Period," *The Modern University*, ed. by Margaret Clapp, p. 75.

CHAPTER EIGHT

EPILOGUE: SOME PROPOSED CONCLUSIONS

The placing of Daniel Coit Gilman in the historical framework of the development of graduate education in the United States in the preceding pages offers the basis for some conclusions and, perhaps, suggests some bases for productive research in the history of American graduate study beyond the defined limitations of this study. The conclusions offered are tripartite, in that, if the major concern has been Daniel Coit Gilman, the study of Gilman has proceeded concomitantly with that of the progress of the graduate disciplines, and both concerns have touched the history of the liberal arts college in America.

Perhaps, the most important result of this study is the historical dimension which has been given Daniel Coit Gilman. His educational service did not begin in 1876 with his election to the presidency of the Johns Hopkins University; rather, his election to this office signalized the culmination of an educational career which had begun twenty years earlier. Gilman's achievement at Hopkins grew out of his experiences gained at Yale College and the University of California and, more distantly, out of his study of European higher education. To suggest, as has been suggested in the most recent history of American higher education, that "it [the Hopkins] sprang like Pallas Athena from the head of Zeus" [1] is not only bad mythology but absolutely in opposition to the facts. Gilman's long experimentation, successfully and unsuccessfully, with the institution of a program of graduate studies before 1876 and the opening of the Hopkins reaffirm the conclusions reached by Professor Richard J. Storr in his monograph on pre-Civil War American graduate education. [2] Professor Storr found that "Of the efforts to found [before 1865] universities in the United States, those which provided in some way for graduate work fall into three distinguishable . . . classes." [3] The first of these efforts imagined the university "as a repository of all knowledge, a living encyclopedia; another view [held] that a university

---

[1] John S. Brubacher and Willis Rudy, *Higher Education in Transition*: *A History of American Colleges and Universities*, 1636-1956, p. 176.

[2] Richard J. Storr, *The Beginnings of American Graduate Education*.

[3] *Ibid.*, p. 131.

was thought to consist of an undergraduate college to which were added distinct graduate ... schools; the third policy ... [was] to give the college the intellectual stature and freedom of a university by expanding the subject matter of the liberal arts course and by loosening up the machinery of instruction." [1] Gilman's subscription to the second of these proposals was no mere accident.

Gilman's experiences at Yale College established and defined the mould into which he was to fit the amorphous graduate impulse of *ante-bellum* America and allow it to take form. Put another way, Gilman's efforts to superimpose a graduate structure over the traditional liberal-arts college at Yale pointed the way, fortuitously or otherwise, to the only practicable solution of the graduate program problem in America. When Gilman was rebuffed at Yale by the conservatism of Noah Porter, he carried his plan for the union of undergraduate-graduate programs to California where he was further checked by the *Zeitgeist* which underlay the principles of the mechanic-arts school and, in a sense, the basis of the American state university idea. But transferred to Baltimore, Gilman's plan took root and the Johns Hopkins University had as its keynote not "the keynote of the German [university] system"[2] but rather the long, indigenous evolution of American educational problem and its eclectic solution. Under Gilman the Hopkins became at once both undergraduate and graduate college, as it could only have become in America; and if it resembled a combination of the German gymnasium and the German university, it was, in point of fact, neither. The Hopkins Ph.D. became the Yale Ph.D. which Gilman had assisted in instituting some two decades earlier, that is, it was an American doctorate, born of the American situation, which almost graphically called to mind Taine's dictum: *race, moment, milieu.* It might not be infelicitous to characterize the Hopkins as a reconstituted Yale minus the antagonistic conservatism of Noah Porter. Certainly, it was this for Gilman. At Hopkins he created a new liberal-arts college, traditional yet tinged with the reform of his "group system," and he made it the reservoir which fed his graduate and professional schools.

Yet, this is not to totally deprecate the so-called German influence on American graduate education. It merely reaffirms the fact that the history of this German influence still remains to be written. As for

---

[1] *Idem.*

[2] Fabian Franklin, *The Life of Daniel Coit Gilman*, p. 196. This statement is repeated in Charles F. Thwing's superficial *The American and the German University*, p. 108.

Gilman, who categorically rejected a German orientation, and as for the Hopkins which fulfilled a half-century of graduate aspiration, the pleading of German model is insufficient. To state that "Johns Hopkins was the nearest thing to a German University yet seen in the United States," [1] is ambiguously so generalized as to avoid the charge of palpable error; the data gathered in this study surely would suggest the statement's modification. The future historian of the influence of the German *Wissenschaftslehre* will do well to remember Gilman's admonition: "At a distance, Germany seems the one country where educational problems are determined; not so, on a nearer look. In following the example of Germany, as we are prone to do in educational matters, we must beware lest we adopt what is there cast off; lest we introduce faults as well as virtues." [2] This future historian will have to do more than speak of an occasional student *Wanderjahr* or attempt the definition of the German concepts of *Lehrfreiheit* and *Lernfreiheit*; he will have to *prove* influence. And influence is Clio's most elusive child.

The Ph.D. which was instituted at Yale College in 1860 "systematized graduate study," [3] and it was the blueprint of the Yale Ph.D. which Gilman carried to Baltimore. The origins of the protean Hopkins Ph.D. are in the earlier Yale doctorate. Gilman was the agency of transmission and connection. The Hopkins doctorate, with its defined minimal residence, foreign language requirements, seminars, thesis, and oral examination became the prototype of the American academic world. Like the graduate structure in which it was granted, it was an indigenous creation. The Ph.D. of Gilman's world answered the needs of that world. In the burgeoning knowledge of 19th century America it gave both direction and definition to research and the frontiers of the age's aspiration. It had the most noble aims which were expressed eloquently by Gilman: "The object of the university is to develop character—to make men. It misses its aim if it produces pedants, or simple artisans, or cunning sophists, or pretentious practitioners." [4] It is tragic irony that the twentieth century has labeled the Ph.D. an octopus, [5] a union card, [6] and a

---

[1] S. Willis Rudy, "The Revolution in American Higher Education, 1865-1900," *Harvard Educational Review*, 21 (Summer 1951), p. 168.

[2] *Addresses at the Inauguration of Daniel C. Gilman as President of the Johns Hopkins University*, pp. 28-29.

[3] Richard J. Storr, *op. cit.*, pp. 58-59.

[4] *Addresses at the Inauguration of Daniel C. Gilman . . .*, p. 38.

[5] William James, "The Ph.D. Octopus," *Harvard Monthly*, March, 1903.

[6] Jaques Barzun, *Teacher in America*, p. 133

fetish.[1] If this study has illuminated the origins of the Ph.D. and the American graduate program in which it was nurtured, it may also have pointed the way to a new clarification of aim and purpose. Gilman's words, spoken on his assumption of the presidency of Hopkins in 1876 patently called for a periodic re-evaluation of objective—a re-evaluation which, unfortunately, Gilman's heirs have not chosen to make.

> It [the graduate school] should prepare for the service of society a class of students who will be wise, thoughtful, progressive guides in whatever department of work or thought they may be engaged. *Universities easily fall into ruts. Almost every epoch requires a fresh start.* [2]

---

[1] John W. Dykstra, "The Ph.D. Fetish," *School and Society*, 86 (May 24, 1958), pp. 237-239.

[2] *Addresses at the Inauguration of Daniel C. Gilman* . . . , p. 38. Italics are added.

APPENDIX ONE

THE SEMINAR AT THE JOHNS HOPKINS UNIVERSITY: THE DEPARTMENT OF HISTORY AND POLITICS (1896).[1]

The Department of History and Politics occupies a suite of seven well-lighted rooms on the third floor of McCoy Hall. The centre of activity is the Bluntschli Library, or Seminary, which contains tables and working desks for graduate students. Here are to be found the books and manuscripts of the late Professor Bluntschli, of Heidelberg, whose library was purchased by German citizens of Baltimore, and generously presented to the University in 1881. With the Bluntschli papers are the MSS. and works of his two friends, Francis Lieber and Edouard Laboulaye. On the tables are the chief periodicals of the world in the domain of History, Politics and Economics. The walls and the cases are decorated with engravings and busts of eminent historians and statesmen. This room is a study, or laboratory, of historical investigation, in which each graduate student has his appointed place. The department has a skilled librarian to give assistance and advice, and a special catalogue is provided for the 18,000 books and 50,000 pamphlets belonging to the historical collection. Noticeable among the books is a case containing the thirty or more volumes of Studies written by graduates of the Historical Departments, including the series published by the University, and the Contributions to American Educational History, published by the United States Bureau of Education. An adjoining room is devoted to the study of European history and another beyond to Economics. In both, the walls are lined with books appropriate to the work and with views of historical monuments and portraits of great men. The rooms are provided with tables and chairs, instead of formal desks or benches, so that the classes meeting here are friendly conferences amid an environment of books. While all of the work of the Department is more or less co-operative, the special Historical Seminary of former years has developed from one weekly meeting into four particular conferences, historical, political, economical, and educational.

Across a broad corridor is a room devoted to the study of Jurisprudence and Comparative Politics. Here the books on English, French, German, American and International Law occupy the available wall space, so that lectures on the English Constitutional History, the Federal State, and kindred subjects, are given with the works of reference immediately at hand. A complete set of the original and the printed documents used in the Alabama case at Geneva was the gift of Mrs. J. A. J. Creswell, whose husband was Counsel of the United States. Adjoining this room is the department of Southern History. The walls and the interior space are taken up with collections of books and materials

---

[1] "Retrospect of Twenty Years," *Twenty-First Annual Report of the President of the Johns Hopkins University* (1896), pp. 34-37.

relating to the history and the literature of the Southern States. Special cases contain a valuable collection on Slavery presented by the late General Birney, of Washington. The central cases exhibit in about 400 pamphlet boxes the printed Americana, given by Colonel J. Thomas Scharf, while closed lockers contain the valuable Colonial and Revolutionary manuscripts also presented by Colonel Scharf. In museum cases are shown interesting documents, autographs, and relics relating to the South, while portraits of the distinguished historians and statesmen of that section are arranged in appropriate groups. Among them are the Calverts, Calhoun, William Wirt, John P. Kennedy, Reverdy Johnson, Chief Justice Taney, General Lee, Jefferson Davis, S. Teackle Wallis, and others. In an adjacent side corridor the public documents of the U.S. Government have been arranged along the walls from floor to ceiling. Thanks to our representatives in Congress and to the generous attention of the superintendent of documents in Washington, this necessary and material aid to the study of American History is unusually complete.

The end of the main corridor has been attractively furnished as a conversation room with carpet, chairs and table, so that students may gather here between classes and cause as little disturbance as possible in the libraries. At this point the walls are adorned with large engraved portraits of the fathers of the Constitution and the great American historians. A bust of Alexander Hamilton, presented by Mr. John M. Glenn, is an original by Houdin. A bas-relief of Chief Justice Marshall is a unique original from which the bronzes of the Marshall Prize have been made. This prize given annually for the best published work by a graduate in the field of History, is one of the most highly valued awards in the gift of the University. This cheerful academic corner forms a convenient connecting link between the Seminary Room and the Lecture Room. Here are not only chairs and tables for the larger classes, but also cases for the greater part of the archaeological museum of the department. The Mayer collection of ancient implements illustrates the development of man through the stone age; the Ellinger collection of relics of the Lake Dwellers shows the traditions and transition from the stone to the bronze age; the Cohen collection of Egyptian antiquities forms a large and representative museum of genuine relics illustrating the life and beliefs of ancient Egypt; barbaric implements of war from various stages of savagery decorate the walls. In this room, devoted to lectures on history, are also portraits of the men who have been the leaders of investigation in classical and European history. Niebur, Ranke, Curtius, Mommsen, Ihne, De Tocqueville, Arnold, Freeman, Stubbs, Seeley, Froude, and others look down upon the men who are studying their works. Additional museum cases in the corridors contain Indian relics presented by the Maryland Academy of Sciences, implements from Alaska, and other illustrations of primitive life. In the Bluntschli Library is the Helbig collection of Greek and Roman coins, a valuable adjunct to the study of classical history. All these collections are kept before the eyes of the students and are used for the information of the classes. In the use of the books there are but few restrictions, the shelves being open at all times to men of all departments of the University.

Connecting with the large lecture room is the office and library of the Director of the Historical Department. This is also the editorial room of the Johns Hopkins Studies in Historical and Political Science, and a convenient place where students may consult Professor Adams in regard to their work. Thus, amid an extensive and pleasant environment of books, documents, and illustrative material, with instructors easily accessible, both in and out of lecture halls, department work is proceeding daily in History, Politics, and Economics. The history of political and social institutions, ancient and modern; the economic life of the Middle Ages and modern times; the theory and practice of government; the history and theory of education, economics, finance, statistics and the practical applications of economic principles are subjects in which both students and professors are engaged in widening the borders of knowledge.

THE PH.D. AT THE JOHNS HOPKINS UNIVERSITY IN THE FIRST DECADE: A CHECKLIST OF DOCTORATES AND THESES, 1878-1886 [1]

Henry Carter Adams (1878). History of Taxation in the United States, 1789-1816.

William John Alexander (1883). Participial Periphrases in Attic Prose.

Francis Greenleaf Allinson (1880). Ionic Forms in the Second Century, A.D., and the Obligations of Lucian to Herodotus.

William Shirley Bayley (1886). Contact Metamorphism in the Slates and Sandstones of Pigion Point, Michigan.

Edward Webster Bemis (1885). Local Government in Michigan and the Northwest.

Louis Bevier (1881). The Genuineness of the First Antiphontean Oration.

Gustav Bissing (1885). Notes on Gauss' Coordinates, and Steiner's Quartic Surface.

Maurice Bloomfield (1879). The Noun-Formation of the Rig Veda.

James Wilson Bright (1882). A Discussion of the Verbal Forms in King Alfred's West Saxon Version of Gregory's Cura Pastoralis.

Adam Todd Bruce (1886). Observations on the Embryology of Insects and Arachnids.

Samuel Fessenden Clarke (1879). (1) The Development of Amblystoma; and (2) A Report on a Collection of Deep Sea Hydroids from the Gulf of Mexico.

Robert Dorsey Coale (1881). Sulphamine and Sulphoisophthalic Acids.

Herbert William Conn (1884). Life-history of Thalassema Mellita.

Thomas Craig (1878). The Representation of One Surface upon another; and on some Points in the Theory of the Curvature of Surfaces.

Ellery William Davis (1884). Parametric Representation of Curves.

David Talbott Day (1884). Changes Effected by Heat in the Constitution of Ethylene.

William Cathcart Day (1883). The Oxidation of Cymenesulphamide.

John Dewey (1884). The Psychology of Kant.

Davis Rich Dewey (1886). History of American Economic Literature previous to the time of Henry C. Carey.

Henry Herbert Donaldson (1885). The Temperature Sense.

James Reynolds Duggan (1884). Fermentation.

Louis Duncan (1885). The Determination of the Ohm by the Lorenz Method.

---

[1] The list is alphabetically arranged with the date of the Ph. D. immediately following the candidates' names. The full title of the thesis is given; since the publication of theses was not required until 1887, none of the theses noted is deposited. The list is reconstructed from Gilman's *Annual Reports* for 1878, 37-38; 1879, 50; 1880, 42; 1881, 45; 1882, 82-83; 1883, 78; 1884, 75; 1885, 40-41; 1886, 73-74. The first four Ph.D.'s were conferred in 1878.

William Pitt Durfee (1883). Symmetric Functions.

George Stetson Ely (1883). Bernouilli's Numbers.

William Henry Emerson (1886). Oxidation in the Aromatic Series.

Edward Allen Fay (1881). Conditional Relations in the Romance Languages.

Lawrence Bunting Fletcher (1881). The Determination of the Mechanical Equivalent of Heat by Electrical Means.

Joseph Auguste Fontaine (1886). History of the Use of the Auxiliaries in the Transitive, Neuter, and Reflexive Verbs of the Romance Languages.

Fabian Franklin (1880). Bipunctual Coordinates [sic].

Samuel Garner (1881). Gerundial Construction in the Romance Languages.

Elgin Ralston Lovell Gould (1886). Local Government in Pennsylvania.

Edwin Herbert Hall (1880). New Action of Magnetism on a Permanent Electric Current.

George Bruce Halsted (1879). Basis for a Dual Logic.

Edward Hart (1879). Nitrosulphobenzoic Acids and their Derivatives.

Edward Mussey Hartwell (1881). Notes on some Points in the Anatomy and Physiology of the Slider Terrapin (Pseudoemys rugosa).

Homer Winthrop Hillyer (1885). Methods of Determining the Relative Stability of the Alkyl Bromides.

William Penn Holcomb (1886). Pennsylvania Boroughs.

William Henry Howell (1884). Experiments upon the Blood and Lymph of the Terrapin and the Origin of the Fibrin formed in Coagulation.

William White Jacques (1879). Distribution of Heat in the Spectra of Various Substances.

Hans Carl Günther von Jagemann (1884). Anglo-Norman Vowel Sounds in Relation to the Norman Words in English.

John Franklin Jameson (1882). Origin and Development of the Municipal Government of New York City.

Joseph Jastrow (1886). The Perception of Space by Disparate Senses.

Edward Harrison Keiser (1884). The Existence of Active Oxygen.

George Theophilus Kemp (1886). The so-called "New Element" of the Blood and its Relation to Coagulation.

Arthur Lalande Kimball (1884). Value of the B.A. Unit of Electrical Resistance in Absolute Measure.

Mitsuru Kuhara (1882). Oxidation of Nitrometaxylene.

Frederic Schiller Lee (1885). Arterial Tonicity.

Charles Herbert Levermore (1886). The Republic of New Haven.

Gustav Adolph Liebig, Jr. (1885). Variation of the Specific Heat of Water.

Gonzales Lodge (1886). The Participle in Euripides.

James Playfair McMurrich (1885). Osteology and Myology of Amiurus catus (L.) Gill.

Robert. W. Mahon (1882). Some investigations on the Benzyl-derivatives of the Sulphamides of Metaxylene.

Allan Marquand (1880). The Logic of the Epicureans.

Charles William Emil Miller (1886). The Participle in Pindar.

Oscar Howard Mitchell (1882). Some Theorems in Numbers with a Generalization of Fermat's and Wilson's Theorems.

Kakichi Mitsukuri (1883). Structure and Significance of Some Aberrant Forms of Lamellibranchiate Gills.

George Frederic Nicolassen (1882). Articular Infinitive In Xenophon.

Henry Barber Nixon (1886). On Lame's Equation.

William Albert Noyes (1882). The Protection from Oxidation of a Group containing two Carbon-atoms.

Bernard Francis O'Connor (1883). The Syntax of Villehardouin.

Henry Leslie Osborn (1884). The Gill in Some Forms of Prosobranchiate Mollusca.

Albert Gallatin Palmer (1885). The Conduct of p-diazo-o-toluene-sulphonic Acid towards Alcohol.

Charles Skeele Palmer (1886). On Benzoyl-Phenyl-Sulphamide and its Derivatives.

Chase Palmer (1882). The Sulphocinnamic Acids.

Charles Albert Perkins (1884). Variation of the Magnetic Permeability of Nickel at different Temperatures.

Burr James Ramage (1886). Local Government and Free Schools in South Carolina.

Henry Fielding Reid (1885). The Distribution of Energy in the Spectrum of Platinum at different Temperatures.

Josiah Royce (1878). Interdependence of the Principles of Human Knowledge. [1]

Shosuke Sato (1886). History of the Land Question in the United States.

William Thompson Sedgwick (1881). Influence of Quinine on the Reflex Excitability of the Spinal Cord.

Henry Sewall (1879). Development and Regeneration of the Gastric Glandular Epithelium during Foetal life and after Birth.

Albert Shaw (1884). Etienne Cabet and the Icarian Community.

Henry Alford Short (1885). The Development and Use of wc Final.

Christian Sihler (1881). The Formation of Bone and Tooth.

Ernest Gottlieb Sihler (1878). Plato's Use of Metaphor and Comparison.

Edward Henry Spieker (1882). The so-called Genitive Absolute and its Use, especially in the Attic Orators.

Henry Newlin Stokes (1884). The Nature of the Sulphinide obtained by Oxidizing a-Naphthalene-Sulphamide.

Washington Irving Stringham (1880). Regular Figures in n-Dimensional Space.

Morrison Isaac Swift (1885). The Ethics of Idealism as represented by Aristotle and Hegel.

Henry Alfred Todd (1885). An Editio Princeps of an Old French Poem, entitled "Dit de la Panthere."

Lewis Webb Wilhelm (1884). Sir George Calvert, Baron of Baltimore.

Edmund Beecher Wilson (1881). The Origin and Significance of the Metamorphosis of Actinotrocha.

Woodrow Wilson (1886). Congressional Government.

Arthur Yager (1884). State and Local Taxation in Kentucky.

---

[1] Signed presentation copy by Royce deposited in the Johns Hopkins University Library.

BIBLIOGRAPHY

The main source of this study has been the various deposits of *Gilman Letters* which are described *infra*; most of the letters reproduced herein or quoted from are nowhere in print. Gilman's annual reports as President of the Johns Hopkins University proved an invaluable source of policy statement and curricular information; in this respect they furnish the only complete record of the early years of the Hopkins since the Hopkins catalogues during Gilman's tenure were only skeletal lists of courses. The *Contributions to American Educational History*, edited by Herbert B. Adams of the Johns Hopkins University (Washington, D.C., Government Printing Office, 1887-1903), furnished some ancillary information.

I. BIBLIOGRAPHICAL AND GENERAL REFERENCES

Bloomfield, Maurice. *Bibliographica Hopkinsiensis*, 1876-1893. Baltimore: Johns Hopkins Press, 1892-94.

Brickman, William W. *Guide to Research in Educational History*. New York: New York University Bookstore, 1949.

——. "Yale, Harvard and the First Ph.D.," *School and Society*, 52 (July 13, 1940), pp. 28-31; "College and University History," *Ibid.*, 64 (December 28, 1946), pp. 465-71; "M. A. and Ph.D. Bibliography," *Ibid.*, 66 (August 30, 1947), pp. 169-74; "History of Colleges and Universities," *Ibid.*, 76 (December 27, 1952), pp. 415-21.

Cordasco, Francesco. *Research and Report Writing*. 3rd Revised Edition. New York: Barnes & Noble, 1958.

Dictionary of American Biography. Ed. by Allen Johnson and Dumas Malone. New York: Charles Scribner's Sons, 1928-37. 21 vols.

Monroe, Paul, ed. *A Cyclopedia of Education*. New York: The Macmillan Company, 1911-13. 5 vols.

II. UNPUBLISHED SOURCE MATERIALS

Will S. Monroe Collection of Henry Barnard Manuscripts. New York University: Washington Square Library.

Letters from Gilman to Henry Barnard in 1856 and 1857. Largely unfiled.

Daniel Coit Gilman Papers. University of California: Doe Memorial Library, Berkeley. Consists largely of letters to Gilman. Includes twenty-two letters from Gilman, and eight mss. The manuscript materials consist of (1) a few pages of notes made on his trip to California in 1872; (2) a typewritten excerpt from a letter on the origin of the Yale School of Fine Arts; (3) a draft of a recommendation to James Lick (a wealthy San Franciscan) to found a "San Francisco Union for the Advancement of Science, Literature and Art"; (4) the draft of a report to the Regents of the University in 1874; (5) the remarks at his farewell dinner; and four manuscripts of confidential comments, notes and statements concerning the dismissal of Professors Carr and Swinton from the University.

The Gilman Family Papers. Yale University Library. With a few exceptions, largely deposited in the Historical Manuscripts Room. Includes letters both from and to Gilman, and the holograph ms. of Gilman's address at the semi-centennial of the Sheffield Scientific School.

Daniel Coit Gilman Papers. Lanier Room, Johns Hopkins University Library.
Includes some 13,000 incoming letters. Letter-press books contain Gilman's outgoing correspondence. Includes Gilman's notebooks, clippings, and ms. drafts (mostly holograph) of speeches and reports. Most of the material is catalogued. The minutes of the meetings of the original Trustees of the Johns Hopkins University are partially indexed and are in the President's office. The collection also includes some 6000 separate documents of the historian, Herbert Baxter Adams and some 4000 documents of the physicist, Henry A. Rowland, largely unworked. Relatively untouched are the papers of the classicist, Basil L. Gildersleeve, which are deposited in the Johns Hopkins University Library stacks.

Miscellaneous Gilman Letters. Houghton Library, Harvard University.
Includes a few letters from Gilman to Francis J. Child, the Chaucerian, and to President Charles W. Eliot.

III. WRITINGS OF DANIEL COIT GILMAN

1. *Books and Monographs*

Scientific Schools in Europe: Considered in Reference to their Prevalence, Utility, Scope and Desirability in America. [Hartford, 1856].
Reprinted from Henry Barnard's *American Journal of Education*, 1 (March 1856), pp. 317-328.

Suggestions Respecting a course of Study for Children between the Ages of six and twelve Years. An Address, delivered in New Haven, February, 1860, before the common-school visitors of the country and the common-school teachers of the city. New Haven: Printed by T. J. Stafford, 1860.

The Library of Yale College. An Historical Sketch. [New Haven?] 1860.

New Phases of the School Question in Connecticut. [New Haven?] 1867.

Our National Schools of Science. Boston, Ticknor and Fields. 1867.

What Sort of Schools ought the State to Keep? [New Haven?] 1868.

The Charities and Reformatories of Connecticut. An Address delivered at the opening of the Connecticut Industrial School for Girls, Middletown, June 30, 1870. New Haven, Printed by Tuttle, Morehouse & Taylor, 1870.

On the Structure of the Earth with some Reference to Human History. A Synopsis of Twelve Geographical Lectures Delivered before the Senior and Junior Classes in the College of New Jersey. February, 1871. Printed for the Students. Princeton, 1871.

The Building of the University. An Inaugural Address Delivered at Oakland, November 7th, 1872. San Francisco, J. H. Carmany & Co., 1872.

Statement of the Progress and Condition of the University of California. Prepared by Request of the Regents of the University. Berkeley, 1875.

The Miscellaneous Writings of Francis Lieber. Philadelphia, J. B. Lippincott & Co., 1881, 2 vols.
Edited by Daniel C. Gilman.

Bluntschli, Lieber and Laboulaye. Privately Printed for a few Friends in Baltimore. [Baltimore, J. Murphy & Co., printers] 1884.

The Benefits which Society Derives from Universities, An Address. Baltimore, Johns Hopkins University, 1885.

Addresses at the Inauguration of Bryn Mawr College, by President Rhoads and President D. C. Gilman of the Johns Hopkins University. Philadelphia, Printed by Sherman & Co., 1886.

An Address before the Phi Beta Kappa Society of Harvard University, July 1, 1886. Baltimore [J. Murphy & Co., printers] 1886.

A Plea for the Training of the Hand. Edited by Nicholas Murray Butler. New York, Industrial Education Association, 1888.

Historical Address. [Development of the Public Library in America] Ithaca, Cornell University, 1891.

The Johns Hopkins University, 1876-1891. Baltimore [1891].
   Reprinted from *Johns Hopkins University Studies in Historical and Political Science,* IV (9th Series) 1891, pp. 39-73.

The Johns Hopkins University from 1873 to 1893. [Baltimore, 1893].

A Study in Black and White: An Address at the opening of the Armstrong-Slater Trade School Building, November 18, 1896. Baltimore [J. Murphy & Co., printers] 1897.

The Sheffield Scientific School of Yale University: a Semi-Centennial Historical Discourse, October 28, 1897. New Haven, Sheffield Scientific School, 1897.

University Problems in the United States. New York, The Century Co., 1898.

Democracy in America. By Alexis de Tocqueville. Translated by Henry Reeve, as revised and annotated from the author's last edition, by Francis Bowen. With an Introduction by Daniel C. Gilman. New York, The Century Co., 1898.

The Life of James Dwight Dana, Scientific Explorer, Mineralogist, Geologist, Zoologist, Professor in Yale University. New York and London, Harper & Brothers, 1899.

Successful Progress. An Address Delivered at the Annual Meeting of the National Civil Service Reform League at Philadelphia, December 11, 1902. [New York] Pub. for the National Civil Service Reform League, 1902.

The Launching of a University, and Other Papers: A Sheaf of Remembrances. New York, Dodd, Mead & Company, 1906.

Memorial of Samuel de Champlain, who discovered the Island of Mt. Desert, Maine, September 5, 1604. [Baltimore?] Privately Printed, 1906.

James Monroe in his Relations to the Public Service during Half a Century, 1776 to 1826. Boston, New York, Houghton Mifflin and company, 1883.
   Reprinted 1892, 1898, 1909, 1911 (*bis*), 1917.

2 *Articles in Periodicals* [A Selection]

"Bishop Berkeley's Gifts to Yale College," *Papers of the New Haven Historical Society,* 1 (1865), pp. 147-70.

"Four College Inaugurals: White, McCosh, Eliot, Porter. By a Graduate of Yale," *Christian Union,* 5 (January 31, 1872), pp. 119-120.

"Education in America, 1776-1876, " *North American Review,* 122 (January 1876), pp. 193-194.

"Present Aspects of College Training," *North American Review,* 136 (June 1883), pp. 327-336.

"The Use and Abuse of Titles," *North American Review,* 140 (March 1885), pp. 267-268.

"The Group System of College Courses in the Johns Hopkins University," *Andover Review,* 37 (June 1886), pp. 13-26.

"The Shortening of the College Curriculum," *Educational Review,* 1 (January 1891), pp. 1-7.

"The Johns Hopkins University," *Cosmopolitan,* 11 (August 1891), pp. 463-466.

"The Future of American Colleges and Universities," *Atlantic Monthly,* 78 (August 1896), pp. 175-179.

"Another University in Washington and how to Secure it," *Century,* 33 (November 1897), pp. 156-157.

"The Carnegie Institution," *Science,* New Series, 15 (February 1902), pp. 201-203.

IV. GENERAL SECONDARY REFERENCES

1. *General Histories of Higher Education*

Brubacher, John S. and Willis Rudy. *Higher Education in Transition*. A History of American Colleges and Universities, 1636-1956. New York: Harper & Brothers [1958].

Butts, R. Freeman. *The College Charts its Course*: Historical Conceptions and Current Proposals. New York: McGraw-Hill, 1939.

Cowlet, W. H. "The University in the United States of America," in Edward Bradby, ed., *The University Outside Europe*, pp. 37-112. London: Oxford University Press, 1939.

Duffus, R. L. *Democracy Enters College*: A Study of the Rise and Decline of the American Lockstep. New York: Scribner, 1936.

Earnest, Ernest. *Academic Procession*: An Informal History of the American College, 1636-1953. Indianapolis: Bobbs-Merrill, 1953.

Hofstadter, Richard and C. De Witt Hardy. *The Development and Scope of Higher Education in the United States*. New York: Columbia University Press, 1952.

Schmidt, George P. *The Liberal Arts College*: A Chapter in American Cultural History. New Brunswick: Rutgers University Press, 1957.

Tewksbury, Donald G. *The Founding of American Colleges and Universities before the Civil War*. New York: Bureau of Publications, Teachers College, Columbia University, 1932.

Thwing, Charles F. *A History of Higher Education in America*. New York: D. Appleton and Company, 1906.

Wills, Elbert V. *The Growth of American Higher Education*. Philadelphia: Dorrance and Company, 1936.

2. *General Histories and Other Aspects of Graduate Education*

Barzun, Jacques. *Graduate Work at Columbia*. New York: Columbia University Press, 1946.

——. "Doctors and Masters—Good and Bad," *Journal of Proceedings and Addresses*, Ninth Annual Conference of the Association of Graduate Schools (1957), pp. 1-7.

Breunig, L. "Graduate Work at Johns Hopkins," *Volta Review*, 39 (April 1937), pp. 205-208.

Deferrari, Roy J. "The Origin and Development of Graduate Studies under Catholic Auspices," in R. J. Deferrari, ed., *Essays on Catholic Education in the United States*, pp. 195-215. Washington, D.C.: Catholic University of America Press, 1942.

Flexner, Abraham. "The Graduate School in the United States," *Proceedings of the Association of American Universities* (1931), pp. 114-115.

Foster, L. *Functions of A Graduate School in a Democratic Society*. New York: Huxley House, 1936.

Good, Carter V. "History of Graduate Instruction in the United States," in Nelson B. Henry, ed., *Graduate Study in Education*, Part I. The 50th Yearbook of the National Society for the Future of Education, pp. 2-12. Chicago: University of Chicago Press, 1951.

Graduate Courses: A Handbook for Graduate Students, 1893-94. Boston: Ginn and Company, 1894.

Graduate Education For Women: The Radcliffe Ph.D. Cambridge: Harvard University Press, 1956.

Hollis, Ernest V. *Toward Improving Ph.D. Programs.* Washington, D.C.: American Council on Education, 1945.

——. "Graduate School," in W. S. Monroe, ed., *Encyclopedia of Educational Research*, pp. 510-519. Revised Edition. New York: The Macmillan Company, 1950.

Horton, Byrne J. *The Origin of the Graduate School and the Development of its Administration.* New York University, School of Education, 1939. Unpublished Ph.D. Thesis.

John, Walton C. *Graduate Study in Universities and Colleges in the United States.* Washington, D.C.: United States Office of Education, 1935.

Kraus, Charles A. "The Evolution of the American Graduate School," Association of University Professors *Bulletin*, 27 (1951), pp. 497-505.

McGrath, Earl J. *The Graduate School and the Decline of Liberal Education.* New York: Bureau of Publications, Teachers College, Columbia University, 1959.

Ness, Frederic W., ed., *A Guide to Graduate Study*: Programs Leading to the Ph.D. Degree. Washington, D.C.: Association of American Colleges, 1957.

Pierson, Mary B. *Graduate Work in the South.* Chapel Hill: The University of North Carolina Press, 1947.

Ryan, W. Carson. *Studies in Early Graduate Education.* New York: Carnegie Foundation for the Advancement of Teaching, 1939.

Storr, Richard J. *The Beginnings of Graduate Study in America.* Chicago: University of Chicago Press, 1953.

Strothmann, F. W. *The Graduate School Today and Tomorrow.* New York: The Fund for the Advancement of Education, 1955.

3. *Selected Miscellaneous Materials*

Ahern, Patrick J. *The Catholic University of America*, 1887-1896. Washington, D.C.: Catholic University of America Press, 1949.

Angell, James B. *Selected Addresses.* New York: D. Appleton Co., 1912.

——. *Reminiscences.* New York: Longmans, Green & Co., 1912.

Angell, James R. *American Education*: Addresses and Articles. New Haven: Yale University Press, 1937.

Archibald, R. C. "Unpublished Letters of JamesJoseph Sylvester and other New Information Concerning his Life and Work," *Osiris* 1 (1936), pp. 93-126.

Atwood, Wallace W. *The First Fifty Years.* Worcester: Clark University Press, 1937.

Baker, James H. *American University Progress.* New York: Longmans, Green & Co., 1916.

Baker, Ray S. *Woodrow Wilson*: Life and Letters. 2 vols. New York: Doubleday, Doran & Co., 1927.

Barzun, Jacques. *Teacher in America.* Boston: Little, Brown and Company, 1945.

Bereday, George Z. F., and J. A. Lauwerys. *Higher Education. Year Book of Education*: 1959. New York: World Book Company, 1959.

Bond, Allen K. *When the Hopkins Came to Baltimore.* Baltimore: Pegasus Press, 1927.

Bredvold, Louis I. "An Outsider Appraises Hopkins," *Johns Hopkins Alumni Magazine*, 26 (April 1938), pp. 22-31.

Burgess, John W. *Reminiscences of an American Scholar.* New York: Columbia University Press, 1934.

Burns, Edward M. *David Starr Jordan*: Apostle of Freedom. Stanford: Stanford University Press, 1953.

Butler, Nicholas Murray. "President Gilman's Administration at the Johns Hopkins University," *American Monthly Review of Reviews*, 23 (January 1901), pp. 49-53.

——. *Across the Busy Years.* 2 vols. New York: Charles Scribner's Sons, 1935.

Carnegie, Andrew. *Autobiography*. Boston: Houghton, Mifflin and Company, 1920.

Caullery, Maurice. *Universities and Scientific Life in the United States*. Cambridge: Harvard University Press, 1922.

Chaffin, Nora C. *Trinity College, 1839-1892*. The Beginnings of Duke University. Durham, N. C.: Duke University Press, 1950.

Cheyney, Edward P. *History of the University of Pennsylvania*. Philadelphia: University of Pennsylvania Press, 1940.

Chittenden, Russell H. *History of the Sheffield Scientific School* of Yale University. 2 vols. New Haven: Yale University Press, 1928.

Clark University, 1889-1899. Decennial Celebration. Worcester: Clark University Press, 1899.

Compayré, Gabriel. *L'Enseignement Supérieur aux Etats-Unis*. Paris: Librairie Hachette et Cie., 1896.

Cope, Jackson I. "The William James Correspondence with Daniel Coit Gilman, 1877-1881," *Journal of the History of Ideas*, 12 (October 1951), pp. 609-627.

Coulter, E. Merton. *College Life in the Old South*. Athens: University of Georgia Press, 1951.

Cross, Wilbur L. *Connecticut Yankee*. An Autobiography. New Haven: Yale University Press, 1943.

Curti, Merle and Vernon Cartensen. *The University of Wisconsin*: A History, 1848-1925. 2 vols. Madison: University of Wisconsin Press, 1949.

Dana, James D. "Science and Scientific Schools," *American Journal of Education*, 2 (1856), pp. 374-376.

——. *The New Haven University*: What it Is and What it Requires. [New Haven] 1871.

Daugherty, Donald H. "The American University," in A. J. Brumbaugh, ed., *American Universities and Colleges*, pp. 49-72. Washington, D.C.: American Council on Education, 1948.

Dexter, Franklin B. *Sketch of the History of Yale University*. New York: Henry Holt Co., 1887.

——. *Documentary History of Yale University*. New Haven: Yale University Press, 1916.

Didier, Eugene L. *The Johns Hopkins University*. [Baltimore] 1897.

Dorfman, Joseph. *Thorstein Veblen and His America*. New York: The Viking Press, 1934.

Draper, Andrew S. *Weaknesses of Universities*. Syracuse: C. W. Bardeen, 1912.

Dwight, Timothy. *Memories of Yale Life and Men, 1845-1899*. New York: Dodd, Mead and Co., 1903.

Eddy, Edward D. *Colleges For Our Land and Time*. The Land-Grant Idea in American Education. New York: Harper & Brothers [1957].

Edmunds, Charles K. "A Half-Century of Johns Hopkins. A Fruitful Fifty Years at the Baltimore University," *American Review of Reviews*, 48 (November 1926), pp. 23-33.

Edwards, Marcia. *Studies in American Graduate Education*. New York: Carnegie Foundation for the Advancement of Teaching, 1944.

Eliot, Charles W. "The New Education," *Atlantic Monthly*, 23 (February, March 1869), pp. 203-220; 358-367.

——. *Educational Reform*: Essays and Addresses. New York: The Century Company, 1898.

Elliott, Orin L. *Stanford University*. The First Twenty-Five Years. Stanford: Stanford University Press, 1937.

Ellis, John T. *The Formative Years of the Catholic University of America*. Washington, D.C.: American Catholic Historical Association, 1946.

Ely, Richard T. "American Colleges and German Universities," *Harper's Magazine*, 61 (July 1880), pp. 253-260.

Ferrier, William W. *Origin and Development of the University of California*. Berkeley: Sather Gate Book Shop, 1930.

——. *Ninety Years of Education in California*. Berkeley: Sather Gate Book Shop, 1940.

——. *Henry Durant*. Berkeley: Published by the Author, 1942.

Fisher, George P. *Life of Benjamin Silliman*. 2 vols. New York: Charles Scribner & Co., 1866.

Fisch, Max H. and Jackson I. Cope. "Peirce at the Johns Hopkins University," in Philip H. Wiener and Frederic H. Young, eds., *Studies in the Philosophy of Charles Sanders Peirce*. Cambridge: Harvard University Press, 1952.

Flexner, Abraham. *The American College*. New York: The Century Co., 1908.

——. *Universities*: American, English, German. New York, Oxford University Press, 1930.

——. "Address," Symposium on the Outlook for Higher Education in the United States. *Proceedings* of the American Philosophical Society, 69 (1930), pp. 257-269.

——. "The Prepared Mind," *School and Society*, 45 (June 26, 1937), pp. 865-872.

——. *I Remember*. New York: Simon & Schuster, 1940.

——. *Daniel Coit Gilman*. New York: Harcourt, Brace, 1946.

——. *Funds and Foundations*: Their Policies Past and Present. New York, Harper Brothers, 1952.

Franklin, Fabian. *An Address* Commemorative of Professor James Joseph Sylvester. [Baltimore 1897].

——. *Daniel Coit Gilman*. New York: Dodd, Mead & Co., 1910.

French, John C. "Johns Hopkins, Founder," *Johns Hopkins Alumni Magazine*, 2 (March 1937), pp. 227-234.

——. *A History of the University Founded by Johns Hopkins*. Baltimore: Johns Hopkins Press, 1946.

Fulton, J. F. and E. H. Thomson. *Benjamin Silliman*, 1779-1864. New York: Columbia University Press, 1947.

Gabriel, Ralph H. *Religion and Learning at Yale*. The Church of Christ in the College and University, 1757-1957. New Haven: Yale University Press, 1958.

Gaw, Allison. *A Sketch of the Development of Graduate Work in the University of Southern California*, 1910-1935. Los Angeles: University of Southern California, 1935.

Getman, Frederick H. *The Life of Ira Remsen*. Easton: Lafayette College, 1940.

Daniel Coit Gilman: First President of the Johns Hopkins University, 1876-1901. Baltimore: Johns Hopkins Press, 1908.

Godkin, Edwin L. "The Johns Hopkins University," New York *Nation*, 20 (January 28, 1875), p. 60.

Goodspeed, Thomas W. *A History of the University of Chicago*. Chicago: University of Chicago Press, 1916.

——. *The Story of the University of Chicago*. Chicago: University of Chicago Press, 1925.

——. *William Rainey Harper*. Chicago: University of Chicago Press, 1928.

Gore, James H. "The Carnegie Institution and the National University," *Popular Science Monthly*, 62 (April 1903), pp. 532-537.

Haines, George. *German Influence Upon English Education and Science*, 1800-1866. New London: Connecticut College, 1957.

Hall, G. Stanley. *Life and Confessions of a Psychologist*. New York: D. Appleton and Co., 1923.

Harper, William Rainey. "The College President," *Educational Record*, 19 (April 1938), pp. 178-186.
　　Originally written in 1904 but not published until 1938.
——. *The Trend in Higher Education*. Chicago: University of Chicago Press, 1905.
Hawkins, Hugh. *The Birth of a University*: A History of the Johns Hopkins University from the Death of the Founder to the End of the First Year of Academic Work (1873-1877). Unpublished Ph.D. Dissertation, Johns Hopkins University, 1954.
Herrick, S. B. "The Johns Hopkins University," *Scribners Monthly*, 19 (December 1879), pp. 202-203.
Hinsdale, B. A. "Notes on the History of Foreign Influence upon Education in the United States," *Report of the Commissioner of Education*, I (1897-98), pp. 610-13.
——. *History of the University of Michigan*. Ann Arbor: University of Michigan Press, 1906.
Hendrick, Burton J. *The Life of Andrew Carnegie*. 2 vols. New York: Doubleday, Doran and Co., 1932.
Hogan, Peter E. *The Catholic University of America*, 1896-1903. Washington, D.C.: Catholic University of America Press, 1949.
Holt, W. Stull, ed. *Historical Scholarship in the United States*, 1876-1901. As Revealed in the Correspondence of Herbert Baxter Adams. Johns Hopkins University Studies in Political and Historical Science, LVI, No. 4. Baltimore: Johns Hopkins Press, 1938.
Holt, W. Stull. "Henry Adams and the Johns Hopkins University: Letters to President Gilman, 1875-78," *New England Quarterly*, 2 (September 1938), pp. 632-638.
Hoyt, John W. "The Proposed National University," *Science*, New Series, 14 (October 1901), pp. 505-517.
Hoxie, R. Gorden, *et al. A History of the Faculty of Political Science*. New York: Columbia University Press, 1955.
Hutchins, Robert M. *The Higher Learning in America*. New Haven: Yale University Press, 1936.
——. *The University of Utopia*. Chicago: The University of Chicago Press, 1953
Huxley, Thomas. *American Addresses*. New York: D. Appleton Co., 1877.
Ingle, Edward. "The First Ten Years at Johns Hopkins," *Johns Hopkins Alumni Magazine*, 4 (November 1915), pp. 7-26.
James, Henry. *Charles W. Eliot*. 2 vols. Boston: Houghton Mifflin, 1930.
James, William. "The Ph.D. Octopus," *Harvard Monthly*, March (1903).
　　Reprinted in *Educational Review*, 55 (February 1918), pp. 149-157.
Johns Hopkins University. *Charter. Extracts of Will. Officers and By-Laws*. Baltimore: John Murphy, 1874.
Johns Hopkins University. *Addresses at the Inauguration of Daniel Coit Gilman as President of the Johns Hopkins University*. Baltimore: John Murphy & Co., 1876.
Johns Hopkins University. *Annual Report of the President*. Baltimore: [1876-1885, John Murphy; 1886-1887, Publication Agency of the Johns Hopkins University; 1888-1902, Johns Hopkins Press] 1876-1902.
Johns Hopkins University. *Celebration of the Twenty-Fifth Anniversary of the Founding of the University and the Inauguration of Ira Remsen as President of the University*. Baltimore: Johns Hopkins Press, 1902.
Johns Hopkins Half-Century Directory, 1876-1926. Baltimore: Johns Hopkins Press, 1926.
Jordan, David Starr. *The Care and Culture of Men*. San Francisco: Whitaker & Ray, 1896.
——. *The Voice of the Scholar*. San Francisco: Elder Company, 1903.
——. *Days of a Man*. 2 vols. Yonkers-on-Hudson: World Book Co., 1922.

Jordan, David Starr. *The Trend of the American University*. Stanford: Stanford University Press, 1929.

The Jubilee of the University of Wisconsin. Madison: The Jubilee Committee, 1904.

Kent, Raymond A., ed. *Higher Education in America*. Boston: Ginn and Company, 1930.

Keppel, Frederick P. *Columbia*. New York: Oxford University Press, 1914.

Knight, Edgar W. *Fifty Years of American Education*. New York: Ronald Press, 1952.

Kuehnemann, Eugen. *Charles W. Eliot*: President of Harvard University. Boston: Houghton Mifflin, 1909.

Lanman, Charles. "Daniel Coit Gilman," *Proceedings* of the American Academy of Arts and Sciences, 52 (1917), pp. 838-840.

Le Conte, Joseph. *Autobiography*. New York: Harper & Brother, 1903.

Le Duc, Thomas. *Piety and Intellect at Amherst College*, 1865-1912. New York: Columbia University Press, 1946.

Lowell, A. Lawrence. "Universities, Graduate Schools, and Colleges," in *At War with Academic Traditions in America*, pp. 206-220. Cambridge: Harvard University Press, 1933.

Macaulay, P. Stewart. "The Group System at Johns Hopkins," *Bulletin* of the Association of American Colleges, 31 (December 1945), pp. 614-615.

McCosh, James. *The New Departure in College Education*. New York: Charles Scribner's Sons, 1885.

Malone, Kemp. "Some Observations on Gilman's Hopkins," *Johns Hopkins Alumni Magazine* 19 (June 1931), pp. 303-320.

Merriam, George S., ed. *Noah Porter*. A Memorial by Friends. New York, Charles Scribner's Sons, 1893.

Morison, Samuel E., ed. *The Development of Harvard University Since the Inauguration of President Eliot*, 1869-1929. Cambridge: Harvard University Press, 1930.

Morison, Samuel E. *Three Centuries of Harvard*, 1636-1936. Cambridge: Harvard University Press, 1936.

Morris, George S. "Philosophy at Johns Hopkins University," *Journal of Speculative Philosophy*, XIII (1879), pp. 398-399.

Nettleton, George H., ed. *The Book of the Yale Pageant*. New Haven: Yale University Press, 1916.

Newcomer, Mabel. *A Century of Higher Education for American Women*. New York: Harper, 1959.

Ouelette, V.A. "Gilman at California," *Pacific Spectator*, 8 (1954), pp. 128-140.

Paulsen, Friedrich. *German Universities*: Their Character and Historical Development. New York: Macmillan and Co., 1895.

——. *An Autobiography*. New York: Columbia University Press, 1938.

Perry, Edward D. "The Ph.D. in the United States," *Columbia University Quarterly*, 6 (June 1904), p. 260.

Peirce, Benjamin. *Working Plan for the Foundation of a University*. [Cambridge, Mass., 1856].

Pierson, George W. "American Universities in the 19th Century: the Formative Period," in Margaret Clapp, ed., *The Modern University*, pp. 59-94. Ithaca: Cornell University Press, 1950.

——. "The Elective System and the Difficulties of College Planning, 1870-1940," *The Journal of General Education*, 4 (April 1950), pp. 165-174.

——. *Yale College*: An Educational History, 1871-1921. New Haven: Yale University Press, 1952.

Pochmann, Henry A. *German Culture in America*: Philosophical and Literary Influences, 1600-1900. Madison: The University of Wisconsin Press, 1957.

Porter, Noah. *The American College and the American Public*. New Haven: Chatfield and Co., 1870.

Power, Edward J. *A History of Catholic Higher Education in the United States*. Milwaukee: The Bruce Publishing Company [1958].

Randall, John H., *et al. A History of the Faculty of Philosophy*. New York: Columbia University Press, 1957.

Rogers, Walter P. *Andrew D. White and the Modern University*. Ithaca: Cornell University Press, 1942.

Royce, Josiah. "Present Ideals of American University Life," *Scribner's Magazine* 10 (September 1891), p. 383.

Rudy, S. Willis. "The Revolution in American Higher Education, 1865-1900," *Harvard Educational Review*, 21 (Summer 1951), pp. 155-174.

——. "Eliot and Gilman: the History of an Academic Friendship," *Teachers College Record*, 54 (March 1953), pp. 307-318.

Schmidt, George P. *The Old Time College President*. New York: Columbia University Press, 1930.

——. "Intellectual Crosscurrents in American Colleges, 1825-1855," *American Historical Review*, 42 (October 1936), pp. 46-67.

Sexson, John A. and John W. Harbson. *The New American College*. New York: Harper and Brothers, 1946.

Shumway, David B. "Göttingen's American Students," *American-German Review*, 3 (June 1937), pp. 21-24.

Smith, Goldwin. "University Education," *Journal of Social Science*, 1 (June 1869), pp. 24-55.

Smith, Munroe. "The Graduate Schools," in *History of Columbia University*, 1754-1904, pp. 267-305. New York: Columbia University Press, 1904.

Smith, Shirley W. *James Burvill Angell*: An American Influence. Ann Arbor: University of Michigan Press, 1955.

Snow, Louis F. *The College Curriculum in the United States*. New York: Department of Publications, Teachers College, 1907.

Steiner, Bernard C. *The History of University Education in Maryland*. Baltimore: Johns Hopkins Press, 1891.

——. *The History of Education in Connecticut*. Washington, D.C.: United States Bureau of Education, 1893.

Stokes, A. P. *Memorials of Eminent Yale Men*. 2 vols. New Haven: Yale University Press, 1914.

Thom, Helen Hopkins. *Johns Hopkins*: A Silhouette. Baltimore: Johns Hopkins Press, 1929.

Thomas, James C. *Brief Review of the Ten Years' Work of the Johns Hopkins University*. Baltimore: John Murphy and Co., 1886.

Thursfield, Richard E. *Henry Barnard's "American Journal of Education"*. Baltimore: Johns Hopkins Press, 1945.

Thwing, Charles F. *The American College*. What it is, and What it may Become. New York: The Platt & Peck Co., 1914.

——. "Daniel Coit Gilman," in *Guides, Philosophers and Friends*, pp. 57-82. New York: The Macmillan Co., 1927.

——. *The American and the German University*. New York: The Macmillan Company, 1928.

Walz, John A. *German Influence in American Education and Culture*. Philadelphia: Carl Schurz Memorial Foundation, 1936.

Warren, Charles H. "The Sheffield Scientific School from 1847 to 1947," in *The Centennial of the Sheffield Scientific School*, ed. by George A. Baitsell, pp. 158-167. New Haven: Yale University Press, 1950.

Wertenbaker, Thomas J. *Princeton*, 1746-1896. Princeton: Princeton University Press, 1946.

Wesley, Edgar B. *Proposed: The University of the United States*. Minneapolis: University of Minnesota Press, 1936.

White, Andrew D. "The Need of Another University," *Forum*, 6 (January 1889), pp. 465-473.

——. *Autobiography*. 2 vols. New York: The Century Co., 1907.

Wilson, Louis N. *G. Stanley Hall*. New York: G. E. Stechert, 1914.

SELECTED ADDITIONAL REFERENCES

Altbach, Philip G., ed. *Academic Super Markets: A Critical Case Study of a Multiversity*. San Francisco: Jossey-Bass, 1971.

[American Council on Education] *Higher Education for Everybody?* Washington: American Council on Education, 1971.

Barzun, Jacques. *The American University: How it Runs, Where it is Going.* New York: Harper, 1968.

Bell, Daniel, ed. *Confrontation: The Student Rebellion and the Universities.* New York: Basic Books, 1969.

Berdahl, Robert O., *et al. Statewide Coordination of Higher Education.* Washington: American Council on Education, 1971.

Berelson, Bernard. *Graduate Education in the United States.* New York: McGraw-Hill, 1960.

Brubacher, John S. *The Courts and Higher Education.* San Francisco: Jossey-Bass, 1971.

Brubacher, John S. and Willis Rudy. *Higher Education in Transition: A History of American Colleges and Universities, 1936-1968.* New York: Harper & Row, 1968. [Includes "A Bibliography of American College and University Histories," pp. 509-518].

Carmichael, Oliver C. *Graduate Education.* New York: Harper & Row, 1961.

Cartter, Allan. *An Assessment of Quality in Graduate Education.* Washington: American Council on Education, 1966.

Chambers, M. M. *Higher Education in the Fifty States.* Danville, Illinois: Interstate, 1970.

Cohen, Arthur, *et al.* eds. *A Constant Variable.* San Francisco: Jossey-Bass, 1971 [Community Colleges].

Cordasco, Francesco and Louis Romano. "The Promethean Ethic: Higher Education and Social Imperatives," *Peabody Journal of Education*, vol. 44 (March 1967), pp. 295-299.

Cross, K. Patricia. *Beyond the Open Door: New Students to Higher Education.* San Francisco: Jossey-Bass, 1971.

Crossland, Fred E. *Minority Access to College.* New York: Schocken Books, 1971.

Curti, Merle and Roderick Nash. *Philanthropy in the Shaping of American Higher Education.* New Brunswick, N. J.: Rutgers University Press, 1965.

Eurich, Alvin C., ed. *Campus 1980: The Shape of the Future in American Higher Education.* New York: Delacorte Press, 1968.

Ferrari, Michael R. *Profiles of American College Presidents.* East Lansing, Michigan: Michigan State University Press, 1970.

Ferrin, Richard I. *A Decade of Change in Free-Access Higher Education.* New York: College Entrance Examination Board, 1971.

Folger, John K., *et al. Human Resources. Staff Report of the Commission on Human Resources and Advanced Education.* New York: Russell Sage Foundation, 1970.

Foote, Caleb, *et al. The Culture of the University: Governance and Education.* San Francisco: Jossey-Bass, 1968.

[Graduate Education] *The Expansion of Graduate Education During the Period, 1966-1980.* New York: Academy for Educational Development, 1969.

Hawkins, Hugh. *Pioneer: A History of The Johns Hopkins University, 1874-1889.* Ithaca: Cornell University Press, 1960.

Hawkins, Hugh. "Charles W. Eliot, Daniel C. Gilman and the Nurture of American Scholarship," *The New England Quarterly,* vol. xxix (September 1966), pp. 291-308.

Heiss, Ann M. *Challenges to Graduate Schools.* San Francisco: Jossey-Bass, 1970.

Hofstadter, Richard and Wilson Smith, eds. *American Higher Education: A Documentary History.* 2 vols. Chicago: University of Chicago Press, 1961.

Jencks, Christopher and David Riesman. *The Academic Revolution.* New York: Doubleday, 1968.

Jerome, Judson. *Culture Out of Anarchy: The Reconstruction of American Higher Learning.* New York: Herder & Herder, 1970.

Kerr, Clark. *The Uses of the University.* Cambridge: Harvard University Press, 1963.

Le Melle, Tilden J. and Wilbert J. Le Melle. *The Black College.* New York: Praeger, 1969.

Letter, Sidney S., ed. *The Time Has Come.* New York: Institute of Higher Education, Columbia University, 1970. [Papers on Higher Education].

McCluskey, Neil. *The Catholic University: A Modern Appraisal.* Notre Dame, Indiana: University of Notre Dame, 1970.

Madsen, David. "Daniel Coit Gilman at the Carnegie Institution of Washington," *History of Education Quarterly,* vol. IX (Summer, 1969), pp. 154-186.

Madsen, David. *The National University.* Detroit: Wayne State University Press, 1966. [The "national" university concept from colonial times to the present.]

Martin, Warren B. *Conformity: Standards and Change in Higher Education.* San Francisco: Jossey-Bass, 1969.

Minter, W. John and Ian M. Thompson. *Colleges and Universities as Agents of Social Change.* Berkeley: University of California, Center for Research and Development in Higher Education, 1968. [Includes an annotated bibliography, pp. 129-146.]

Nevens, Allan. *The State Universities and Democracy.* Urbana: University of Illinois Press, 1962.

Parker, Garland G. *The Enrollment Explosion: A Half Century of Attendance in U.S. Colleges and Universities.* New York: School & Society Books, 1971.

Pattillo, Manning M. and Donald M. Mackenzie. *Church-Sponsored Higher Education in the United States.* Washington: American Council on Education, 1966.

Pentony, De Vere, *et al. Unfinished Rebellions.* San Francisco: Jossey-Bass, 1971. [The revolutionary struggle at San Francisco State College]. See Smith, *infra.*

Perkins, James A. *The University in Transition.* Princeton: Princeton University Press, 1966.

Reinert, Paul C. *The Urban Catholic University.* New York: Sheed & Ward, 1970.

Rudolph, Frederick. *The American College and University.* New York: Knopf, 1962.

Sanford, Nevitt, ed. *The American College.* New York: John Wiley, 1962.

Sloan, Douglas. *The Scottish Enlightenment and the American College Ideal.* New York: Teachers College Press, 1971.

Smith, Robert, *et al. By Any Means Necessary: The Revolutionary Struggle at San Francisco State College.* San Francisco: Jossey-Bass, 1970. See Pentony, *supra.*

Stone, James C. and Donald P. DeNevi. *Portraits of the American University, 1890-1910.* San Francisco: Jossey-Bass, 1971. [A collection of contemporary periodical pieces with photographs, woodcuts, etc.]

Storr, Richard J. *Harper's University: The Beginnings: A History of the University of Chicago.* Chicago: University of Chicago Press, 1966.

Veysey, Laurence R. *The Emergence of the American University.* Chicago: University of Chicago Press, 1965. See *Review,* F. Cordasco, *History of Education Quarterly,* vol. VI (Spring 1966), pp. 73-75; and *Ibid.,* vol. VI (Summer 1966), pp. 105-106.

Wallerstein, Immanuel. *University in Turmoil: The Politics of Change.* New York: Atheneum, 1969.

Walters, Everett, ed. *Graduate Education Today.* Washington: American Council on Education, 1965.

Willingham, Warren W. *Free-Access Higher Education.* New York: College Entrance Examination Board, 1970. See Ferrin, *supra.*

Zyskind, Harold and Robert Sternfield. *The Voiceless University.* San Francisco: Jossey-Bass, 1971.